NEIL POWELL is originally [from]
Newcastle, County Down[n]
Mountains, with his wife [and ...]
he trained Ireland's first mountain rescue dog, and since then
has gone on to train drowned victim recovery dogs,
collapsed structure search dogs and is a founder member of
British International Rescue Dogs. Neil's dogs have been
the recipients of awards for animal gallantry and devotion
to duty.

SACRAMENTO PUBLIC LIBRARY
828 "I" Street
Sacramento, CA 95814
05/12

D0360842

NEIL POWELL

SEARCH DOGS and Me

One Man and his
Life-saving Dogs

BLACKSTAFF
PRESS
BELFAST

First published in 2011 by
Blackstaff Press
4c Heron Wharf, Sydenham Business Park
Belfast, BT3 9LE
with the assistance of
The Arts Council of Northern Ireland

© Text and Images, Neil Powell, 2011

All rights reserved

Neil Powell has reserved his right under
the Copyright, Designs and Patents act 1988
to be identified as the author of this work.

Typeset by CJWT Solutions, St Helens, Merseyside

Printed in Great Britain by the MPG Books Group

A CIP catalogue record for this book
is available from the British library

ISBN 978 0 85640 867 0

www.blackstaffpress.com

I would like to dedicate this book to all the wonderful search and rescue dogs around the world who live, and often die, for humanity, and especially to the dogs which have been so much a part of my own life, but are now gone: Trixie, Pete, Kim, Kelly, Jessie, Mac, Lucy, Manny, Misty, Missy, Charlie, Pepper, Cuisle, Dylan and Cracker.

In life I loved you dearly,
In death I love you still.
In my heart you hold a place
no one could ever fill.

From 'I Only Wanted You', VICKY HOLDER

Introduction

In 1972, when I first began to discover the delights of the mountains and then became involved with search and rescue, I found that I could combine my love for dogs with this new passion for the great outdoors. The chapters which follow are an attempt to chart part of a journey which has taken me and my dogs from the mountains of Mourne, Donegal, Kerry and the Lake District to Kashmir, Turkey and Algeria.

This odyssey has allowed me to share a little of the joy of those who have survived an ordeal on the mountains or a major disaster, and, on occasion, the pain of those left behind when someone dear to them has not been so fortunate. I believe it has also allowed me to grow as a human being and to appreciate life more fully but, above all, it has given me the opportunity and the sheer delight of working with dogs. They have been a constant source of pleasure as I have watched them mature from eager boisterous pups to strong, independent, hard-working adults, whose single drive in life is to find missing people. There is no doubt – I love working with them and being in their company.

Chapter 1

When I was nine years of age, my family and I moved from our home in Cobh, County Cork, to begin a new life just outside Belfast, in what was then a new and very small Housing Executive estate called Rathcoole. As I tried to come to terms with a very different lifestyle, not to mention the very strange accent of the local people, two dogs became very special to me – Pete and Trixie.

Pete lived with Peggy and Kevin Martin, about three doors from our house. He was a small, bearded, wiry-coated, black-and-white, belligerent, overweight Scottish-terrier mix, with a tail curling menacingly over a short stocky back. He thoroughly disliked people, except his owners.

Pete was not impressed when I first started wandering into the Martins' house, drawn there like a moth to a light by the cakes and fancy biscuits Peggy would dish out to all the kids in the street. He grumbled and snarled, he complained and he huffed, and he made it very clear that I was not welcome in *his* house – I was not to go near his bed or his toys and I was most certainly never, ever to go near him! Pete also became enraged by anyone who might venture too close to his Peggy or Kevin, irrespective of age, colour or creed. The thing was that neither Peggy nor Kevin tried to stop him because, to tell the truth, I don't think they were really too bothered. They loved him warts and all – he was like a son to them.

After a while, I took to visiting Peggy and Kevin every day until, in effect, their house became my second home. I had my lunch and dinner there and in the evening, could generally be found watching kids' television when Kevin came home from work. I often stayed on to have supper too, before finally being packed off to my own house to sleep. I suppose I was a real pain in the ass, but I was too young to see it. Mr Pete, however, was getting well ticked off with all of this cosiness. He grumbled and he guarded and he barked for weeks and weeks.

Then, completely out of the blue, Pete and I became mates. I don't know how or why – he just suddenly melted. It started with him *not barking at me* when I went into his house one day – in fact, he actually wagged his tail, slowly and a bit uncertainly, but he did wag it just the same. When I went outside, he followed me, and when I sat on the low wall at the front of his garden, he sat at my feet.

A day or two later, he followed me down to the shop and eventually I was allowed to sit on his favourite chair, play with his toys and, most astonishingly of all, stand close to Peggy without him barking at me! He even took to hanging around our door at home (on the odd occasion I was there), waiting for me to come out. My mother, who Pete also disliked, often had to get me to move him so she could go round the back to bring in the washing. Everyone was gobsmacked by Pete's sudden and totally unexpected change of disposition. It was the equivalent of seeing Dr Paisley sitting down to tea and crumpets with His Holiness, the Pope. Pete, Martin and I had become virtually inseparable.

I was now the only person apart from Peggy and Kevin that he liked, and there were to be no other exceptions. I learned, though, that the price of this new friendship was that I had to play on my own – my friends were all afraid of Pete so they gave us a very wide berth.

One day while he was eating his dinner, I made a big, painful mistake. I got down on my hands and knees beside him and pretended to share his food. Without realising it, I had stepped way over the mark and, in a flash, Pete bit me on the upper lip, removing a chunk from it. There was blood everywhere. I ran around, holding my mouth and screaming.

Poor Peggy, who had been out enjoying the peace and quiet of her garden, heard all the commotion and came charging in. She scooped me up and rushed me into the bathroom to try to find something to stop the flow of blood. She then ran with me next door to Mrs Downey, a very motherly neighbour, who took one look and hurried me off down the road to Dr Canavan's surgery. Nobody had a family car in those days – we either walked or got a bus and on that day we walked.

Doctor Canavan was a lovely, gentle man, someone I liked and trusted, and I was so glad to hear him say, 'I can fix that. I'll put this new stuff into that hole to make it heal more quickly. Now if you would just hold him still Mrs Downey, I'll stitch his lip.'

Until that moment, I had never heard of stitching up the human body. My mother was forever doing repair jobs on my clothes and I was familiar enough with needles to know they really hurt when they stuck in you. The good doctor reached for my lip with an encouraging smile on his face and a funny-shaped needle between his fingers. I saw the needle coming closer and then I felt it being pushed into my skin. My God did it hurt! It was so painful that I thrashed around and Mrs Downey had to sit on me to keep me still. When he eventually finished, he smiled and told me I would soon be as good as new and that I was to stop stealing Pete's dinner.

When we got home I went straight to Pete's house and, as ever, he was overjoyed to see me. I suppose he thought there was no harm done – he had just disciplined a young upstart in his pack. He had needed to teach me a lesson and that was the end of it. He enjoyed the position of pack leader and all of us were merely his subjects. Peace returned. I gave him a hug and we remained the best of friends until the day he died – yet, oddly, I have no memory of that part at all.

The very first dog I ever owned myself was Trixie, a little female cairn terrier. My parents bought her for me for my tenth birthday after we'd spotted her in the window of a pet shop at Smithfield Market in the heart of Belfast. Although I had always wanted an Alsatian, Trixie was so tiny and so cute that I fell in love with her on the way home on the bus. I have no doubt that we formed the beginnings of a very special and lifelong bond that day, which grew and grew as the weeks went by. Just as it had been with Pete, wherever I went, Trixie went – when I sat down, she was on my lap and when I was in bed, she was there too. When I was upset, say because my dad had given me a box around the ears for some misdemeanour, she was at my feet, staring anxiously up at me. I swear she could read my thoughts.

At eighteen, I went off to study at a college in Kilkenny and for the first time the two of us were apart. I hated being away from her, not seeing her every day – it made me feel empty and shadowless. Things were just as bad for Trixie, my mother told me – she immediately went off her food and took to moping around the house, or sleeping all day in my bedroom.

One night, I had this really bad dream in which I saw Trixie being knocked down by a car on the road outside our house. I could see her lying motionless and then being taken, all bloodied and broken, to the vet's. Later on I could see wires and tubes attached to her while she struggled to stay alive. It was so real ... I woke with a shout and sat bolt upright in bed, gasping for breath and soaked in sweat.

At half past six in the morning, I rang home and blurted out, 'Mam! What has happened to Trix?'

'Nothing at all, boy. She's grand. Why are you ringing at this hour?'

'I'm sorry, Mam. I couldn't help it. I had a terrible dream last night. I saw her being run over by a car. She's all right then? You're sure?'

'Don't worry, boy. She's fine. It was only a dream.'

I should have felt better hearing that, but somewhere at the back of my mind was a niggle that things weren't quite right.

A week later, my best friend Chris Craig, who had not been well enough to start with the rest of us, came to college. The very first thing he asked me when he saw me was how I'd known about Trixie being knocked down.

'What?' I replied.

'How did you know? Your mum couldn't believe it, you ringing her at six-thirty in the morning.'

'What are you on about?' I asked him.

'Trixie, you twat! You were right! She was knocked down and badly injured. She ended up in intensive care at the vet's on the

Antrim Road. Your mum lied because she knew that if she had told you, you would have been on the next bus home.'

I have never forgotten that dream and, although some of the details have faded, the fact that it happened at all will never leave me. Happily, she made a full recovery. She was a fighter who lived life to the full, and when a few years later her life came to an end by the natural order of things, I cried for weeks. We all did.

Chapter 2

In March 1972, when I was twenty-eight and in my last year at St Joseph's College of Education, studying to be a secondary school teacher of general science, I got married to Kate. We had met nine years earlier on the day that I went for an interview with the Doagh Spinning Company. Kate was one of the secretaries there, and had welcomed me and showed me where to wait. I was struck by her kindness and completely bowled over by her good looks.

Soon after our wedding I landed my first teaching job working as a science teacher in a brand new school called St Mark's. It was in a beautiful setting on the outskirts of Warrenpoint, County Down, a sleepy seaside town at the inner end of Carlingford Lough.

Its near neighbour Carlingford, a small village on the far side of Narrow Water, separates north from south. The Newry Canal – a once very busy water highway carrying coal boats from the sea almost to the centre of Newry – further divides the two jurisdictions.

We lived four miles from the school in a tiny village called Killowen, built on the shores of the lough. It was just a group of houses, really, boasting a post-office-cum-shop. People there were kind and accepting, and their kindness was particularly evident during the Troubles when the many people from Belfast who sought sanctuary in the area were welcomed with open arms by the locals.

It was so peaceful there, the quiet punctuated only by the sound of the sea as it rolled in to caress the shores of the forest-clad mountains soaring skywards in a splash of green and purple. It is a beautiful part of the world – a place where people are born, live their lives, die and then don't have to travel too far to get to heaven.

After living there a few months, I began to explore the open spaces and craggy tops surrounding us. On Sundays, Kate, now expecting our first baby, Clair, would often come with me, climbing slowly to the top of Cloughmore, one of the high points above Rostrevor, our neighbouring village. There were times when I needed to help her up the steeper parts as she clung fast to a dog lead tightly stretched between us. She stubbornly refused to give up and go back to more even ground. Where I went, she went – and she still does thirty-eight years later.

One Monday morning, a teacher who was heavily into mountaineering invited me to go climbing with him and his mates the following weekend. He said there would be three going, all teachers from other schools. They met every Saturday at ten in the morning and spent the day in the mountains. I jumped at the chance, not knowing that it was to be my initiation into a new way of life. That first excursion into the hill hooked me on the whole experience of mountaineering and rock climbing – it was the perfect antidote to teaching, a profession not normally associated with risk and excitement. Climbing with the lads became a Saturday ritual. Kate would make up a few sandwiches and a flask for me, which I crammed into an old rucksack with wet-weather gear and all sorts of other mountaineering paraphernalia.

As the weeks went by, I learned to navigate using map and compass – to trust the dictates of this small trembling magnetic needle, however much I might think it was wrong and that I knew better. There was rock climbing too: balancing the risk of scaling a cliff face against the degree of safety offered by carefully placed pitons, running belays and one hundred and twenty feet of climbing rope was exhilarating!

In early 1973 I decided to apply to join the Mourne mountain rescue team, a relatively new group, small in number, made up of local farming people and instructors who worked in the nearby outdoor pursuit centres. It was not a busy team in terms of mountain rescue, but the members met once a month to train for the possibility that they might someday have to deal with a mountain calamity. Occasionally they would be asked by the police to go searching for people who had got lost or injured in the mountains at night or in bad weather.

It was not without its moments of humour. Once we were searching the mountain for someone reported to be lost, when, out of the blue, a man asked if he could join us. He said he had some spare time and would be glad to give us a hand with the search. After an hour or two, somebody in the team thought to ask him his name. Surprisingly enough, it was exactly the same name as that of the guy we were out there searching for. This man had spent hours helping us to look for himself!

I had been in the team for a year or so when I came up with an idea, an idea which has grown and stayed with me for the last forty years. It started off one day when I found myself thinking about how to make searching for missing persons easier and more effective. After all, there was nothing particularly nice about clumping around in the dark, sloshing through rain and mist and inevitably losing the battle of trying to stay dry. It was hard, monotonous work.

After one particularly hard night's searching, a flash of inspiration hit me. Surely life would be much easier if I could train a dog to help with the search work. It was so obvious and I couldn't understand why no one in the mountain rescue team had come up with the idea before. After all, a dog could fly over the ground, way faster than any of us. And what about his fantastic sense of smell? Darkness and poor visibility would no longer be a problem – all we would have to do would be to follow the dog.

Now, as it happened, I had a dog at the time, a very lovable but dim-witted Doberman called Kelly. I had absolutely no idea how to train him for this new career and he had absolutely no desire to learn. He was, as we say here in Northern Ireland, a dose. Let me give one illustration to explain what I mean.

I have always had real difficulty about going anywhere on holidays without my dogs, then and now, so we take them with us.

We go to the west of Ireland, the perfect location for a pet-loving family. It is wild and uncrowded, with miles and miles of empty, safe beaches where dogs can run around without upsetting anyone.

On this particular holiday, we went to Spanish Point in County Clare, a truly magical part of the world where everything happens slowly: 'Ah sure there's no hurry. Can't it wait until tomorrow, sir?' At the end of the first week, on a Sunday morning, I went to Mass in the beautiful village church. Time there seemed to have stood still and peace oozed from every stone. Kelly was with me in the car. It was a nice car. We had bought it a few months earlier in Warrenpoint and, although a few years old, it was our pride and joy.

Anyway, it was almost time for Mass when I parked in the adjoining car park and opened the two front windows to give Kelly some air. I glanced over my shoulder and saw he was fast asleep, curled up nice and comfy on the back seat, the cheeky sod. He knew his place was in the boot part of the hatchback, but Kate wasn't there to remind him, so that was okay. I locked him in, went up the steps and into the chapel. It was full of worshippers, most of them locals, judging by the number of cars parked outside bearing Southern Irish number plates. I had hardly knelt down in the only empty space, which just happened to be right at the front, when the strident note of a car horn came from outside. It went on and on for a while and then as suddenly as it had started, it stopped. The horn began again, the difference now being that it only blew when the priest, Father John Horgan, was saying something. It was uncanny. It was a deafening din and it soon became plain for all to see that his Reverence was struggling to keep his cool. Everyone became agitated, tutting and shaking their heads. Even at the end, when poor Father Horgan began to give his final blessing, we couldn't hear one word. The noise vandal decided to keep his hand on the horn in one long, loud continuous blast! The chapel was buzzing with indignation and outrage.

Now these were sensitive times in Ireland. Tensions had grown between some Catholics and Protestants in the north of the island, and occasionally trouble spilled over into the south, so people there were on their guard for troublemakers from the north.

So as I left the chapel with two or three hundred locals, everyone was scanning around to see if they could identify where the noise had been coming from. However, by then, it had become more sporadic, so it wasn't easy to pinpoint the car.

As I walked down the steps of the chapel, I became acutely aware that the noise was coming from somewhere very close to my car. In fact, the closer I got, the more I realised that the blaring was coming from mine. Our car – the one with the Northern Irish registration plates. 'Oh loving Mother of God, what has that bastard of a dog done?' I gasped to myself. 'Oh my dear, sweet loving Mother of God! Noooooo!!'

I broke into a cold sweat as I sped over the last few steps, trying desperately to act casually, knowing that dozens of locals were still looking around for the culprit.

When I got to the car Kelly was on the driver's seat, his front paws dancing around the steering wheel, and his great big mouth putting the finishing touches to a complete redesign of the car's dashboard. 'Blast, blast!' went the horn while he snapped at the tiny fragments of dashboard floating past his head in the air currents. 'You little shit!' I shouted, and watched him jump with shock. But then I had to bite my tongue for fear of drawing attention to myself. I unlocked the driver's door and got in, seething with rage, embarrassment, shock and fear. Yes, fear. What was I going to tell Kate and how was I going to prevent Kelly and me from getting lynched? The car was a wreck but there were still people milling about all over the place trying to source the offending vehicle. A great deal of discretion was called for. I took a deep breath and pulled slowly out of the car park. Behind me, dancing about from seat to seat was an ecstatic Doberman, beside himself with joy to be on the move again.

When we got to the house and herself saw the damage he had wreaked, her jaw dropped and my universe imploded. My ass was grass. I don't know what was worse, the experience I had just come through, or the ear bashing I got that day. It was, however, classic Kelly and gives just a taste of the kind of dog he was. But I digress …

How was I going to get this idea of training a dog to help our mountain rescue team off the ground? I thought about it long and hard and then decided to bite the bullet. I would go and talk it over with Teddy Hawkins, the leader of the Mourne mountain rescue team. Teddy was well known in the local community as a great cyclist, and a formidable rock climber and mountaineer. He was a living legend in the mountaineering world of Northern Ireland and a very capable mountain rescue team leader. However, Teddy's moods tended to be a bit unpredictable. He could cut anyone to the bone with a razor-sharp comment and he was not open to new ideas.

He answered my very timid knock on his front door one evening. 'Yes?' he said.

'Hi, Teddy. Sorry for disturbing you,' I stammered.

'Yes?' he repeated.

'Well, I wanted to ask what you might think about me training a mountain search dog,' I blurted out. He listened with a smile of strained patience to my hasty, stumbling, garbled proposition and then replied, 'Do ye now? Do ye know anything about it? Have ye ever even seen one of them working?' he asked in his broad Castlewellan accent.

'Well, I know about dogs,' I stuttered.

'Hmmm …' He scratched his head, stared at the ground for a minute and then reluctantly muttered, 'If ye want to have a go at it, I won't stop ye. Bye.' He shut the door and my interview was over. He had given me a green light, albeit a very low-powered one, and I walked away from his house that night, thinking ecstatically, 'Yes … Teddy said yes … I'm going to train a mountain search dog. Now all I have to do is find the right one.'

Kelly, for reasons already stated, would not fit the bill, so I neither had a suitable dog nor the slightest idea of how to begin to train one.

Chapter 3

1978 was a very significant year for two reasons. Firstly our younger daughter Emma was born. She always loved the dogs, and now works with me at the dog-training classes that I run. 1978 was also the year in which I finally found the right dog for mountain rescue work. I had been looking for more than three years at this point, having had no real idea what I was looking for and not wanting to jump in too quickly. Then along came a German shepherd misfit. He was found abandoned in a garage by Joe Boyd, a police dog handler friend of mine, who rang and said, 'Young Neil, I have the very dog for you. He's a cracking two-year-old shepherd called Kim. He's in need of a good home and you're the very man to give it to him. Why not come and have a look?'

Come and have a look? How could I just go and have a look? I was sold and he knew it. He needed a home for this dog and I needed a candidate to be trained for mountain search work.

I arranged to meet Kim at Joe's house on a Friday evening so that if I did decide to take him home, we would have the whole weekend to get to know each other. I was so looking forward to meeting Kim, this super dog, shining like a shilling and ready for work, but when I saw him I was shocked. He was a sorry sight with a bedraggled and matted coat, long, curved-over toenails and his ribs sticking out. The poor thing had clearly endured weeks of neglect. Joe said that, according to reports from neighbours, his owner had also beaten him quite a bit, never mind not socialising him or taking him for walks. But there was one other minor detail which at the time he 'forgot to tell me' and I didn't hear about until six months later. Kim had bitten a coalman. The coalman had been making a delivery to the owner's house, walked straight into the garage carrying a bag of coal, and – wham – Kim nailed him.

Oh joy! I had a nervous wreck of a dog, with no social skills, who thought human beings in general were shits and who had a previous record of GBH (although I didn't know about that until further down the line)! The cards were well stacked against us. I had no idea how to train a mountain rescue search dog and Kim, my student, was a refugee from skid row who thought humanity stank.

In any event, he came home with me that Friday night, but when I brought him into the house, another problem emerged – Kelly. The two dogs took an instant dislike to each other, circling and sniffing and signalling, 'Don't mess with me.'

So there we were – me, Kate, our toddler Clair, our new baby Emma and two fully-grown male dogs, both of them certain they were the pack leader in a house where, until that day, Kelly had ruled supreme. But Kim was a survivor. He had made it this far against all the odds and he was not going to be intimidated by anyone or anything. We watched and waited with bated breath. They postured and strutted, they growled and stared daggers, but they didn't actually fight.

And then it was over. For the time being at least they seemed to have come to some kind of arrangement with Kelly as temporary boss. Kim, on the other hand, had flagged up that he was more than available to take him on for that position, anytime, anywhere. The scene was set for the showdown, and, as it happened, we did not have too long to wait.

Three weeks later Kate was on the way to the shops in Warrenpoint in our small Renault 6 with Clair strapped into the back seat and the two lads in the boot section (why she chose to bring them both that day will never be known). Suddenly, the dogs decided that the pressing matter of leadership needed to be sorted out there and then. A huge fight started. Kate hurriedly pulled the car over and yanked Clair out. The two gladiators were locked in battle and the little Renault 6 bounced and shook in time to the conflict. It must have looked pretty bad because cars began to pull in behind and people got out to watch the action. Nothing much happened around that part of the world so this had the makings of a good distraction. Some offered completely unhelpful suggestions like 'Throw a bucket of water over them, missus' or 'Jam a stick between their jaws' or 'Squeeze one of them by the … oh sorry …', after a dig in the ribs from his wife.

Meanwhile Kate, red-faced and helpless, holding Clair in her arms, was standing there mortified. 'Aren't those the new master's dogs?' she heard somebody ask.

'Aye, they are,' someone replied in a stage whisper and added, 'Bloody hell, I hope he puts better manners on the youngsters than he's done on them dogs.'

This got the approval of everyone standing around, judging by the synchronised nodding of heads which followed.

When the fight eventually stopped, an uneasy silence descended in the car and the dogs seemed to declare a temporary suspension of hostilities. Amazingly, neither dog was injured, and in time the crowds dispersed, traffic started flowing again and Kate got the family home in one piece.

When I arrived back later and was bombarded with the blow-by-blow account, I nodded and clucked my sympathy. Kate was still steaming over what the dogs had put Clair and her through, and made it very clear that if Kim was going to stay, he'd better behave …

In the weeks that followed it became obvious Kim was not only a very clever dog but also a one-man dog. He became fanatically attached to me: if I went outside to get coal for the fire, I tripped over him as I returned; when I was cutting grass, he was never more than a couple of paces behind. He even took to waiting outside the toilet door, front legs crossed, head resting on them, his anxiety turning to delight when I reappeared. I suppose that, not having had anybody for so long, he was not going to lose the one friend he had found. The feeling was mutual because I had become very attached to him.

However, the bottom line was that I got him for mountain rescue work and as yet I still had no idea how to begin to train him. I sat down and wrote to the Royal Ulster Constabulary for advice and after a long delay, due no doubt to the fact that we were in the middle of the Troubles, I received a reply. It said that the RUC would be happy to assist me and had instructed none other than Joe – my old mate and their twice National Police Dog Trials champion – to work with me every Saturday for twelve months. What a break! I would have the best police dog trainer and handler in the UK to help me train Kim. He was a very good instructor also and had an amazing ability to connect with the mind of a dog. He seemed to know exactly what they were thinking and just by studying a dog's body language, he could predict exactly what they were going to do.

After twelve months he had taught me the basics of dog training, by helping me to train Kim for working trials, the civilian version of police-dog tests. The dogs compete in stakes, each one at a slightly higher level than the last, beginning with companion, followed by utility, working, patrol and tracking. We went as far as the working-dog stake, to give Kim and me a thorough grounding.

Near the end of these training sessions and quite by chance I got to hear of a man in Glencoe called Hamish MacInnes. He was the inventor of a special stretcher for use in mountain rescue (the MacInnes Stretcher) and the leader of the famous Glencoe mountain rescue team, a very busy and highly professional lot. The Mourne mountain rescue team was given one of Hamish's stretchers, which led to a conversation about his other particular area of expertise – mountain search dogs. Apparently he was already working with them in the Scottish Highlands. I contacted him and he invited me to go to Scotland to meet him. On the map, Glencoe seemed to be at the other end of the world, hundreds of miles away, but I would happily have travelled to the moon to meet him.

I got off the ferry in Stranraer, turned towards the north and began a long slow journey that twisted and turned through unfamiliar places with strange-sounding names. North of Glasgow, the beauty and harshness of the magical snow-covered mountains and valleys of the Highlands blew me away.

After what seemed like an eternity, I arrived in Glencoe and knocked on the door of Hamish's solitary cottage, perched high above Ballachulish. Meeting him was a life-changing moment. We shook hands, he brought me in and – over several cups of tea – he had me spellbound as he told the story of how he had become involved in the search dog world.

He said that in 1963, while on a visit to Switzerland at the request of the International Red Cross, he had watched avalanche dogs working on a training exercise. They had impressed him very much by the way they quartered the snow as they searched for a hidden person. He said that when they made a find, they would come to a stop and dig excitedly to uncover the 'casualty'. He became convinced that dogs like that would be of real benefit to mountain rescue teams in Scotland and indeed the rest of the UK. So when he got back to Scotland, Hamish set the ball in motion by training his two German shepherds, Rangi and Tikki. He adapted the training he had seen in Switzerland, where the dogs worked very close to the handlers, to a system more suited to the Highlands. Here wind, rain, snow and large open areas were the norm, so his dogs needed to be able to range a long way off from the handler in order to search effectively.

In December 1964, after many months of training, probably driven by trial and error more than anything else, Rangi and Tikki became the very first search and rescue dogs in the British Isles. Then four months later, in May 1965, the Search and Rescue Dog Association (SARDA) was formed and it was agreed by all who attended this initial meeting to hold a course each December at which new dogs could be assessed.

Hearing about Hamish's work with the dogs in Scotland was heady stuff and when I went back home to the wet and definitely not snow-covered hills of Ireland, I started thinking about how I was going to put all I had learned into training Kim, my own search and rescue dog.

Chapter 4

For months I spent hours setting up training scenarios for Kim, sometimes getting it right and sometimes getting it hopelessly wrong and then having to start all over. A big difficulty was finding people willing to go out on the mountain and wait to be found by a dog. Nobody in their right mind wants to sit on a wet and windy hillside for a couple of hours, twiddling their thumbs, waiting for a dog to appear.

One day, completely out of the blue, a highly unlikely volunteer offered to help me. It was none other than team leader Teddy himself. 'Sure I'll do body for you,' he answered when I jokingly asked him to help me out. 'Call up to the mountain centre on Friday night and we'll get some training done.' Not sure what to expect, I duly turned up. I knocked on the door, went in and – surprise, surprise – Teddy was nowhere to be seen. He had gone home early, but had asked his deputy, Willy Annett, to stand in for him.

Like Teddy, Willy had become a sort of legend in the mountaineering circles of Northern Ireland and we all treated him with deferential respect. His mystique was enhanced by the story of an accident he had survived in Scotland. It was said that while ice climbing in the Highlands, he had fallen and broken his leg, suffering a compound fracture. He spent some time convalescing in hospital, but before he was fully well again, he had gone back to work as a mountaineering instructor. Apparently he was none the worse for the experience. A man in a thousand, and I was in awe of him.

Willy was not known for his love of dogs and he particularly disliked German shepherds. I tried my best to reassure him that Kim did not conform to the German shepherd stereotype, but he was not convinced. I changed tack and gave him a short briefing about what I wanted him to do and, more especially, what Kim would do when he found him. None of that seemed to put him at ease either.

'Okay! Let's get on with it,' he said in a resigned and perfunctory manner, as, with torch in one hand and Kim's ball clutched tightly in the other, he disappeared into the darkness of Tollymore Forest. After a short wait, I sent Kim off, giving a good loud 'Find him, son', so that Willy would get an early warning Kim was on his way. Kim launched himself into the forest with excitement but, as I listened to him crashing through the trees, I knew that Willy was not going to be happy.

Suddenly Kim started to bark. The barking grew more and more intense and a bit frenetic. I began running towards the sound until, as I drew near, I could just about make out the shape of Willy in my torch light, six feet tall, well built, but now cowering against a tree, with his arms over his head bellowing, 'Get that fucking dog off me for fuck's sake!'

It was clear that Kim had got really into it by then. He was very loud and very, very excited.

'Just give him his ball, Willy, and he'll stop barking,' I shouted.

'You give him his fucking ball, you bastard, before he fucking kills me,' he screamed.

I tossed Kim the spare ball I carried and the barking stopped instantly as he chomped on his prize and threw it all over the place. Willy stumped off into the darkness muttering about bloody Alsatians and the mad people who own them. Not my best training session.

Training Kim in hide-and-seek games like that was the basis of search dog training, but was not the only thing I had to do. I also desperately needed to find a sheep farmer who would be willing to let me train Kim to ignore sheep when he was working. It took a lot of research but eventually I found the very man: John Magin, a sheep farmer and sheepdog trials expert, who lived near Newcastle in Glassdrumman.

He was helpful, patient and knowledgeable and spent many hours helping me. The time came for Kim to be tested. John warned me that if Kim showed the slightest interest in chasing sheep, his search dog days would be over. Using one of his own champion sheepdogs, John set the sheep up so that they were gathered in the centre of a large meadow. I was at one end and a friend of mine was at the opposite end. The wind was blowing from my friend towards where Kim and I were waiting and the sheep were right between us. This was it.

With bated breath and John watching closely, I gave Kim the command 'Find him'. He shot off straight like an arrow, straight into the wind, running through the panicking woolly bundles as they scattered in all directions. But he looked neither to his right nor his left and was interested only in getting to the casualty. When he arrived, he stayed there barking at him. Job done!

John was satisfied and gave me a piece of paper to confirm it, adding, 'A wee word of advice, Neil. Kim should wear a bright coat when he's working, otherwise he could get shot by some of the sheep men. There's a lot of sheep-worrying going on this last while and they won't know about you. It'll take time for the word to spread.'

In a couple of days, I got Kim a bright orange coat with the words *Search Dog* printed on both sides and hoped it would be sufficient to let the other farmers know he was okay around sheep and was not to be harmed. Week by week, I watched this big German shepherd whom I had adopted all those months ago grow and blossom into a steady, balanced, self-assured dog with purpose. He and I were ready for assessment as a search dog team.

In 1979, exactly one year after I had taken him home, I asked the Search and Rescue Dog Association (Scotland) if we could have a go at the next novice search dog grading. The man in charge was a wily police dog handler called Sergeant Kenny MacKenzie, a close friend of Hamish MacInnes's. He said that I was welcome to come and that the December assessment would take place at the King's House Hotel on Rannoch Moor.

The journey went quickly, and was as magical as on the first occasion I had been in the Highlands. It was not just the place that was special though – the people who live there, with their ready wit and banter, bring a sparkle and a glow too. On the Friday and Saturday nights of the assessment the bar was filled with the haunting sound of wonderful Scottish airs as a piper in full Highland costume strutted his stuff. His brother followed this performance with one of his own – he'd play the fiddle and tell stories of life-and-death rescues with the Glencoe mountain rescue team. The craic was outstanding but the reality of the assessment was looming so, at four in the morning, I slipped away to bed.

At eight-thirty sharp, Kenny was waiting outside the front door with two other assessors. There they stood, booted and suited, Kenny with a clipboard in one gloved hand and a mountain rescue radio in the other. As we tumbled outside he bellowed, 'And what time of the day do you call this? Get yourselves into the wagons!'

If I was nervous before, I was positively shitting bricks now. I was still half asleep, it was my first assessment, there was snow everywhere and the main assessor was already pissed off! To make things worse, I could hear the cracking sounds of small and not-so-small avalanches going off in the hills all around us. It didn't seem to bother Kenny and the others at all and so I had to pretend I was fine too.

We parked in a lay-by near the base of Beinn Fhada (which means Long Hill), the most easterly of the Three Sisters of Glencoe. Kenny explained that we were going to climb part of the snow-covered monster to its right, Gearr Aonach (Short Ridge), and then traverse round into the Lost Valley to its left. Now remember that up to this point I'd had all my mountaineering experience in the benign Mountains of Mourne where snow is a fleeting visitor to only the highest peaks. Now I was faced with what looked to me like a vertical wall of ice-covered rocks, guarded by an approach of waist-deep snow.

What was more, Tom Middlemas, one of the Scottish dog handlers, with whom I had struck up an immediate friendship, told me something about the history of the place. He said that in former times, this was where the Macdonalds had hidden cattle they had stolen from the Campbells. And he then went on to tell me in great detail the story of the 1692 massacre of the Macdonald clan by the

Campbells. The noise of avalanches all around was loud and was only just matched by the sound of the wind as it whipped down the icy crags and blasted over snowdrifts, flinging ice crystals in our faces. So before we were even halfway up the face of the mountain, I was well freaked-out.

The first of the dogs was sent out across the wide expanse of the valley floor to begin its assessment. Bodies had been 'buried' in the snow. The dog had to locate them as quickly as possible and to let its handler know. I could hear occasional snippets of shouted instructions from the dog's owner. The tension built and built.

Eventually it was our turn. I was shown the search area, told not to go beyond certain boundaries, and to let Kenny know when I had finished searching. I looked out over the white ocean of snowdrifts, rolling off into the distance. Steep mountain walls pressed in on all sides: with the dark sky and howling wind, it made a bleak picture.

I sent Kim off and watched as he plunged shoulder-deep into the new snow. I blundered after him, sweating hard. It was such an effort moving forward. And then in minutes, he had found his first body. 'Bark, bark, bark.' What a relief to hear that wonderful noise on the wind.

'Good lad, Kimmy! Good lad!' I roared with relief as I crashed through the snow towards him, exhaustion forgotten. I arrived, covered in sweat, to see that he was looking down at the snow. I could see no one. 'Oh my God! He's made a mistake,' I thought in horror. But the body was there all right – so well hidden that without Kim, I would never have known. Over the radio Kenny said, 'Well done. Make your way back here.'

Elated, I floated back over the snow that had been so difficult to get through half an hour earlier. When I got back, Kenny told me to take a breather and then 'do a bit of bodying' before my next search. This being my very first experience of mountain rescue work outside Ireland, I had not expected to be asked to 'body'. At home, I was the only person training a search and rescue dog and so always pressed others into service for Kim to find. But apparently it was the rule at the assessments that everyone took turns at being 'casualty' for the other dog handlers. In other words, we had to be buried in a snow grave for anything up to two hours. The floor of the grave was about three feet below the surface and was narrow, giving just enough room for a person to lie flat. Now I had two problems with that. Firstly, I am claustrophobic, so the thought of being buried in a snow grave, with no escape until someone dug me out, was a waking, living, screaming nightmare. Secondly, I had a gut-wrenching fear of one of the Scottish police dogs … a large, snarling black Alsatian called Robert. He was a monster who hated all human beings, with the exception of his handler, who was himself very big and in way resembled Robert. I had twice passed too close to Robert over the weekend, and he had lunged at me with malicious intent. And so when my turn came to act as casualty and the assessor told me I was to be buried for none other than PC Robert, my anxiety reading went off the scale.

Robert's handler came over to where I was standing trembling and, in a very serious voice, gave me a 'survive the beast' guide to bodying for Robert: 'Now remember, Neil, the very second he finds you, stuff that hedgehog in his bloody mouth. It'll keep him busy until I get there. If you do that, you won't come to any harm. Got it?'

'Got it,' I whispered weakly.

I have no recollection of being taken to the snow hole, and instructed to lie down on a mat and stretch out while they covered me with blocks of snow. The grave was so restrictive that I could barely move my hand to scratch my itchy nose, or anything else for that matter. And although there was slightly more space around my head to prevent suffocation, breathing was difficult. As I lay there, I degenerated into a virtual basket-case, besieged by the twin terrors of claustrophobia and the thought of PC Robert. Then I heard it … the unmistakable sound of snuffling. I knew the moment I had been dreading had arrived.

Desperately I hunted around for the hedgehog, ready to jam it into alligator jaws packed with very large, very white, very sharp teeth. I was shaking so much that the hedgehog had slipped from my hand. Frantically I scrabbled around for it when suddenly, just inches above me, a huge snarling mouth pushed through the roof of the icy tomb. Despite the freezing cold, sweat poured from every inch of my body. 'Where the hell is the bloody thing … where is it?' I was shrieking. My feverishly searching fingers found the hedgehog and, in blind panic, I shoved it into his jaws and saw it snatched away!

I listened with a mixture of shock and relief as Robert shredded the squeaking, unfortunate toy. Then I heard the sound of his handler stumping and puffing through the thigh-deep snow. He stopped outside. At last it was over. Relief flooded my whole being as I waited impatiently to be released from the snow grave.

'Good lad, Jet,' I heard the handler say. 'Well done, Jet.'

Jet? Jet? Who the hell was Jet?

'You all right there, mate?' shouted the ecstatic handler from somewhere above. 'Sorry about the hedgehog. This bastard's totalled it. It's now an ex-hedgehog! Ha ha ha.'

I got my voice back and croaked, 'What? What are you talking about? That was Robert's hedgehog! Tell me that was Robert just then!'

'There was a slight change of plan. They squeezed Jet and me in now, to make up a bit of time like. Robert's next. Oh! Did you say that was his hedgehog?' he asked innocently.

'Oh Jesus! Yes! Of course it was his fucking hedgehog,' I shouted, a sea of panic engulfing me all over again. I was drowning in it. 'Stop! Stop! Come back! Come back!'

But there was just silence again, broken only by the moaning of the wind, blowing my cries away over an uncaring, desolate Rannoch Moor.

'Oh Christ Almighty. I'm dead!'

I passed the next thirty minutes or so in a paroxysm of fear knowing that at any second Robert was going to find my hiding place, my tomb. Then sure enough I heard those sounds again – the heavy footfall, the eager sniffing, the sounds of a dog pinpointing my position. Just as it had been with Jet, the icy roof disintegrated, to be replaced by the very large face of Robert. Our eyes locked, I held my breath, and then to my total astonishment, I felt a large wet tongue licking my face clean. No snarling, no bared fangs, just a sloppy wet tongue. I could hardly believe it.

Robert's head withdrew and was replaced by a clear blue sky

and bright sunlight. Life began again and living was so sweet. Outside Robert was barking enthusiastically, beside himself with excitement, his attention having switched entirely to the approach of his puffing, panting handler. 'Good lad, Robert. Good lad,' he was shouting.

'Squeak, squeak,' responded Robert's spare hedgehog, which had no doubt been tossed into his mouth from afar. I was ecstatic. I had miraculously survived my very close encounter with Robert. Although I seemed to have been forgotten in my snow hole, I didn't give a hoot.

The searching and the burying went on all day, with just a very brief stop for lunch. Then, as darkness fell and the temperature plunged, the assessors were satisfied. It was over for today. We could go back to the King's House for a shower and a pint.

I was on the point of collapse by the time I sat down to a dinner that night. It was a spread that would have choked a donkey. Then back to the bar where the music and smoke and storytelling started all over again, just like the night before. It was mad, bad and brilliant fun, but at eight-thirty next morning, just like before, Kenny and his assessors were standing outside the front door saying, 'And what time of the day do you call this?'

At last the weekend drew to a close and I learned that Kim and I had done enough to get our novice search dog grade. To top it all, the certificates were to be presented by Hamish MacInnes. Wow! It did not get better than that.

The place was packed with members of the fabled Glencoe and Lochaber mountain rescue teams. I was beside myself with joy and eventually, my name was called and I went up to be awarded my certificate and a warm handshake from the great man. We had made it, Kim and I. We were the first search and rescue dog team in Ireland!

Chapter 5

Not long after Kim and I returned from Scotland, I was invited to give a presentation on search dogs to the newly formed Northern Ireland mountain and cave rescue coordinating committee. The committee comprised representatives from the various rescue teams in Northern Ireland, both voluntary and statutory, as well as officials from the Sports Council for Northern Ireland. I accepted straightaway.

Bert Slater, a neighbour of ours, represented the Sports Council on the committee and gave me a lift to the meeting in Derry. A wise, humble and unassuming man, Bert was highly respected as a mountaineer and explorer, his accomplishments a byword for excellence within the mountaineering circles of Ireland and beyond, and I respected his opinion immensely. On the journey, he warned me that I might get a bit of stick over the search dog idea – he had heard that some people in the mountain rescue world felt that dogs would find casualties too quickly and make the human searchers redundant. I couldn't believe that people would be resistant to an idea that would enable casualties to be found more quickly and felt pretty apprehensive about the presentation I was about to give. In the event, however, my talk seemed to be well received – I spoke about SARDA and how search dogs could assist mountain rescue teams by significantly reducing the time it took to find a missing person, as well as the huge savings in man-hours and money to be made by using SARDA dogs and the significantly reduced risk factor to team members.

An officer from the RUC dog section had also been invited to give a presentation. In fact, he had hardly prepared anything, beginning his talk with, 'What do youse want to know?' From the officer's attitude towards me – presumably because he took the view that search and rescue dogs were a waste of time; a threat to a role that had been dominated by police dogs up to now – I had a feeling that from that day a line was drawn in the sand: I was inadvertently on one side and the police dog representative was on the other.

Later that year the police spokesman on the mountain rescue committee engineered that Kim and I should be formally assessed for competency by members of the RUC dog section. The implication was that the assessment already conducted by SARDA was not sufficient. I had no doubt that Kim and I would sail through any test they might set but was glad to have advance warning from a policeman friend of mine that the test was going to be much harder than I might have expected. Most importantly, he warned me, 'Now, look, they'll tell you that you're only going to be looking for one guy in the forest, but I've heard that they're going to plant three of them.'

Kim and I arrived at Stormont for the test, as arranged. The RUC officer who sat on the mountain rescue committee and two representatives from the dog section – including the man I'd met at the presentation in Derry – were waiting for me.

'Right, Neil,' the police dog section boss said, 'we want you to search the forest here for one man we have hidden. When you find him, come out and tell us where he is. That's all there is to it. Okay?' We found the first of the three bodies in seconds, so I wrote down his name and carried on. Within seconds, Kim found the second man and then the third not far away. I noted their names too, and, for good measure, I searched the remainder of the forest, just in case they had been even more sneaky than my informant realised. It was all clear, so we made our way back to our waiting critics.

'Good lad. We heard the dog barking,' said one of police dog section guys. 'Did you find him then?'

'Well actually, I found three men,' I said innocently. They all exchanged glances but when he looked back at me, he made no comment. However, he wasn't quite finished yet … 'Right, now, can you now show us your dog doing a send-away please?'

He wanted to see if I could get Kim to run directly away from me in a straight line. It can be a difficult exercise but because it was a fundamental exercise for working trials, Kim had been well schooled and was a master at it. A two-hundred-metre send-away was nothing to him. I pointed him in the direction he had indicated and said, 'Away, Kim.' He shot off, running non-stop until he reached the tree line that bordered the open ground. I stopped him and made him lie down. He had done the perfect send-away, but there was silence from my assessors.

The mountain rescue committee representative muttered that I was free to go. I called Kim and we walked away. To this day, I haven't heard whether we passed or failed the test, but I knew I had not won any new friends.

I had to get Kim through the next level of his search dog training: full search dog. We worked every day, hail, rain or shine, and as the December deadline approached, Kenny MacKenzie rang and, in his broad Scottish burr, said, unnecessarily, 'Neil, it's me, Kenny.'

'How are you, Kenny?' I said, already knowing the reason for his call.

'Are you ready for the Cairngorms, Neil?' he asked, referring to the place where the grading was going to take place. I jumped in with both feet and said, 'Yes certainly, Kenny. We'll be there.'

For full search dog grade, we would be expected to demonstrate we could operate safely alone in the Scottish mountains in winter and find all the bodies that were hidden. I would not be told how many there were and so when I finished an area and reported that all missing persons had been located, I had better be right!

The assessment was based at the ski cottages of Glenmore Lodge and, to be fair to them, the new Northern Ireland mountain rescue coordinating committee agreed to cover my travel costs. Progress was being made, however slowly.

When we got to Scotland, conditions were ideal but the snow was deep and very taxing. On our last day, having passed the assessment, we were called out to search for a man and woman who were late returning from a skiing excursion. I worked with a navigator from the Cairngorms mountain rescue team. He was a very nice lad and, despite partying most of the night before and being a heavy smoker, he led me a merry dance in the deep snow that smothered Corrie An Sneachta.

Kim did indicate at an object he found in the snow but it turned out to be the top of a weather station which someone had recently visited. Of the missing couple we found no trace, but they later walked out safely – tired, wet, embarrassed and very sheepish. They had been trying to avoid publicity because they were married to different people and wanted to keep their weekend secret. Oops.

Kim had performed faultlessly during his assessment, finding all the hidden bodies, and by Sunday lunchtime it was all over. That evening, we were formally awarded the coveted full search dog certificate. Kim and I had arrived.

Back in Northern Ireland, the bond between Kim and me, which was already intense, deepened to a new and rare degree when we were part of a training exercise on the 2,084-foot Eagle Mountain on the western side of the Mournes. This mountain has vertical crags and steep gullies along much of its eastern face. We were near the top in dense mist and visibility was down to two metres, sometimes even less than that. As we made our way into a strong north-easterly wind that was hammering us with sleet and rain, Kim was constantly checking for scent just ahead. Suddenly he stopped and would go no further. He was about one metre in front of me. 'Get on Kim, you silly bugger,' I shouted. He stood quite still and turned and looked directly at me, with his ears pricked and his head cocked to one side. I was baffled – this was so unlike him. In a moment of suspended time, the clouds were torn aside like a giant curtain and to my shocked eyes, revealed the valley directly below us! We were about two metres from a three-hundred-foot drop to what would have been certain death. 'Oh my God! Good lad, Kim,' I croaked. I owed my life to him that day.

Weeks' more training went by, and then a problem emerged. I had been taught in Scotland that, while carrying out search and rescue work, when the dog found the casualty, he had to stand beside it and bark until the handler arrived. But because Kim was working at long distances from me, there were times when I didn't know he had made a find. Distance made it hard to hear him barking, especially when the wind was blowing away from me. That this system was totally inappropriate for the mountains was made cruelly clear during one particular training episode. It was another day of howling winds and low cloud. The mist, swirling and dense, reduced visibility to almost zero and the stinging rain was being driven horizontally into my face. I was at the bottom of a steep gully which leads out of the Glen River valley. In the bedlam, I could hardly hear my own shouts of encouragement to Kim, let alone hear him bark should he make a find up there.

He had been searching for some time and I knew he must be near the top of the gully. Then, in a brief lull, I heard him, but the wind started up again, completely drowning out all sounds. I scrambled up the gully, but when I reached the top, the noise was even more deafening as the gale screamed around the small crags and fissures that abound there. If I was right about Kim barking, it meant he had made a find, but where was he? My anxiety levels started climbing off the scale. Why? Because the individual who we were searching for was none other than the police officer who had been one of the assessors at my sham test at Stormont.

In another momentary lull, somewhere to the east of me, I heard Kim barking again. As fast as I could, I scrambled over the rough ground towards the sound. Gasping for breath I eventually found them and saw Kim standing beside the policeman who, although swathed in a bivvy bag, was clearly soaking wet and very angry. He shouted, 'That stupid bloody dog of yours has been barking at me for nearly half an hour and you still couldn't find me. You're both bloody useless! Useless!'

'Hi,' I managed lamely. He ignored that, got to his feet seething and mumbling, stuffed his gear into his rucksack, threw it over his shoulder and stumped off towards the gully shouting, 'You're fucking useless! Both of you!'

His words stung and, as I followed him dejected back to base, I could not stop the moment playing and replaying in my mind. All the way down the Glen River, I was on the very edge of quitting.

I agonised over his hurtful words and wondered if he had a point after all. Maybe this search dog idea was indeed all a load of nonsense.

Later, after a shower and some dinner, when I could think more rationally, one of those moments of inspiration that sometimes strike from the blue hit me. My belligerent colleague had quite unwittingly done me – and, as it later transpired, search dogs all over the world – a huge favour. I realised in shock it was not Kim and me that were useless; the problem lay with the method that we were using to indicate a find. What was the point of Kim barking at the casualty? Surely it would make far more sense to train him to come back to me and then bark. All I'd have to do would be to train him to take me back to wherever the casualty was. It seemed so simple and so obvious. I was ecstatic and decided to raise my new idea at the next training weekend in Glencoe.

That chance arrived a few weeks later. After a day's training on the hill we went to the team pub in Fort William. The training officer, Bill Michie, was a very experienced and very able police-dog instructor but, like his counterpart in Northern Ireland, he was not open to new ideas. I somewhat hesitantly put my suggestion to him but his response was predictable. 'That's daft,' he said. 'How'll you be able to tell the difference between the dog just barking at you and the dog telling you he's made a find? It's just not possible. Forget it.' Bill, like all police dog handlers, was trained in a certain way and, as regards criminal work, it was the best way – tried and trusted. But I knew, and I'm sure that others did too, that it was not right for mountain rescue dogs. At that time, there wasn't any point trying to explain it, so I let the matter drop.

However, when I got back home I set about figuring out how to teach Kim this new method. He already knew how to bark on command so that was a good start. Now I all had to train him to do was to come straight back to me and bark at me when he had made a find. When he'd got that nailed, the next bit would be to train him to take me to the person he'd found.

For weeks I worked and worked at it and when I knew Kim was ready, I arranged to go back to Scotland to show Bill Michie. He set up the exercise and watched in astonishment as Kim found the hidden person, came back and indicated to me and then led me all the way back to him. It was magic. As far as I know, that method had never been used anywhere before in mountain rescue. Now, of course, it is commonplace and is called the re-find or the bounce back. At any rate, it is Kim's and my small claim to fame.

Chapter 6

By 1982, although Kim was only around six years old, he had developed a bit of lameness in his back legs which, although I didn't know it at the time, was the beginning of a degenerative spinal condition for which there is no known cure. But he was as determined as ever to go where I went and to carry on as a search dog. He was definitely slowing down on the hill, but his heart was as strong as ever, and I wanted him to keep going as long as he could.

Late one evening in January, the wife of one of our local GPs rang our house in a very distressed state. She told me that her husband had gone for a walk in the mountains early that morning and had not returned, and now it was nearly dark. It was completely unlike him and she was convinced that something terrible must have happened. I asked for more details: where in the mountains she thought he might have gone, what equipment he might have taken with him, how he was dressed, whether he had food and so on. 'He said he was going to the top of Slieve Donard,' she said. (Slieve Donard is a 2,750-foot mountain – the highest peak in the Mournes – near Newcastle.) 'Okay. Leave it with me and I'll get things started,' I replied.

'Thank you. I'm sure he won't be pleased with me for calling you like this but … ' she tailed off.

'I know. I'll let you know as soon as I find anything out, okay? Bye for now.'

I knew the doc well. I was one of his patients. He was – and indeed still is – a jovial, happy-go-lucky sort, with a caustic sense of humour, well liked by all who know him. I was deputy leader of the mountain rescue team at the time and, because the team leader Willy Holmes wasn't available, I rang the police and asked them to call the rest of the lads out. I bundled my kit and Kim into the back of the car and in ten minutes we were at the police station. It was raining heavily as I ran in through the gates and the wind was powerful enough to throw big waves over the sea-wall close by. What were conditions going to be like at two and a half thousand feet?

In the operations room, I assessed where I thought the Doc was most likely to be. Given the time, I reasoned it was most probably going to be somewhere on the lower part of the path up to Slieve Donard. The Glen River track, as it is called, is not a difficult path to walk but in some places there are very steep banks on one side. I worked out a rough search plan for the team and then rang my good friend James McEvoy, also a member of the team. He lived near me in Newcastle, and so I knew that he would be able to get to the station quickly. Having given him a summary of what I was planning, I suggested that while the rest of the team was gathering, he and I could use Kim to do a very quick initial search of the Glen River track. 'I'm on my way,' he said, without hesitation.

When the next team member arrived at the station, I briefed him and asked him to take over the planning of the search, based on my initial assessment. I knew I could safely leave it to him sort out the lads when they got there and put them into various search groups. He would also organise the usual equipment, such as the stretcher and casualty bag, and arrange for an ambulance to be on standby should it be needed. Very soon after that James arrived, and he, Kim and I were driven in the police Land-Rover to the top bridge, which marks the point where the Glen River track leaves Donard Forest and meets the open mountainside.

As expected, conditions were far worse than at sea level with visibility down to a few metres. I sent Kim off up the track into the weather as, lifting our rucksacks, James and I followed. After twenty minutes or so, we were about half a mile up the valley. The river on our left was boiling and dashing its way down the narrow gorge, throwing up a fine mist and making a deafening, thunderous noise. Hunched against the wind, it was difficult to avoid slipping on the greasy boulders underfoot, never mind watching where Kim was going or indeed how he was coping. But he seemed to be bearing up well, given the appalling weather and his less than full health.

Suddenly he paused, head in the air as he checked whatever it was he was smelling, and then took off, swallowed quickly by the mist. Could he have found the Doc already, I wondered, hardly daring to hope? Indeed he had … in no time, he had returned, barking excitedly. Despite his age and condition, Kim had managed the almost impossible. 'Show me, Kim,' I shouted against the noise. He needed no second bidding. He turned and led back up the track where finally, through the mist and rain, I could just make out the shape of the very large figure of the missing doctor stumbling around close to the edge of a steep drop. The river was waiting noisily below as millions of gallons of water crashed and tumbled off the mountain.

Kim had found him – his first casualty since qualifying. James and I ran to stop the Doc from teetering over the edge, which was just feet from where he was standing. I shouted, 'Doc! Stand still! Stand still!'

James steadied him, holding his arm and shouting over the bedlam, 'You're all right, Doc,' knowing full well that this was far from true.

But the good doctor shouted back, 'Piss off! Leave me alone! I need to contact my wife. I've got to let her know I'm okay. Where the fuck am I? Who the fuck are you?'

James tried to calm him, and explained who we were and why we were there, but it seemed not to register at all. He tried telling the Doc that he was almost certainly suffering from hypothermia (the symptoms of which include confusion and loss of reasoning). He wasn't having any of that, so we tried to persuade him to eat a Mars bar to replace lost energy, but he didn't want that either. He shouted again that he wanted to get home to his family and we were not going to stop him. He began nodding to himself and tried to push past us. But then he saw Kim blocking the way, alert and curious, puzzled by this bizarre behaviour. The Doc seemed to calm down a little at that and decided he would eat the Mars bar after all.

Meanwhile James, speaking over the radio to the police, told them we had found the Doc alive, and that he was receiving some first aid treatment. He asked them to send an ambulance to meet us at the top bridge. They acknowledged and said the rest of the team was on its way up to our location, and that the ambulance was already there waiting for us. They promised to let the Doc's wife know right away.

Much less agitated now, our still-complaining patient finished the Mars bar and started to tell us what had happened. He said he had reached the top of Slieve Donard by early afternoon, and that was when the weather had changed so dramatically. Being the man he is, he decided a little bit of rain was not going to stop him and, rather than taking shelter until the squall had passed, he headed back down the mountain. He then got disorientated in the low cloud and soon after became wet through as he ploughed on in the lashing rain. He said that the wind had been horrendous, so he tried to find his way back down the mountain. Unfortunately, he only managed to get as far as the col between Slieve Donard and its neighbour Slieve Commedagh. Then for some unknown reason, instead of continuing to descend, he chose to turn round and climb to the top of Commedagh.

At the summit, he found an old stone hut which offered him some shelter from the howling gale that was trying to fling him off the mountain, but unfortunately its door was facing directly into the worst of the weather. He said he remembered trying to work out his options as he shivered uncontrollably from the wet and the cold, totally exhausted. He thought that this must be the end: he almost decided to give up the fight and just stay there and die.

After a while – he had no idea how long – he regained his senses and decided that he must make one last-ditch effort to get home to his wife and family. He got to his feet, left the hut and fought his way through the storm, back down the mountain to the col. This time, he found the path that led him to the valley floor and that was where we found him.

The Doc was determined to walk to the top bridge unaided, so it took us a while to get there. When we finally arrived the Doc – protesting – was bundled into the warmth of the waiting ambulance and whisked off to hospital where happily, after a few hours, he was pronounced well enough to be sent home. Apart from hurt pride, our stalwart GP was apparently none the worse for wear. To have endured what he did and keep going made him in all our eyes a very brave and very strong man. However, for some time afterwards, he had to put up with a fair bit of stick from certain close friends and colleagues in the practice. As for Kim, he was the toast of the local press and was awarded the certificate of merit by SARDA (Scotland), endorsed by the mountain rescue committee of Scotland.

But in what seemed to be such a short time, Kim had slowed down even more and had become much less steady on his back legs. He was only about seven or eight years old. Our vet said that his illness would progress to a gradual shutting down of all feeling to his back end, whereupon he would completely lose the ability to walk. He would also become incontinent. Kate, Clair, Emma and I were devastated. Kim's illness turned out to be exactly as the vet had diagnosed, and in just a few short months, my big brave, strong lad had reached the point where he was no longer able to stand up. His legs just stopped working.

I knew I should have done the right thing by him then, but I couldn't. It was summer, the weather was dry and warm, birds were singing and all should have been right with the world. Kim still thought he was fine and wanted to be with me wherever I went. But he couldn't walk, so he had to drag himself along and for a while, became quite good at it. In time, though, the constant dragging wore away all the fur on his back legs.

I developed a system of 'wheelbarrowing' him out into the garden for a pee or just to be near me while I was doing a rare bit of gardening (I hate gardening but sometimes it is necessary). I held his back legs off the ground while he walked forward on his two good front legs. When we got to where he wanted, he would flop down and watch or would occasionally try to dig if I was digging.

And all the while, he was on guard, just in case something or someone might be about to do me some mischief. He just didn't know he couldn't do anything about it. I can still see his big brown eyes, bright and intelligent, holding silent conversations with me.

He could not or would not accept that he had now become permanently disabled. He was still my minder and my mate, no matter what.

Eventually his condition worsened to the point when, as the vet had predicted, he became incontinent. He was starting to lie in his own mess and he hated that. But Kate and I both kept cleaning him and drying him and putting off the inevitable. I was torn apart by guilt but I couldn't face up to what I knew had to be done. Kate felt equally bad but she hid her feelings from me. Then one awful day, I said to her, 'Look, Kate, I can't do this any more. Please take Kimmy to the vet on one of the days next week when I'm at work. I don't want to know when but please do this for him and for me. I can't face it.'

A couple of days later, when I came home and looked for Kim, he was nowhere to be seen. 'Where's Kim?' I asked.

She kept her face turned away from me and said, 'He's gone, Neil.'

'Gone? Gone where?'

'I took him up to the vet this afternoon. He's there now.'

'What?' I raced to the phone, dialled the vet and shouted, 'This is Neil Powell. I'm ringing about Kim. Don't do anything to him. I'm coming up to get him.'

'It's too late, Neil,' the vet said gently. 'I have had to put Kim out of his misery.'

I dropped the phone and cried my eyes out. My old mate was gone and my heart was broken in two. He was more than just my first mountain rescue dog and my minder. He was Kim my best friend, and he had burrowed his way deep into all of our hearts.

I know there will be those who will think I was a cowardly bastard for not being with Kim when he was being put to sleep. I know I should have been there for him, as he always was for me. But I can't help the way I am, and the pain and the grief I felt then – and indeed every time one of my dogs dies – is beyond description. I just could not do it.

For weeks and months afterwards, our house was so sad. We live at the foot of the Mourne Mountains, but I couldn't bear to look at them, let alone go near them. I even suspended my membership of the mountain rescue team.

Then, one day in the late summer of 1982, when I was aimlessly turning the pages of a German shepherd dog club magazine, I saw that a fancy breeding kennel somewhere in the south of England was advertising pups. Kate and I agreed that we needed another shepherd. Yes! I rang the breeder and told her about our loss, and explained that Kim had been the first mountain search dog in Ireland. She listened sympathetically and said she had the very pup for me. He was big for his age and just ten weeks old. Mac, as we later called him, came from a really impressive working background. Seemingly, some of his predecessors had gone to the Hong Kong, Singapore and Metropolitan police forces, the RAF and so on. Thinking back on it, I suppose this genetic predisposition to police work should have been a bit of a warning sign to me – although police dogs and mountain rescue dogs share many of the same characteristics, such as high intelligence, a powerful scenting ability and a willingness to please their handler, police dogs tend to be more intense characters, often selected from specific bloodlines which are bred specifically for police work. Police dogs tend to be very 'alpha' in temperament and unlikely to back down when provoked or when they consider their handler to be in danger. Mac was a case in point, but love is blind and he sounded perfect, a really strong prospect as a new mountain search dog. I knew he could never replace Kim – the old boy's shadow was everywhere – but he would give me a chance to start again. We sent the breeder a cheque the next day.

When he finally arrived at the airport and all the paperwork had been completed, I opened his sky kennel and was absolutely amazed. Mac was big and almost jet black. Even at that young age he looked impressive and had police dog written all over him. A hint of things to come. I couldn't wait to get him home to show him to the girls and Kate. 'Right, young man, let's go!' I said to the bright little eyes peering at me from the front of the sky kennel. I carried on a conversation with him the whole way home, a journey which took about an hour.

As we pulled into our drive, the front door of the house burst open and out poured my three ladies, Kate, Clair and Emma. They took one look at this big black furry bear of a pup and were in raptures. Mac accepted all of this attention with a kind of aloof indifference, which – in retrospect – was another hint of things to come. For a while, he seemed to fit into our family perfectly, but then, after about eight weeks, it looked as though young Mr Mac had certain issues. He didn't like the girls coming near him when he was eating or, especially, when he had a bone or a toy in his mouth. He would growl deep in his throat, warning them they had come far enough. The signs of trouble ahead were all there but I'm afraid I didn't read them correctly.

By the age of twelve months, Mac had become a big, powerful, almost intimidating dog, still nearly completely black. His behaviour seemed to have improved, but it was actually a false impression – the girls had merely learned to stay away from him when he was eating or when he had something in his mouth. In any event, I kept working hard to socialise him and I genuinely thought I was getting somewhere. He clearly enjoyed our training for mountain search work, and showed great promise, hunting happily until he found his 'missing person'.

In the early winter of 1983, when he was eighteen months old, I took him to SARDA Scotland for the novice grade search dog test. We had the usual heavy snow that weekend, making walking and searching a real pain. None of it bothered Mac though. He found all his hidden bodies and everyone at the assessment commented that he looked the part, his black colouring standing out starkly against the blue-white highland snow. When the two and a half days of testing ended, his performance had been without fault, so he was given novice grade and I was thrilled. We went home on the crest of a wave.

I was already planning ahead to the following year when I hoped to have him assessed at full search dog grade. But then disaster struck. The problem came to light in the early part of the new year when the sheep had been let back out on the mountain. Mac encountered them unexpectedly while we were out training and he didn't like what he saw. In fact it was obvious that he intended to make it his life's work to drive them all off the hill. His hill!

I was shocked and for about six weeks tried everything I could think of to stop him from wanting to chase sheep, but nothing worked. I contacted other dog trainers for help and even phoned John Cree, the author of one of my favourite books on dog training (*Training the Alsatian*). He was very sympathetic and offered various training suggestions but it was all for nothing. Mac had absolutely no intention of changing his behaviour. Then a sheep farmer told me about an 'electric collar' he had. The way it works is that when the handler presses the 'send' button on the little transmitter, the receiver on the dog's collar emits a mild static shock through two metal prongs that touch the dog's coat. I experimented with it on myself because I wanted to know exactly what it was going to feel like. As it turned out, it wasn't too bad — similar to the kind of shock you get from an electric fence, but not as severe. The farmer said that the collar would cure sheep-worrying instantly and at the time it sounded like it might be the only solution to Mac's problem. I decided to borrow it.

I headed off up into the mountains with Mac and James McEvoy, who was going to 'body'. In a while we spotted some sheep in the distance, so James took a wide detour to a position where the sheep were between him and us. There was a good strong breeze blowing directly from James's hiding place, which would give Mac every opportunity to find him if he wanted to. I put the collar on Mac, gave him the command 'find him' and watched with bated breath as he galloped off.

He quickly picked up the scent of James and, of course, the scent of the sheep. Mac had to make a choice. Unfortunately, he opted for the sheep. Away he went after the flock which, at the sight of a large black Alsatian dog bearing down on them, went into headlong flight. Nightmare! I pressed the button to activate the collar. Mac checked for a moment, but then continued running. I tried pressing it again, but with precisely the same result. It was obvious that not even the electric collar was going to stop this bucko.

As luck would have it, the whole flock and Mac were heading straight for James. James jumped up and managed to grab him as he shot past. The sheep were safe and the experiment was over. We packed up and went home. Mac's search dog career was over. It was a terrible blow.

I phoned SARDA Scotland and told them I was withdrawing Mac as a search dog and why. They were very sympathetic and offered all sorts of well-meaning suggestions but it really was over. As for the electric collar, I have never used one of them since.

Then one day, some time later and completely out of the blue, Mac charged at a little girl who was walking past our front gate. Although he did no physical damage to the child, she was badly shaken. It was an entirely unprovoked attack which was quite unforgivable and marked the end of the line for him in our family.

I called to the little girl's house to apologise for what had happened, and her mother was very nice about it. She didn't want Mac to be put to sleep because of a one-off incident, but she did say that she would prefer to see him rehomed. I was relieved because I don't know how I would have coped with bringing him to the vet for the last time. I phoned a police dog handler friend of mine to tell him about Mac. He had good contacts, and eventually was able to have Mac accepted by HM Prison Service as one of their trainee patrol dogs. I never saw him again but I heard that he eventually became an exceptionally good Prison Service dog that none of the inmates ever challenged.

I know now that the fault for Mac's behaviour lay not with him but with me. I had failed to give him clear, unequivocal leadership and, for an alpha male like Mac, that was a sign of weakness. He was not doing anything wrong in his world – he had simply assumed the position of pack leader to make up for my shortcomings. Clearly that little child was no threat to him, but in the dog world, there is no distinction between adult and child, and Mac had wrongly believed that he had to drive her off his territory. It was wrong and inexcusable but, in light of what I have said about leadership, understandable. Of course an attack on anyone is totally unacceptable but the blame for Mac's behaviour lay entirely with me.

Chapter 7

A few months before Mac went off the rails, I had put out some feelers among local sheep farmers for a collie. One of the men I had spoken to was Sammy Holmes, a local character who had developed a sort of cult following around the Mournes. Sammy was as hard as nails and forever had his shirt open all the way down to his belly button, summer and winter alike. His ability as a dog trainer was legendary: people from the area said he once had a German shepherd which could gather sheep as well as any collie. Better than that, it could even open and close gates for them as they made their way home. This dog was once reputed to have been seen sitting quite comfortably on a horse's back.

One day in October 1985 Sammy rang to say that he had the very pup for me. 'His Ma is a bearded collie owned by Frankie McCullough and his Da is my old champion dog Tam.' Frankie, just like Sammy, was renowned in the Mournes for his top-class dogs and his sheepdog trial successes. With breeding like that, I was on to a winner before I had even started. I went straight down to Sammy's to meet the pup.

Sammy's was a typical farm, with outhouses, feeding troughs, old machinery and sheep all over the place. It was March, so ewes were busy lambing and the air was filled with the sound of bleating. As I peered over the fence, I saw Sam examining one of the ewes in a holding pen. He looked up and said, 'Come on in, Neil. The pups are all over the place, but that one there ... you see him? The wee long-haired black-and-white one – that's the one I was telling you about.'

In the middle of the pen were six or seven pups scampering

around, tumbling over and chasing each other. When I opened the gate to go in, all of them fled except the one Sammy had pointed to. He came straight over and looked up at me as though to say, 'Yes? Can I help you?' This was to be Pepper, my new boy.

'What do you think, Neil?' said Sammy, the hairs on his chest blowing this way and that in the light breeze. 'Will he do?'

'Sammy, I'd love him. He's not a bit bothered by all the commotion. He looks absolutely perfect. I'll go home, let her ladyship know and be right back.'

'Well, he'll be here for you … I'll see you later,' and he turned back to his work with the ewes.

Off I went with a spring in my step, but not to tell Kate. Not yet. She might have said no. Instead I went down town to buy Sam a half bottle of whiskey by way of saying thanks. Then I called for my friend James McEvoy, knowing that he would want to see my new pup.

Ten minutes later we were back at Sammy's farm. Bursting with excitement, I knocked on the door. 'Sammy,' I said when he opened it, 'I've brought James along to see the pup and I've a little something to say thanks because I know you won't take any money.'

'Shh! Don't let the wife hear you,' he whispered conspiratorially. 'She's dead against drink. Come on. This way.' We joined him in the semi-darkness of the byre and he said quietly, 'Right then men, let's have a wee dram.' I opened the bottle and handed it over. Sammy savoured the moment, took a swig and handed it back.

Now, I'm not a whiskey drinker. I hate the stuff, but to be sociable, I took the bottle and had a little nip. James very wisely said no because he was driving us home. He passed it back to Sam. Another swig and then it was my turn again. 'Oh God! He's expecting me to go drink for drink with him,' I thought. Another little sip from me and the level fell ever so slightly. Sammy's turn again. I was becoming desperate and already, even after such a short time, my head was starting to spin. I tried to distract him for a second, so that I could pour some of it into the hay bale I was sitting on. He was watching me closely. It was hopeless! I spotted my new pup staring at us from under the lower rail of the byre's gate. The ewes were milling around him but he took no notice. He was mesmerised by what the weirdo humans were up to. He *knew things*, even at that early age.

With relief and gratitude to a merciful God, I watched joyously as Sammy finally drained the last few drops from the bottle and handed it back. 'Here Neil, hide that. Good lad. I don't want the wife to know,' he whispered, touching the side of his nose.

'Right you are, Sam,' I managed in relief. 'We'll just gather up young Pepper and we'll be off.'

But Sammy hissed in that same conspiratorial voice he had used earlier, 'Hold on a wee minute, young Neil. I've another one here somewhere.' Whereupon he went to the wall of the byre, slid out a loose brick and produced another half bottle, exactly like the one we'd just finished!

'Oh sweet Jesus,' I thought. 'I'm going to die.'

'There we go, boys! Cheers,' he said and tilted the bottle to his mouth.

I don't really remember very much more about what happened after that. James told me that he drove me home and when I broke the glad tidings of the new arrival to Kate, all I got was, 'You're drunk! Get out to hell and don't come back till you've sobered up. And you can take that pup with you.'

Poor James had to take me into Donard Park in Newcastle and walk me round for ages until the worst effects of the whiskey had worn off. It was a very long night for both of us, but that is the true story of how Pepper came to be my new mountain rescue search dog.

From the beginning it was obvious that Pepper had star quality. He was a special dog, one in a million. He was super-inquisitive and never tired of playing with a ball, or a piece of grass – in fact, anything he could lift and persuade someone to throw for him.

When he was young I devised a method of bringing him up the mountain by carrying him in my rucksack. It had a gap in the top for his head to poke out, but the hole was not big enough for him to fall from or jump out of.

One particularly beautiful day, when snow covered the hills and the sun shone from a clear blue sky, three of us – James, another mate of ours, Mike Starret, and I – went out to do some snow and ice climbing, because James and I, being members of the mountain rescue team, had some basic knowledge of it. On days like this, we liked to attempt the odd route up some snow or ice climb, but never tried anything too adventurous. At the top of the Glen River is a gully, which leads steeply to the col between Slieve Commedagh and Slieve Donard. On the right side of the gully, when conditions are right, there is a snow route of about sixty feet. On that particular day, the snow was perfect and the route was definitely on. It was close to vertical for the first thirty feet and then tapered off to a less-steep angle leading to the top.

We fitted on crampons, hefted ice axes and, with James in the lead, were good to go. Michael was climbing behind me and Pepper was in my rucksack, head sticking out the top, surveying the proceedings with interest. As we made our way slowly upwards, Michael said Pepper was looking very excited and he was a bit worried he might wriggle out. I assured him he was snug as a bug and told him not to worry.

When I got to the top of the vertical section I took my rucksack off and lifted the wriggling joyful Pepper out. I put him down on the snow and let him scamper off up the easy slope towards James, now some twenty feet above me. Unfortunately, up where James was, the snow had developed a hard crust and was very slippery.

For some unknown reason, Pepper, now well above James's position, decided to take a roll in the snow. On his back, he no longer had the advantage of those little canine crampons. His body started very slowly to slide downhill then accelerated as it gathered momentum. In seconds he was travelling at the speed of light. James shouted, 'Neil! Neil! Look at Pepper … he's falling! Grab him!' I looked up in shock and saw my little search dog protégé hurtling down the slope like a torpedo. James, teetering on his crampons, one hand holding the ice axe, reached out to try to stop him, but missed. Pep went straight past, going faster and faster, heading for me at a phenomenal speed. I leaned forward, dropped my axe and tried to snatch the rocketing ball of fur, but I missed him as well.

That left one last hope – Mike. If Pepper was going to survive, it all depended on Mike. But he was in a really precarious position having just come to the top of the vertical section of ice. All that was preventing him from falling were the front four points of his crampons and his ice axe pick, buried deep in the snow.

As I watched Pepper plunging towards the edge, it was like looking at an action replay in slow motion, except this was happening in real time. 'Mike! Grab him for Christ's sake!' I screamed. There was a blur of movement as, like the tongue of a giant anteater catching some hapless insect, Mike's right arm flashed out and snatched my doomed pup, scooping him up to his chest. He had done the impossible. He had saved Pepper. What an escape!

The protesting pup was stuffed unceremoniously deep inside Mike's duvet jacket and the zip done up to the top. I don't think he even considered the possibility that Pepper might suffocate! Mike – badly shaken and his face running with sweat – climbed slowly up to where I was waiting, now speechless and in shock. We shook hands, said nothing and carried on to the top in stunned silence. When we got to James, Mike unzipped Pepper from his cocoon, only to discover he had fallen fast asleep, seemingly none the worse for his near-death experience. He zipped him back up again. It was time to go home.

For the rest of his life, Pepper loved climbing and was never bothered by heights or steep ground.

By the time he was twelve weeks old, I had taught him to bark on command, to come when he was called and that 'find it' meant he had to go and search for a tennis ball. By six months he had learned that 'find him' meant he had to search for a person hidden upwind. Then he quickly grasped the next stage, which was that having found the person, he had to come back to me and bark to let me know that he had made the find. Later still, I taught him that having come back and barked, the new command 'show me' meant he then had to run back to wherever the person was hiding, leading me to the body. Pepper loved it and thought this whole searching thing was great fun. He couldn't get enough of it. Next he had to be taught directional work which began with him learning to run directly away from me in a straight line when he heard the command 'get on'. That was no problem and soon I could send him up to quarter of a mile away. Once he had grasped the send-away, he next had to learn to go left, right, up or down, all on different commands.

All in all, Pepper was shaping up to be the perfect mountain search dog except for one fatal flaw: he hated other dogs with a vengeance. I think they reminded him that he was actually a dog himself and not the human being he considered himself to be. The presence of other dogs might possibly have been seen by him as a threat to the certainty of that mistaken belief!

But on the other hand, Pepper loved people to distraction. He appeared to develop the notion that all men, women and children were placed on this earth just to play with him. No one was exempt.

Let me give one example. I used to have a second, part-time, job in a small mountaineering shop in Newcastle, called Hilltrekker. Pepper loved Hilltrekker and always came with me when I was working there because, as long as the customers kept coming in, he was assured of unlimited playmates. No one escaped. When the door opened, he would immediately dive into the waste-paper bin, pull out whatever screwed-up paper ball he could find, and drop it at the customer's feet. His beseeching brown eyes and pricked-up ears said loud and clear, 'Please play with me.' If the customer tried to ignore him, he would launch himself into persistent mode. He'd pick the paper ball up and, again and again, continue to drop it in front of them, demanding that they throw it for him.

One day, an elderly man and his wife came in to the shop. Pepper went through his usual routine but didn't get a response. He became very agitated. It was quite unheard of for any member of his beloved human race to refuse to cooperate with him. I watched his antics for a while and was getting ready to call a halt, when he made the ultimate attention-grabbing move. He deliberately shoved the paper ball right up between the elderly man's legs from behind. And I do mean right up!

He got a response then all right. The venerable gentleman turned quickly, saw the culprit staring up at him bold as brass with big appealing brown eyes and, after the briefest of pauses, he reacted as everyone else eventually did – he threw the paper ball. Pepper had cracked it yet again. Game on!

The two of them played for nearly half an hour, Pepper ducking and diving and charging round the shop like something possessed and the customer every bit as bad, chasing him in and out through the clothing stands, behind the table that served as a desk, and out into the middle of the shop again. Pepper went wild with excitement, until in the end, I just had to step in and call a halt. I took him out to the car because it was the only thing I could think of to give us all a bit of peace.

In the small parking area outside the shop, I noticed that close to my jalopy was a big powerful expensive-looking shiny black car. Its motor was running quietly and two stern-faced guys were sitting inside watching me closely from behind very thick-looking glass.

Meanwhile, inside the shop, the venerable gentleman was waiting at the cash desk to pay for whatever purchases he had made. I apologised for Pepper having stepped over the mark as he had, but the man laughed and said, 'Not at all. That was the best fun I've had in a long time.' We talked for a bit about Pepper and the work he was being trained to do, then we said goodbye. As the man shut the door of the shop, one of the heavies waiting in the big car leapt out and opened the rear door. Then the car slid out into the traffic and was gone.

Some time later, a BBC news flash reported that a high court judge and his wife had been killed by an IRA bomb blast on the road between Dublin and Belfast. There was a picture of the man to accompany the story. I recognised him immediately: it was Pepper's friend. That explained the very special type of car that had been parked outside the shop that day, and the two men who had been with him were obviously his bodyguards. What a pointless and tragic waste of life his death was, and for what? I hope we never return to those brutal days in the name of any cause.

Chapter 8

In 1986, after months of training – and with the help of stalwarts of the rescue team such as Paul Houricane and Dennis Chambers who bodied for us – I felt that it was time to enter Pepper for the novice search dog grade. He loved everything about being a mountain search dog and was, by then, very good at it.

I got in touch with one of my SARDA friends, Phil Haigh, to ask when the next novice grading was being held in the Lakes. I had met Phil on a course a few years before. We shared the same sense of humour, were obsessive about search dog training and were less enthusiastic drinkers than many in the mountain rescue world of those days. Phil came from West Yorkshire and he too was a teacher, although I didn't know that for many years – he liked to give the impression that he was a bit thick and that he had a manual-working-type background. It was a kind of inverse snobbery. I eventually discovered that he worked in a school for disruptive boys who had been excluded from mainstream education, so he must have been an exceptionally talented teacher. Phil was planning to enter his dog Scherne into the novice grading, so he was able to give me all the details.

Once I'd found out about the test, I asked my mate Mike Starret if he would like to come with us. I knew his dog Barney was not yet ready for assessment, but Mike had said the experience of just being there would be very helpful for him – a sort of preview. A month later, Mike and I got the Larne-to-Stranraer ferry. We had no car because mine was needed at home and Mike only drove a works vehicle which he would not have been allowed to take across the Irish Sea for a non-business trip. So we decided to hitchhike from Stranraer to Keswick, a distance of about 140 miles. We packed everything we needed into rucksacks, including food for Pepper, his bowl and a bottle of water.

So when we arrived in Stranraer, the first thing we had to do was find someone willing to take two men and a dog as far as the turn-off to Keswick. A van driver we had met on the ferry spotted us thumbing a lift just outside the harbour gates and our problem was sorted. He took us as far as the turn-off and said he would have liked to take us all the way but he was under pressure to get his delivery made in Penrith. We thanked him and crossed to the much narrower Keswick road. Twenty minutes later, an estate car stopped and – joy of joys – the driver turned out to be a member of the Penrith mountain rescue team. He told us he was going to the assessment to act as 'body' for the search dogs. Happy days.

We arrived at the Crow Park Hotel in Keswick at about teatime. Just as I got Pepper out of the car for a drink, a pee and some food, he immediately spotted four Border collies running around loose about fifty yards away. That was the end of his drink and his dinner. He went clean boogaloo and made a complete fool of himself and of me. He launched an ambush on the nearest of the dogs, only to realise he had made a mistake – it was female and he didn't do fighting with females. He reverted to trying to make amends by licking her face, bowing in front of her and cocking his leg on anything stationary. Unfortunately, one of the stationary things he peed on was a shiny new rucksack. He sprinkled all over one side of it and for good measure gave another little squirt on the lid at the top. 'Pepper. You little shit. What have you done?' I hissed. 'Oh my God, Mike. Look what the little prick has just done to that bag. We've only arrived and he's dropped me right in it.'

'I don't think anyone saw him,' Mike whispered. 'Quick! Put the wee frigger back in the car and say nothing. Here, give me the bottle of water and I'll wash it off.'

He hurriedly rinsed the bag and dried it as best he could, using Pepper's blanket. He worked at a phenomenal speed, trying to get it done before the owner got back.

'Mike, I'll have to tell him or her.'

51

'Are you raving mad? Get a grip! They'll never notice,' Mike said confidently.

I didn't know how I was going to keep it quiet. I was bound to see the owner carrying his bag sometime during the weekend and I knew guilt would be written all over my face. I promised myself I was going to own up before the weekend was over. But right then, I just grabbed my own bag and ran up the steps of the hotel after Mike.

When we opened the front door, we were plunged into a fug of tobacco smoke, beer, cooking and noise. The reception area was filled with fit-looking people, most of them holding full beer glasses and all shouting to each other at once. There were Welsh accents, Scottish accents, the broad drawl of the West Country and, of course, the local Cumbrian drawl. I shouted hello to some of the guys I knew, and introduced Mike. In an instant, we were drawn into the mêlée and I felt again that peculiar sense of belonging, of feeling part of an elite brotherhood.

After a while, Mike and I excused ourselves and headed to our rooms. Mine looked over over the road – and as I looked out of the window I spotted my good friend Andy Collau. Andy was seen by some as eccentric, even somewhat 'off the wall', but he was one of the most talented dog trainers I knew. Anyhow, as I watched, there he was, innocently lifting his shiny new rucksack onto his shoulder, the very same rucksack Pepper had christened earlier …

It was soon time to go and eat, and when we got down to reception, someone was shouting that everyone should go to the dining room for a briefing. This was to let us know who our assessors were going to be and what search areas we had been assigned for the following morning. I spotted Andy just ahead of me so I decided that I would have to face the music.

'Andy. How are you mate?'

'Neil,' he shouted. 'Good to see you. Is Pepper with you?'

I guiltily wondered why he was asking but said only, 'Yes. He's in the car of one of the Penrith guys,' as I waited for him to give me the bollocking I deserved.

'Right, well, look I have to find Alison. I'll see you later. Bye for now.'

And he was lost in the crowd as we funnelled into the dining area. Phew!

Maps of the search areas were pinned up and we were told which area to report to the following morning. We were also reminded that every dog and handler would have to complete two two-hour searches on Friday and the same again on Saturday. If someone was borderline following those searches, they would have to undertake a further two-hour search on Sunday. Finally the organisers reminded us that before any searching was done, before we were allowed to go anywhere near the hill, every dog would be subjected to the dreaded stock test.

Charlie Relph, a well-known Lake District sheep man, was an honorary member of SARDA (England) and had been appointed their final arbiter in the stock test. For our assessment he would be assisted by Neville Sharpe, a police dog handler and a senior member of SARDA (England). If Charlie gave any dog the thumbs down, that was it – the dog and handler were immediately sent home. He hated any hint of 'sheep-eye' in a mountain search dog – a reference to the behaviour of a dog which, on seeing sheep, assumed a fixed stare and crouched body, all signs of an impending chase. Sheep-eye was enough to make Charlie send that dog and his handler packing immediately.

I hunted around for Phil and finally found him propping up the bar. Wow – Phil at the bar. Things must be bad. We sat at a table near the window looking out over the stunning views of the Lake District fells, as they call them in that part of the world. It was clear that Phil was seriously wound up about the stock test. As ever, he tried to play it down and act like he was Mr Cool, but I knew that he was worried about how Scherne would perform, and he wasn't fooling me. We took up our friendship from where we had left it off twelve months earlier. It was always like that with Phil and me – the suspension of time between SARDA training sessions marked a type of punctuation that seemed only seconds long in our conversations. Mike wandered over and I introduced the two of them, then headed outside to feed Pepper.

Pepper was always funny about eating when he was away from home and this time was no different. He just looked at the dish, smelled the food disdainfully and cocked his leg. He was so predictable. It was time to smuggle him up to the room. I put his lead on and went back to the front door of the hotel. When the reception was clear, I sneaked him upstairs. He was 'human' after all and needed a decent place to sleep. No one would ever know.

Dinner over, it was back to the bar where the drink flowed and the place got noisier and noisier. Out came a couple of guitars and the singing and craic built … It went on until two in the morning. By that time, the hotel owner and his wife had gone off to bed, leaving the bar in our hands. It looked like a mad idea, but there was an unwritten law in the Crow Park that everyone scrupulously paid for their drinks.

On and on the partying went, into the small hours. I was getting anxious – I had to have some sleep before my assessment. Of course as soon as the crowd spotted anyone trying to slip off to bed, they would all break into a very loud and mocking song to direct everyone's attention to them. But I had to go to bed. Tomorrow was important and it was already five in the morning. Mike had escaped unnoticed, the crafty sod, so I just waved to my tormentors, bowed obsequiously and legged it.

Morning came. It was time to give Pepper his breakfast, which of course he would not eat. I went in to get some breakfast myself. Mike had already finished his and, having only managed to get one hour's sleep more than me, asked in amazement, 'How the hell do they ever get anything done here? Some of these lunatics must have been at it all night!'

'Now you know why you needed to come here and see for yourself,' I said.

The first order of business was, of course, the dreaded stock test. No sign of Phil so we cadged a lift with the lad from Penrith, who took us the few miles out of the village, to the test. Now where was Phil? I looked everywhere and finally saw him standing near the gate, staring miserably over the stone wall into the test field. He fidgeted and fretted, waiting anxiously for the test to start. As the first of the new dogs was called in, he watched every move the dog made, mumbling to himself all the while, holding Scherne by her lead.

Suddenly I spotted some sneaky movement behind Phil. One of the other handlers crept towards him and, as I looked on speechless, untied Scherne. Phil didn't notice a thing but everyone else did. The thief led her nice and quietly to the other side of the watching spluttering crowd of spectators who were beside themselves with suppressed laughter. It was like watching the Roman guards in the *Life of Brian* when Michael Palin was telling them that his cousin's wife was called Incontinentia Buttocks. Poor Phil was so uptight that he didn't notice a thing, and was now holding a dog lead with nothing attached. When at last his turn came to do the test, Neville shouted, 'Okay Phil. You're next. Let's be having you, lad!' Phil jumped and, almost tripping over himself, went through the gate, already kindly held open for him by someone. Out he marched, empty dog lead clutched tightly in his hand, head held high. He strode right to the middle of the field where Charlie and Neville were waiting.

The sheep being used for the test were gathered behind the assessors, held there by two of Charlie's own sheepdogs. Neither of the men gave anything away.

'Okay, lad. You're Phil Haigh – is that right?' asked Charlie, straight-faced and reading from a sheet.

'Yes, Charlie,' said Phil, in trance-like state.

'All right. Are you ready for this then?'

'Ready as I'll ever be,' Phil managed, trying hard to sound jaunty.

'Well … is it just me, or are there not supposed to be two of you doing this test?'

'What? What do you mean two?' stammered Phil, jauntiness fast evaporating.

'Well, where's your dog, lad?'

'She's here,' he said pointing to an empty lead. 'Oh my God! Where's she foooking gone?'

The penny dropped.

'You shower of bastards!' he roared and the place erupted. It was priceless and one of the few times I ever saw anyone get the better of my mate Phil Haigh. When he finally retrieved Scherne, cracking little dog that she was, she passed the test without a problem.

Pepper's stock test came and went without a hitch. What a

bloody relief, because my little chap was not that averse to showing a bit of the famous sheep-eye either. However, on that day, he was a gentleman. In fact, nobody failed the test so we were all told to go on to our search areas. Mine was a valley called Langstrath, and the first of my searches was to be on the right-hand side of it. The ground was steep and had small, nasty-looking crags scattered throughout it. There were also little bundles of woolly animals wandering around all over the place, so Pepper would get another stock test, albeit by default.

My assessor pointed out the enormous section of mountain that was to be our search area. He gave me some time to think about how to carry out the search – I had to think about wind direction, trying to work out what it might be doing higher up and especially the little crags that could disrupt air- and therefore scent-flow. If I didn't get the plan right then Pepper wouldn't be able to find the bodies within the allocated two hours, and that would mean a big black mark beside my name. I outlined my plan to the assessor and then got started. I had no idea how many bodies I was looking for, but one thing was certain – when I had finished the search, I'd better be absolutely certain that I hadn't missed anyone.

It took us one hour and thirty-five minutes to complete our search. We had one terrifying moment when Pepper came to the edge of a frozen ledge and seemed to be thinking of continuing the search by going over the edge, but generally he performed brilliantly – racing across the hill as though floating through the snow, with me blundering along behind. Pepper found three bodies, which had all been well hidden. I radioed back to the assessors that I had finished and that my area was clear. With no indication as to how we'd done, they asked me to return to their location.

It is always nerve-racking walking back the last few yards, worrying that you may have got it wrong and missed someone. I was torturing myself, thinking, 'Dear God, please don't let them say, "I'm afraid you have missed a body, mate" or "Do you realise that you missed a huge part of your search area?"' But there was none of that. Pepper had found all the bodies and we hadn't missed any of the area. What a relief. Then it was on to the next set of assessors and another area.

At the end of day one, everyone went back to the hotel for a shower, a pint and dinner, and the talk and banter were mighty. But, as always at the assessment weekends, the thought that tomorrow we do it all over again was niggling away – two more massive areas to search and another set of assessors to impress. Just before dinner each evening, the assessors go to a private meeting where they compare notes on the day's performances. The assessors discuss and score each candidate (each should receive a minimum score of 60 per cent). Afterwards, everyone troops into the bar where the dog handlers and their assessors have a few drinks and some banter. Phil and I usually end up as the entertainers, me playing my guitar and him singing his folk songs.

By Saturday evening, with all the searches complete, the assessors decided who had passed and who would have to come back again next year. If someone had missed a body but was able to justify why – for example because of very poor and variable wind conditions – then he might be given the benefit of the doubt and asked to do a decider search first thing on Sunday morning. Muck that one up and it was definitely curtains until next year. But, back in 1986, most of us, including Pepper and me, were told that we had passed and that we were officially search dog handlers of SARDA.

Chapter 9

Then the unexpected happened – a genuine callout. A skier had been reported missing, overdue by four or five hours. Darkness had fallen and it had begun to snow. All available dogs and handlers were asked to assist, including those who had just passed their assessment. I could not believe my luck.

I was assigned to work with John Brown and his dog Sam who had been made famous by Cumbrian writer, Angela Locke. Angela, an admirer of search dogs for years, had written two wonderful books about John and Sam entitled *Search Dog* and *Sam & Co.* Everyone in SARDA had read the books and we all greatly admired both John and the legendary Sam. Now here I was, going out on a real shout with two of my top heroes.

Sam was ten years old by then and nearing retirement but he still loved to go out on searches. We'd been tasked to search the high ground above Coniston Water so, in the hallway of the Crow Park, we had a quick discussion about what gear we might need and so on. We arranged to meet in the car park in ten minutes. I was ecstatic. In my room, while I was throwing things into my rucksack, Pepper, who was even more wound up than me, was dancing and jumping around like a mad thing. I was certain people would hear him downstairs and maybe they did, but nobody said a thing. We were all dog lovers.

I checked my rucksack again, making certain I had put in my warm gear, bivvy bag, Karrimat (a closed-cell foam mat which gives insulation from the ground), torch, map, compass and so on. It could be a long night. Then it was off to find John. He was putting his rucksack on the back seat to make more room in his very smart four-wheel-drive Subaru estate car. When he opened the boot for Pepper to jump in, there was Sam, swathed in a wool rug, one eye open, silently asking, 'Who is this whippersnapper bothering me at this time of night?'

Now as I've said before, Pepper had a problem with other dogs and here he was, being asked to share the boot of a car with a complete stranger, and another dog at that! John, unaware of Pepper's profound animosity, grunted, 'Move over, Sam, and let Pep in.'

'Here we go,' I thought. But Pepper nimbly jumped in, curled up in a ball with his back to Sam and pretended to fall asleep. Relieved and amazed, I said nothing and tossed my rucksack on the back seat beside John's.

Cautiously John edged us out of the car park and, as he skilfully negotiated the treacherous, un gritted roads, proposed a search plan. Because Sam was ten years old and not as capable of working over difficult ground as he used to be, John thought it best that Pepper and I search the steep gullies. He and Sam would work along the top of the crags where the going would be a bit easier but where he could take most advantage of the wind direction. I didn't care what I did: I was delighted to be in such well-known and highly regarded company.

We slithered to a stop in a small lay-by at the start of our search area. We hoisted on our rucksacks, switched on head torches and made one final check of our equipment. It could be a long night and it was no good remembering some essential piece of kit a couple of miles away in the dark. As we set off, John suggested that I should radio him as soon as Pepper and I got to the start of our area and then begin searching immediately. John and Sam would wait a few minutes when they reached their area so that John's scent wouldn't confuse Pepper.

We parted company and set off for our respective areas. No navigators to accompany us, just us, our dogs, a map, a compass, a head torch and a more powerful hand torch – 'No GPS or owt like that,' as Phil would put it. I kept on a compass bearing to bring Pepper and me to the bottom of a steep, snow-choked gully, which marked the start point for us. 'Ready, young man?' I asked Pep, who was absolutely frantic with excitement. I struggled to get his green coat on – it held a glowing cyalume stick, which would let me see him in the dark, assuming the night didn't throw any more snow at us. For now it had stopped, but an icy wind was blasting straight down from the high ground where John and Sam would soon be arriving. I called John on the radio and he confirmed that he and Sam would reach the start of their area in ten minutes, which kept us right for scent.

I made my final safety checks – ensuring my ice-axe was secured, that I had no slack laces, that my extra torch was accessible, that my compass was secured, etc. – and then it was time to go. 'Find him, Pep!' I shouted. Away he ran, caught in the powerful beam of my torch ploughing through the deep snow, as he made his way into the first gully. It was steep and intensely cold, the high walls covered in a thick coat of black shiny ice. Not a place to spend a night in good health, let alone if you were lying injured. I shuddered at the thought of it.

We finished our first gully and I began to work my way round to the next one, but to do that I had to climb a bit higher. The wind was very strong and seemed to be gaining in strength as I climbed. John must be in a real shit-hole of a white-out up there, I thought. We found nobody. On and on we went until the radio hissed and John came on: 'Neil from John.'

'Go ahead, John.'

'Neil, conditions are really bad up here now. We're going to have to stop for the night,' he said.

'Roger, John. Are you able to come down to me?'

'Too difficult to estimate exactly where I am,' he replied. 'It would be only too easy to go down the wrong gully.'

I knew what he meant: the last two we had searched were lethal.

'Roger, John. The gully I am in now seems not too bad, so I'll come up to you.'

'Roger, Neil. Take care man!'

I shone the torch upwards and could just make out a line up the gully which looked safe enough.

'Right Pep, let's go,' I said, stepping out much less confidently than I might have sounded.

It was a bit of a struggle, but we got to the top. As we broke out of the gully's limited shelter, we were plunged into a world of noise and pain. The wind was shrieking like a banshee, whipping the snow and ice fragments into a stinging, blinding blizzard. I had no idea how John had been able to work Sam and navigate in conditions like that.

'John from Neil,' I said into the radio.

'Go ahead,' he replied.

'John, we are at the top now. Do you have any idea how far along you've gone?' I asked.

'I estimate grid reference ... ,' and he read off a six-figure set of numbers. Now, under less severe conditions, I could have transferred the numbers easily to my map and I would have had his exact location. But that night, there was no easy way to use the map. I needed to find shelter to stop it blowing away, and I needed to take my gloves off. 'Wait one, John,' I asked him as I got down out of the wind into a fold in the rocks. I got the map and a small notebook out and was ready to copy down his position.

'John, this is Neil. Say again your position,' I asked. As he called out the same six figures I scribbled them down ready to convert them to the map. Fighting the wind, I was eventually able to see where he was waiting. Having just left my gully, I knew exactly where I was on the map, so I could work out the bearing from me to him. I estimated that we were about three hundred yards from each other.

Calling Pepper to my side again, I set the bearing on the compass and pushed out into the wind. But Pep, as usual, had his own agenda. In his mind, he was still working and he took off into the white-out. In no time he was back, barking to tell me had had found someone. 'Good lad! Show me, Pep.' He went a few feet, waited for me to catch up, turned and went a few feet more, always making sure I was following. Eventually we got to John and Sam. And of course, Pep started his crazy dancing and barking, taking no notice of the blizzard raging all around us. Blizzard or no blizzard, he was demanding his ball – he had done his job and found a missing person. 'Here, John. Give him the frigging ball quick!' I shouted, handing him a tatty tennis ball. John tossed it into Pepper's mouth and Pepper was happy.

However, we were now potentially in very deep shit – way over our heads and far beyond, in fact. I suggested back-tracking and just heading down the way that Pepper and I had come up, but John pointed out that there would be too great a risk of our going down the wrong gully. If that had happened, then it would have been 'good night from me and good night from him'.

So John got on the radio again and told the controller we were going to have to stay put. He also gave our estimated position, in case things deteriorated more. They replied that they would maintain a listening watch (someone back at base would monitor the radio all night in case any of us got into difficulties) and wished us good luck. We were definitely on our own now.

There was no chance of digging a snow hole because the snow wasn't deep enough. What we were standing on was a mixture of rock, ice and frozen snow and we were both knackered anyway. So we hunted around for a bit of a windbreak – not as easy as it sounds. The light from the torches was being reflected back in the blizzard, and the wind was still blasting tiny ice fragments into our faces, making looking ahead far too painful, even with snow goggles on.

Eventually, we stumbled across a big boulder, standing strong and defiant against all that the night could throw at it. It became our haven. Now the emergency gear we had so carefully checked was going to be worth its weight in gold. We fished around for bivvy bags. I found mine but had to hang on to it with all my might. In the odd sneak attack around our boulder the gale was trying to snatch it away into the darkness. I stuffed a Karrimat into it, to lie on. I then slid well down into the bag and wrestled myself into my duvet jacket. 'Come here, Pep,' I shouted. He was standing with the ball still in his mouth, ready for more play. 'Here. Get in here you dopey sod,' I shouted. He did as he was told and burrowed down into the bag beside me. I jammed my rucksack into the opening to stop the snow coming in and we were ready for the night. 'Are you okay, Neil?' John bellowed from beside me.

'All's well, John,' I shouted back over the roar of the wind.

'Goodnight then,' he said. And so began one of the longest and coldest nights of my life.

My bivvy bag was of the bright orange plastic variety. Condensation ran everywhere inside it and soaked my clothes, but at least we were out of the wind. I was so glad I had brought my duvet jacket as without it I think I would have frozen to death that night. However, while it kept the upper part of my body warm, my legs and feet had no such insulation and they were soon freezing cold. The solution came in the form of my little black-and-white mate. Pepper lay on my legs and that way both of us could stay warm. Magic, but the flapping of the plastic bivvy bag and the noise of the storm blasting a couple of feet above made sleep impossible. Every now and then, the wind would reach us and make the bag shake and slap around like a loose sail. Hour after hour the night wore on.

John and I would check that the other was okay from time to time, and then at last the first weak signs of daylight started to filter through the darkness. We had made it!

'Morning, John,' I ventured.

'Ah. Morning, Neil. Sleep all right?'

'Not really. I'm bloody frozen!'

'Me too, but at least we're still here, eh?'

Slowly, we emerged from the bags to find we were both covered in an insulating layer of snow. Maybe that was why I had stopped shivering earlier. But for now, the wind had died away to a whisper and the snow had stopped falling. 'Let's find that gully and get the hell out of here,' John suggested.

'I'm right with you!' I laughed.

John let base know we were safe and that we were about to make our way down the nearest descent gully. He gave our position again, and then with the two dogs close by, looked for the way down. We very quickly discovered that the safest descent gully was indeed right where we had suspected it to be the night before.

We made a slow careful descent in the deep snow, and were soon safely back in the car and on our way to the Crow Park. Over the radio we were told that the missing skier had been found safe and well. He was miles from where we'd been searching but John said that was often the way these things worked out.

Although we had not found the guy, I was proud. We had survived the mother of all storms and, best of all, Pepper was now a novice grade mountain search dog with his first search under his belt. Not only that, but I had met John Brown and Sam and been on a real live search with him. I was over the proverbial moon.

By Sunday lunchtime, everyone had gathered in the dining room to hear the official announcement of the results of the assessment. When it was our turn, the assessors told me that, had Pepper and I been in SARDA (England), we would have tied for the coveted 'Novice Shield', an award made to the best young dog on the assessment. Wow!! Good lad, Pep. It doesn't get any better than that. And who had we tied with? None other than Andy Collau!

I was given my SARDA handler licence and a new dog jacket for Pepper with the words 'Search Dog' emblazoned on each side. I also got a brand new set of expensive wet-weather gear, consisting of a jacket which had the SARDA dog handler logo on it and a pair of waterproof trousers. It was magical.

The following year, 1987, we went back to Keswick to do the full search dog grade, sometimes called the upgrade. On one of the assessment searches, Pepper and I were walking along a ridge looking into a valley hundreds of feet below. We had been searching for our second body for about an hour and were coming close to the cut-off time. I gave him the command to go down, which sent him towards the riverbank way down in the valley floor. It looked like it was 'miles' away, but he went down and down until he was finally there. He looked around and then began running along the riverbank with purpose. Could it be? Had he picked up the scent of our last body? He plunged over the bank and disappeared for a minute or two. I thought he'd fallen in the water. In panic I began scrambling down the steep ground towards where I'd seen him vanish. I was about halfway there when he climbed back up onto the bank and started running towards me. He arrived, caught his breath for a few seconds and then started barking like mad. He's done it! I thought. He's found the last one. I shouted, 'Show me, Pep!'

Off he ran again, legging it all the way back down into the valley, with me charging along behind. Over the riverbank he went and when I followed, I saw him standing beside a deep hole, a dark recess in the bank itself. I peered inside and could just make out the shape of a body. What a result! I radioed back to the assessors and was told to bring the body out and make our way back to their location. The day's searching was over.

Sunday meant the last search exercise of the assessment, generally looked on as a 'belt and braces' event. Even though all the dog teams might have performed impeccably up to then, they were given this final hurdle just to be sure. However, those handlers whose dogs had had a hiccup during the assessment would be scrutinised much more closely on this Sunday morning and for them it was make or break.

Having done well on Friday and Saturday, I was feeling a bit complacent, always a foolish attitude to have during an assessment. My assessor was Neville Sharpe, the same man who had wound Phil up during his stock test the previous year and, because he was up there with the best, I wanted to impress him.

He gave me an area of very steep hillside which led down to a quarry to search. I sent Pepper to clear the hillside first and while he was working, I angled upwards across the slope, eventually arriving at a position where I could look down into the quarry. I saw Neville watching, so I sent Pep into the quarry, smugly thinking what a great opportunity it was to let Neville see just how good a dog Pepper was at distance control.

I directed Pep to go from one side of the quarry to the other, making him look a bit like a little remote-controlled vehicle. He was perfect and I was delighted. However, as he was crossing, I noticed him hesitate, stop, go back a few steps and look at a pile of stones. I roared at him to get on, but he didn't want to obey and just stood there. I shouted again and to my immense relief he reluctantly dragged himself from the stone pile and ran to the far end of the quarry. He stopped there and looked up towards me, waiting for his next order. I was sure he hadn't found anyone and that the area was clear, so I radioed Neville and said I was coming out. Job done.

I was feeling pretty satisfied and was convinced Neville had deliberately given me an area with nobody hidden in it – a negative search. Such searches test the handler's confidence in his dog and in himself. When I reached him, Neville said, 'Well, how do you think that went, Neil?'

'Oh, I think it was okay, Nev. There was nobody there.'

If ever the old adage about pride coming before a fall applied to anybody, it applied to me at that moment.

'Well I have to tell you that there was a body hidden in the quarry and your dog actually found him. But you were so busy bloody grandstanding that you called him off. He was looking at the guy and would have gone back to tell you, but you sent him on, you stupid bastard. You were showing off, weren't you?'

'Oh my God,' I groaned. 'Yes I was. Oh shit.'

Shaking his wise head, Neville said, 'Don't you ever do anything as stupid as that again. I'm not going to give you a fail because I know how well that little dog has done over the whole assessment. But you, you daft bastard, you really let him down this morning. Take this as a warning and learn from it!'

'Thanks Nev. I'm very sorry and it will never happen again,' I promised weakly.

He allowed the barest of smiles as he said, 'Right. See that it doesn't. Now bugger off.'

That was how I ended my full search dog assessment. We passed, but what a nerd I had been. I never doubted my dog again, so it was a valuable lesson learned.

Chapter 10

In 1987, Northern Ireland was facing one of its worst winters in years. It seemed as though snow fell constantly, and the Mournes and all the surrounding lowlands were under at least three feet. One evening, at around seven o'clock, I got a call from Newcastle police asking me come to the station urgently. They said they had a person had been reported missing, and should have been home about five hours previously. I looked out of the window to see a blizzard blocking the light from the street lamps and the snow almost up to the car's wheel arches. There was no way I could drive in those conditions, but as we only lived about fifteen minutes' walk from the station, I could go on foot.

I got all my warm gear and a couple of torches into the rucksack, called Pepper and made for the front door. When Kate saw the weather conditions, she wasn't at all happy about us going out, let alone up the hill. To me it was a challenge and the kind of thing that we'd been training for in the mountain rescue team. But to Kate it looked threatening and dangerous. Days later she told me that as she had watched Pepper and me heading off into the snow that night, she thought she would never see us alive again.

Shortly after I got to the station and checked in, three more of the team arrived. They were Trevor Spiers, James McEvoy and Eunan Jackson. They all lived locally and were very experienced – good mountain lads. The duty inspector called us into his office for a briefing. 'What we've got is a teenage boy, with a slight learning disability. His name is Paul Fitzpatrick and he's from Newcastle. His mum tells me that he went out for a walk in the mountains early this morning and hasn't come home. There's still no sign and it's now …' looking at the wall clock, 'nine o'clock.' Apparently the lad had told his mother that he was going up the hill to look at a frozen waterfall, one he could see from his bedroom window. He had only been wearing town clothes and trainers, all completely inadequate for the sort of weather we were experiencing.

The inspector looked at us with a hopeless expression on his face and then turned to stare out the window as the wind defiantly hurled heavy snow against it. He seemed to come to a decision, shook his head, turned back towards us and said, 'He's now seven hours overdue. You know far better than me what the conditions must be like up there. There's no way he is going to survive. I'm not prepared to take the responsibility of calling the team out. Anyway, how could they even get here, for God's sake? The snow is getting worse by the minute. In my opinion it's far too dangerous and for that matter, I don't even want you guys to go out.'

'It's bad all right, Inspector …' my voice tailed off. But he had made his decision.

'The young fella's Mum and Dad are out at the desk,' he went on. 'I'm going to have to tell them.' He got up and went out to the front desk to break the bad news.

I was having second thoughts about what he had said and I could see from the expressions on the faces of the three other lads, that they felt the same. 'I think we should give it a try,' I said and, without hesitation, they all agreed.

'The inspector can only advise us,' one of them said, 'but he can't actually stop us from going.'

'He's probably right about not calling out the rest of the team though,' agreed another. 'With the roads as bad as they are how are they going to get here? Some of them live over twenty miles away.'

We decided to go for a compromise: we'd ask the inspector to put the rest of the team on standby until the blizzards stopped, or at least eased off. When that happened, they should come to the station. In the meantime the four of us, and of course Pepper, would get the ball rolling and start the search. Minutes later, the inspector came back to the office and his face told its own story. He said that when he had told Paul's parents that he could not risk sending anyone out on the hill that night because of the weather, they had broken down. They both begged him not to write their son off as dead. How could the inspector know he was dead, Mrs Fitzpatrick kept asking. He told her he'd talk it over again with the mountain rescue team and would go with their best advice.

He sat down heavily in a chair, looked pointedly at us and said, 'Look, it's up to you lads. If you want to have a shot at it, go ahead, but I'm not telling you to. I'm not even asking you to, and I am not calling out the rest of the team.'

'What about putting them on standby until the weather improves, then?' I asked him.

'Okay. I'll do that,' he agreed.

'And the police mountain rescue team? Could you put them on standby too?' asked James.

'I've already done that,' he said. 'They're going to make their way here as soon as they can.'

'Right then. Let's go talk to Mr and Mrs Fitzpatrick and see if we can work out where Paul might have gone to,' I said.

We went to the front desk to find Paul's parents, who were still in a terrible way, but who were overcome with relief and gratitude when we told them we'd decided to go out and search. 'We need to work out where he might have gone … maybe we could do that from what he told you this morning,' James said. Paul's mum tried to remember as much as she could. 'He said he wanted to go up the hill and look at a waterfall,' she said very quietly.

Our problem was figuring out which one. There were a few likely candidates up there. The Fitzpatricks showed us where they lived on the map and, using that information, we tried to narrow down the search area. We worked out that there were two possible waterfalls he could have seen. That at least gave us a start point. Now, how to get there?

The police mountain rescue Land-Rover was being warmed up as we spoke and the inspector had put the most experienced police driver he had behind the wheel. We piled in and he drove us, with great difficulty, slipping and sliding in axle-deep snow, to what is called the top bridge. There we decided to split into pairs: James and I would go on up on to the mountain with Pepper, while Trevor and Eunan would search the top edge of the tree line to the right and left of our drop-off point.

Having cleared the trees we were in the full force of the wind. Snow was driving horizontally into our faces and with each step we plunged waist-deep into the drifts. Pepper was having a slightly easier time – he could skip over the top – but, eventually, even he started to slow. His long hair was balling up with ice and we had to keep stopping to break it off. We crossed the Glen River and carried on towards the waterfall known as the Black Stairs, a vertical gully about fifty feet high. As we got closer, we could see the water had actually frozen solid in its plunge to earth. How does water do that as it is falling, I wondered. James was behind me, struggling. He told me he'd been out cross-country skiing all day and was knackered.

Pepper searched around the base of the waterfall and as far up the side of it as he could, but there was no sign of the young lad, no footsteps, nothing. We carried on for a further half-mile until we reached a small hut which used to be a stonecutter's shelter. By then, James was looking really tired. I suggested he should wait there and take a breather while Pepper and I went on a bit further to check out a second waterfall in an old quarry. He reluctantly agreed.

Pepper and I got to the other waterfall but still found no trace of the teenager. By the time we'd returned to the hut, I was getting really tired. My legs were aching and Pepper was not looking too happy either. James and I now had to consider our options seriously. We talked it over and decided there was really only one thing left to do – a really long hard push of about another mile to the valley head. It had to be searched because it led the way up to another waterfall and then on up to the col and the much higher ground above it.

The radio James carried hissed to life: 'Neil, this is Trevor, over.'

James pressed his mic key and replied, 'Trevor, this is James. Go ahead, over.'

'Roger, James,' came Trevor's voice, distorted by the wind clamouring for attention as he spoke. 'We are ready to head up to the top end of the Glen River now. Nothing found so far, over.'

'Roger, Trevor. We have found nothing either. We are heading for the top end of the valley too. We will stay this side of the river and you keep to that side. Roger?' instructed James.

'Will do, James. See you up there. Trevor out,' and the radio went quiet again.

Time to move on. James and I put our heads down and pushed against the wind, the snow still blasting and swirling into our faces. Away above us, we could hear the banshee-like howling of the wind in the crags that rimmed the Glen River valley. When we reached the halfway point, we were nearly exhausted from constantly hauling ourselves out of deep snow only to plunge thigh-deep again with the next step.

Pepper had been criss-crossing in front, covering maybe four times as much ground as us. He was all in too. We had to stop for a break. I fished out a Mars bar from my rucksack and tried to break it, but it was rock hard. I warmed it under my arm to soften it and divided it into three. Pepper had the third bit. After five minutes or so, I could feel the energy creeping back into my muscles. James said he had the same feeling and even Pepper seemed perkier. We set off again.

The snow stopped falling as we got near the valley head, where Pepper took off like a bat, running and sometimes disappearing from sight in the drifts. He ran straight towards the base of the steep head wall, vanished for a minute and then came running back towards us, barking excitedly. 'Bloody hell. He must have got him,' I said. With that, we could both just hear a very faint call – 'Help!'

It was coming from the direction where Pepper had been.

'Show me, Pep,' I shouted. He turned and ran towards the sound.

'Help! Help!' we heard again.

We were floundering and thrashing through the snow until suddenly there he was. We could just make out the figure of a man. He was spreadeagled against a steep high bank of snow, arms outstretched as though crucified. We couldn't believe it. We ran to him and found he was alive but almost frozen solid.

'Okay! You're safe now,' I gasped.

James, thinking fast, got on the radio (manned by a police officer in the mountain rescue Land-Rover): 'Base, this is James. Base, this is James, over.'

'James, this is base. Go ahead, over.'

'Base, this is James. We have located the missing person. He is alive but looks to be hypothermic. He is very cold and his hands are frozen solid. I'd say his feet are just as bad. We're about to get him under shelter and check him over properly.'

'Roger, James. What is your location? Over.'

'We are at the base of the ascent gully, at the top end of the Glen River. Over.'

'Roger that. We've got the rest of the team coming in. They'll be on their way as soon as they get here. Over.'

'Many thanks, base. Are any of the local doctors available? Over.'

'We'll check that for you. Wait out.'

While we were waiting for the reply, Trevor and Eunan arrived looking like two abominable snowmen. They took in the situation at a glance but said nothing. Trevor came over and we both tried to put the casualty's arms down by his side but they refused to move. He was locked solid in that position. Meanwhile James got out the bothy, a three-man emergency shelter tent I carried in my rucksack: it gave us the best chance of warming up the youngster. Eunan had been hunting around and shouted that he had found a sheltered place out of the wind. At least here we would not be fighting the powerful gusts which seemed to be trying to yank the shelter from our hands.

Eventually, and with great difficulty, we got Paul's arms down by his sides. We lay him on a Karrimat and pulled the bothy – which has no base to it for this very purpose – over Paul, James and me. We tucked it in under our rucksacks and bums and when we were sure it was well anchored, turned our attention to Paul. We could see that his clothes were wet through and had frozen on him. Both his hands were frozen solid also. In fact I was able to tap the back of each of them with my knuckle and it sounded as though I was tapping plastic. This must be what frostbite looks like, I thought. James was clearly thinking the same. I had never seen anything like it before. We urgently needed to start warming him from the inside, so we got him to drink some warm tea from a flask.

He wasn't that happy about it but he managed a few sips. Then we encouraged him to nibble on a Mars bar, although he didn't really want to cooperate over that either. If he was going to survive, he was going to have to start warming up, so a bit of gentle persuasion did the trick. Base came on the radio and told us that Doctor Walsh, a well respected GP from Newcastle, would guide us on what to do for Paul. Although we had first aid training, frostbite in the Mournes was new to us, and so advice from the doctor would be invaluable. They also gave us the good news that the two teams (the police team and the rest of our own guys) were on their way. The radio hissed again and we heard the Doc come on. He calmly guided us through the early stage of treatment for the frostbitten teenager to try to prevent any loss of limbs. Pepper was curled up beside Paul to try to give him some warmth. The Doc meanwhile told us to place the frostbitten hands and feet under our armpits. That was really cold. Brrrrrrrrrrrr.

As he started to warm up, we needed to change Paul's clothes because the ice in them was melting. We all carried extra clothing and so were able to cannibalise a complete change for him. A couple of hours passed and at last we could hear the others approaching. Thank God for that. Now we had a plentiful supply of armpits to warm up Paul's hands and feet.

At first light, the eagerly awaited RAF Wessex helicopter arrived, filling the valley with the swish, swish of rotor blades and the roar of twin Rolls Royce engines. The green monster descended slowly in a cloud of swirling spindrift, landing about fifty metres from us. Paul, now looking a lot better, was stretchered to the open door and slid inside. The door closed, the engine noise gradually increased and the whirling blades slowly pulled the Wessex back up into the air. It turned, lowered its nose and sped away quickly, on course for Downpatrick Hospital.

Amazingly, an Egyptian doctor who was working at the hospital at the time specialised in frostbite cases, which was a godsend for Paul. Over the following weeks he made a full recovery, suffering no loss of fingers or toes. Today he is alive and well and living near Newcastle.

Chapter 11

On 21 December 1988, Pan Am Flight 103 – *Clipper Maid of the Seas* – was brought crashing to the ground by a terrorist bomb, which killed all the 243 passengers and 16 crew on board, and 11 people on the ground. I was glued to the television set and, like everyone else in the country, was barely able to take in the enormity of it. The images were shocking, the scale of the disaster overwhelming, all those poor people dead. Just like that. Even a couple of children had been killed. Who would want to put a bomb on a plane at any time, let alone at Christmas?

Like millions of others, I was sitting at home, wishing I could do something to help. I tried to ring Phil Haig because if anyone would know what to do, Phil would. But his wife told me he had already left for Lockerbie. 'He's been there since the twenty-second,' she said. 'I haven't heard from him since then.' Unfortunately, we didn't have mobile phones then so I couldn't get in touch with him. Frustration. I so badly wanted to help but who could I ring?

On Christmas Eve I had a call from another good friend, Stan Tanner, a dog handler from SARDA (Scotland).

'Neil. Have you seen it?'

'Yes Stan. I've seen it. Are you guys helping?'

'We are. That's why I'm ringing. Can you come over to give us a hand?' he asked.

'Of course, but how am I going to get there? There won't be any ferries running at this time of the year.'

'What about trying the RAF?' he suggested.

'God yes! It's worth a try. Right, I'll ask them. Listen, Stan, before you go, do you want me to bring Vicky and Mitch as well?'

They were two other dog handlers in SARDA (Ireland) who lived up in Bushmills, on the north coast. 'We could do with as many dogs as you can bring, Neil,' he answered quietly. 'Some of the lads have been here since early morning on the twenty-second. We are all knackered.'

Then he really surprised me. 'Look Neil, I have to ask you this – will you be able to handle it? It is very, very bad here.'

'How the hell do I know?' I said, because I didn't know and I really didn't want to think too much about it. I had always been a bit squeamish if things got messy in a road accident, say, but I could never admit to that. I couldn't let Stan even suspect it or I'd be going nowhere.

'Right,' he said with finality, 'let me know when you get here.' The phone went dead.

My mind in a whirl of things to do, I rang Vicky and Mitch. Like everyone else in the country, they too had been watching the news, horrified at the sights being shown and without hesitation they agreed to come. Transport to Lockerbie was next on the list. Only the police would be able to help with that. I rang the local RUC station in Newcastle, but because of the ongoing IRA campaign, they were understandably very cautious with me. Car bombs, shootings and clever plots to lure unsuspecting members of the security forces into an ambush were a daily occurrence, so the police trusted virtually no one.

'Newcastle Police. Who is this?'

'Hello, officer. It's Neil Powell, the search dog guy,' I started off.

'Oh … right, Neil,' the voice at the other end said carefully.

'It's about the Lockerbie air crash. Three of us have been asked to take our dogs over to help in the search,' I said, 'but we have no way of getting there.'

'Lockerbie? You've been asked to go to that?' he asked incredulously and then added, 'How're you going to do that at this time of year?'

'I know. That's what I'm ringing about. Is there any chance the police could help us? Could you speak to someone in the military about a helicopter maybe?'

'Bloody hell. That's a tall order,' he said helplessly. 'Bloody hell.'

Then – obviously at a loss as to what to do next – he said that he would have to ask his inspector. I thanked him and hung up. I needed to decide what gear I would have to bring with me, so started throwing things into a rucksack and a small kit bag.

Ten minutes later, the duty inspector rang. 'Neil? Inspector Johnston here. You need to get to Lockerbie?'

At last! I knew the inspector very well and if anyone could work a transport miracle that day, it was going to be him.

'I do, Inspector. The lads are having a bad time over there and all the dogs are knackered. Can you help?'

'You're in luck. I've contacted the military. They say they need to check with their counterparts in Scotland but they're certain they'll be able to help. As soon as I hear back from them I'll ring you. You'll be at this number all evening, will you?'

'I will, Inspector, and thanks so much,' I replied, astonished at the goodwill and generosity that everyone was showing.

Twenty minutes later, he rang back to tell me that a helicopter had been arranged and that the three of us were to get to RAF Aldergrove as quickly as possible. He had even arranged for a police car to take me from Newcastle straight to the airfield. After thanking him again, I rang Vicky and Mitch to tell them it was on, and to ask them to get to the airfield as quickly as they could. I just hoped that they had as good a contact in the police up in Bushmills as I had in Newcastle.

Pepper knew something was in the air because he was standing barring the door, his ears cocked and his head on one side, questioningly. I grabbed my kit and his dog food. 'Let's go, mate,' I said, and went out to the car. Its back door was already open and, needing no second bidding, Pepper jumped in. With five minutes to spare, Kate drove us down to meet the police car. Just as promised, they were waiting at the roundabout on the Belfast road and as we pulled in behind them, the blue lights came on. I piled Pepper and my gear into the car, and after a hurried goodbye to Kate, we were off. The police car covered the forty or so miles to RAF Aldergrove quickly and, in what seemed like minutes, we arrived at the main gate in a flurry.

The police told the guard who I was. He nodded, having already been warned I was on my way. He directed the driver to the flights area then we were through the gate and on to the camp. At the main door I piled out of the car into the cold of a December night. I said a heartfelt thanks and goodbye to the police lads and shut the car door. Another RAF guard appeared and led Pepper and me to the 'ready room' where I was met by an RAF officer. He informed me that when the other two arrived, he would be giving us a pre-flight briefing.

Vicky and Mitch and their two dogs showed up forty minutes later, having made amazing time from where they lived. The officer, in a matter-of-fact voice, calmly explained the safety procedures we were supposed to observe in the event of the aircraft ditching in the sea. Whoa – this was becoming very serious now. For some reason, given that I hate flying, I hadn't even thought about that eventuality. Not giving us time to ponder too much, the same officer led the way to a store room where we were told to put on cold water immersion suits. Apparently, they would help our chances of survival if we did end up in the sea, assuming of course that we survived the crash. The suits felt clumsy and stifling, but I was happy to wear mine.

We were led out to the waiting helicopter, a light shining from its open door and the winch-man waving at us to hurry. Pepper had forgotten the other two dogs in his excitement and was straining to be first to jump in. What was it about him that he just delighted at the prospect of flying?

The winch-man took our kit from us and tossed it into the back of the madly vibrating machine. We were given the signal to climb aboard and he pointed to where he wanted us to sit. We strapped ourselves in and were handed a set of earphones each. Over the earphones I heard the pilots talking to a controller. They got the all-clear and we lifted off. The door was slammed shut, but the noise was as bad as ever. Over the headphones the pilot said our flight path was going to be directly across the North Channel to Lockerbie. When we were close to the site, he would approach from the south so that we could see the crash area and get a better idea of what we were about to do. I thanked him. I said a silent prayer to ask that I be given the strength and the skill I needed to get me through the next few days so that Pepper and I could make a difference. I'm sure Vicky and Mitch were doing the same thing.

I have no idea how long the flight took and then we were over Scotland. I listened to one of the pilots talking about some road he was looking at below,

'That's the one we need. It'll take us straight into the town.'

'Got it,' replied the one flying the aircraft.

'Keep a sharp lookout for electrical wires everybody,' he urged.

A couple more minutes passed.

'Wires to port,' I heard someone say.

'Roger that. I see them,' acknowledged the pilot.

Then he said to us, 'If you guys look out the windows now, you'll see the crater of the main crash site.'

I did as he asked and saw this huge ugly scar right in the middle of rows of small houses.

'Do you want me to go round again?' he asked.

'No thanks,' I said, speaking up before Vicky or Mitch could say yes. 'We've seen enough.'

It was terrible looking and I didn't want to get too freaked out before I even landed. The Wessex began a slow descent, skirting the town's southern tip.

'Right then,' said our pilot, 'I'll put you down near those buildings on the left there. I've been told that's the operation centre. Good luck!'

We thanked the pilots and the crew and, having been given the thumbs-up from the winch-man, jumped out of the helicopter, with the dogs following close behind. When we were a safe distance from the aircraft, the engine noise increased as it climbed, turned west and disappeared from sight.

A man came out of the centre to bring us to meet Bill Parr, a senior dog handler in SARDA (Scotland) and now the controller for all search dog teams at the crash site. Vicky, Mitch and I had known him for years. He was a jolly and easygoing person with a ready smile. He met us with a really sombre expression on his face, the strain of the last few days clear to see. This morning he was a changed man.

'Welcome,' he said with outstretched hand. 'Glad you could make it. We're under serious pressure here.'

'Things are bad then?' asked Mitch.

'Bad is not the word for it,' he replied quietly. 'To be honest, it's bloody carnage. Horrendous. Do you want a cup of tea or do you want to get started?'

'I think we'd prefer to make a start, Bill,' I said. The other two nodded.

He brought us to a large table where there was an enormous map spread out. It was marked out in search areas, each one numbered. Some were shaded in, to indicate they had been searched, while others were clear of any marks – still waiting. The task was enormous, he said, the wreckage from the plane having been scattered over huge swathes of countryside in Scotland and across the border into England.

He showed us where he wanted us to concentrate. Vicky and Mitch were to go to a big section of Calder Forest and I was to report to Sherwood Crescent, the site of the main impact crater. This is it then, I thought. Now I'll know what Stan was alluding to. I just hope I am able to do this.

When I got to my assigned area, I was met by Roland Leyland, another friend of mine and one of the Welsh search and rescue dog handlers. He and his German shepherd had been working in and around the crater for days.

'Hi, Neil,' he said quietly. 'What a shit-hole. Will Pepper be all right doing this work?'

'Dunno, Roly,' I replied. 'Is there anything I can sort of let him practise on first?'

'Look around you, Neil. See over there in the bushes. Do you see all that stuff? Well those are human remains. Start him off on that.'

I had never seen anything like it. I couldn't comprehend that what I was looking at had once been a human being. But this was no time to be shocked. I said, 'Find him, Pep,' and pointed in the general direction of the hedge nearby. He went straight over and smelled intensely at what was in front of him. I praised him enthusiastically and asked, 'What have you got, Pep?'

He caught on quickly and started to bark. I gave him his ball. He had known straight away that this was what I needed him to find. Nodding in approval, Roly called me over and pointed to a police constable standing near the very edge of the main crater. He suggested I go to him.

'He'll show you where he wants you to search, mate,' he said, patting my back.

As I picked my way over to the policeman I looked around and saw that the area was crowded with people in military uniforms, picking their way through the debris of what was once Sherwood Crescent. I introduced myself to the young cop and asked him where he wanted us to search. 'Probably down there, mate,' he said, directing me to the bottom of the crater. I looked and suddenly became aware of the intense smell of aviation fuel as it rose on a light breeze from this huge hole. I looked at the policeman again. 'It's bad isn't it?' he said, shaking his head in disbelief.

Just then, I noticed Pepper scratching at the ground close to my feet. 'I wonder why he's doing that?' I said, more to myself than anyone else. As I was watching, Phil Haigh suddenly appeared and slapped me on the back. 'How are you, you Irish twat?' he asked, trying to sound his usual carefree self. Then more quietly he added, 'This is a real shit-hole isn't it?' – just as Roly had described it minutes before.

Knowing Phil the way I did, I knew that the more stressed he was, the more jocular he would pretend to be. I could see he had been through hell and was doing his best to hide it from me. Things must be really bad. I replied, 'Phil! Good to see you mate. This is way worse than I thought it was going to be.'

'Yes. When I got here, the place was still ablaze. I was sent out along the fields and came across bodies still strapped to their seats. It was awful.' He went on to describe in detail what he had seen and it truly was shocking. I could see how hard it was for him to talk about it.

'The smell of aircraft fuel, Phil … ugh! How can the dogs work around that?' I asked.

'That's not the worst of it, mate,' he said soberly and I discovered later exactly what he meant.

Meanwhile, Pepper was showing even more interest in whatever he could smell in the ground below him and was digging frenziedly. I pulled him back by the collar. I asked Phil to pass me a nearby fork. With Pepper watching closely – head to one side, ears pricked – I dug into the ground where he had been so busy. I had probably dug about a foot deep when I felt something soft meet the prongs of the fork. I called the cop over. More gently now, I probed further. The smell of fuel was suddenly replaced by what I came to recognise over the next few days as the smell of burned flesh. I levered the fork up a little bit more and was confronted with a sight I will never forget as long as I live. It was the head and upper torso of a human being. Shocking is not a strong enough word. Horrific is closer. 'Oh dear God,' the police officer exclaimed quietly.

The three of us stood there stunned until the policeman turned and picked up a plastic bag lying at his feet. 'Put it into this,' he said. Gently, we did as he asked. The bag was tagged and laid beside a pile of other similar bags nearby. The contents were to be identified later on.

Pepper began to sniff around a partly collapsed house. Two walls were lying at an impossible angle. Between them was a narrow, steeply sloping gap, like the letter V lying on its side. I could see that the space between the walls became steeper and much narrower the further in it went. Pepper disappeared into the gap, slithering on his belly, until he was out of sight. 'Pep,' I shouted, 'come out of that!' Seconds went by and then he emerged, dragging with him the bones of an arm, all still connected – radius, ulna and humerus – but no flesh at all.

'Leave it, Pep,' I said, shocked.

'Hey, officer. Have you got another bag?'

That was how it was to be over the next few days at that crater. We found human remains all over the place, buried just beneath the sticky, clinging, fuel-soaked clay. Pepper and the other dogs worked tirelessly. Meanwhile another friend of ours, Neville Sharpe, the police dog handler who had been one of my assessors a hundred years earlier, suddenly collapsed and had to be rushed to hospital. Nev had been working almost non-stop with his little cadaver dog in the destroyed buildings nearby. Later that evening, we were told he had been overcome by a combination of fuel vapours and exhaustion, but that he would make a full recovery. It shook everyone up because Neville was one of the SARDA greats. A superman.

As night fell, the teams carried on searching under floodlight but the dogs could only do so much. They needed to eat and rest so Phil and I took our two to the school assembly hall which was to be our base for the next few days. We washed the stinking, sticky clay from our two exhausted collies, dried, fed and watered them, and then found something to eat ourselves.

Word went around the room that a lady from the Samaritans was on hand in case any of us felt the need to talk. 'Bloody counsellors,' Phil muttered. 'What the hell do they know?' He and I thought counselling was a load of crap. We believed we were above all that and had not been touched by anything we'd seen or done. We were both perfectly capable of taking it all in our stride. We were invincible – rough, tough, hairy-arsed mountain rescue guys! But the truth was, and is, that no one is immune from the effects of working in those kinds of circumstances. We all suffered, including the Samaritan volunteer – we heard later that this very brave lady had eventually left the hall in floods of tears, overcome by the nightmares being unloaded onto her by stressed-out rescuers.

Nevertheless, the assembly hall was a vital source of strength and recovery. All the search people sat around in groups, telling each other what they had done and what they had seen, trying to exorcise the demons that were playing hell with their emotions. But the rule of confidentiality took a severe blow one day. In fact, it was smashed to pieces.

A journalist from some sensationalist newspaper in London had been eavesdropping on the conversations in the hall. He then phoned his editor and, the next day, much of what had been disclosed privately was plastered all over the front page of this rag! To take advantage of the atmosphere of trust that existed between the rescue workers in such a callous way was an outrageous act. To prevent any recurrence of such underhand and unethical practices, the authorities issued each of us with a special badge of identification without which you could not enter the assembly hall. We were urged to be extremely careful about when and where we let our guard down. In essence, things had to be bottled up.

The dog handlers were put up in a small hotel on the outskirts of Lockerbie. Phil and I shared a room where we would joke and laugh a lot as a way of coping. We had become almost like brothers during this shared horror story. We worked in different places but I hoped Phil would be spared from too much more. He had seen more than enough for any man, God love him.

One day I was asked with some others to search an area for whatever we could find. As we were walking across open fields with the dogs out in front of us, Pepper stopped and stared at something on the ground and then looked back at me. He had found a wallet. I picked it up, knowing it must have belonged to one of the passengers. I opened it and found myself looking at a photograph of a young couple on their wedding day. The man was wearing an army uniform and his young bride was dressed in white. They both looked radiantly happy. At that moment, a sense of almost overwhelming sadness hit me. There, on a windswept field in southern Scotland, that wallet with its photograph formed an invisible thread linking me to a young American couple who I had never met. I noted the position where I had found it, put it in an evidence bag and carried on, lost in my thoughts.

Passing by a wood a few minutes later, Pepper ran off down into the trees and disappeared from my sight. A couple of minutes went by, and then he came back carrying a red high-heeled shoe in his mouth. I gently took it from him and noticed it was size 6 and almost unused. It was not a very significant find I know, but again, unbidden thoughts and questions started creeping into my imagination. I wondered what the young lady looked like? Had she suffered much before she died? Did she have a family at home waiting anxiously for news that she had somehow miraculously survived? Other thoughts too started crowding in, tearing at my heart, like the children's toys and items of clothing we had found. I stood stock still for ages, staring at that shoe, lost in a world of sadness, until eventually Pepper nudged me, his shining brown eyes seeming to say, 'Come on, Dad. Let's get on with it.' He was right of course – it was time to get a grip and put thoughts like that firmly behind the large steel shutter I had learned to create in my mind – a very simple but effective system of coping.

An hour or so later Pepper found a suitcase. It was not a big one, and it was still closed. I didn't open it, but again I noted its location and brought it with me back to the centre. Days later I heard in one of the debriefs that it had contained what they described as 'vital information' leading to a deeper understanding of how the plane had crashed. That was good news, I supposed.

And then, as if things were not bad enough, as if our faith in humanity had not been tested to breaking point, we heard that strangers had been arriving in the district, some from as far away as England, with the sole purpose of stealing from dead passengers. We heard that they had been taking wallets and watches from bodies as they lay there waiting to be removed. No right-thinking person could ever understand such depraved behaviour and for us, already emotionally drained and raw, it twisted the knife even more deeply.

Five days after arriving in Lockerbie, Vicky, Mitch and I went home with our exhausted dogs. We travelled by the Stranraer–Larne ferry and when the crew members somehow learned that we had been working in Lockerbie, they absolutely showered us with kindness. It was wonderful, and another example of how humanity joins forces against the powers of darkness. I have witnessed things like that all over the world.

When I got home, I was treated to a delayed Christmas and Boxing Day celebration which Kate and the family had arranged as a surprise for me. It was lovely and was going very well until someone innocently asked, 'What was it like, Neil?' What a complete shock that simple question was. It made me feel like I had been punched in the stomach. I tried very hard to find the right words but I couldn't. There were no words to explain what it was like. Instead, I found myself in floods of tears and running from the room. I was losing the plot.

A couple of days later, and quite by chance, I found a pamphlet which Strathclyde and Galloway Social Services had issued everyone before they left for home. I opened it in desperation and suddenly felt I had been thrown a lifeline. It explained that some of us might find ourselves experiencing a condition known as post-traumatic stress. It outlined the symptoms of the disorder and went on to say that feeling as though you were going mad was, in fact, a symptom in itself. Apparently it was a well known illness, albeit a temporary one, but it could be cured they said. Thank God! I no longer felt I was drowning and alone – I had an illness. I was not going mad after all. What a relief.

Months later, when the entire recovery operation in Lockerbie had finished, Phil and I arranged to return with some of the lads we had worked with. We had all been invited to attend a memorial service which was going to take place at the newly opened Lockerbie Memorial Garden of Remembrance where all the dead from that fateful night would be honoured and remembered for future generations.

We met in the centre of town, near the school which had acted as the control centre. The police were there when we arrived and one officer came over and said, 'Lads, if you don't mind, we'd prefer you to leave your dogs in the vehicles. What they did here was outstanding, but we cannot afford the chance they might still find human remains. The difficulties that would cause would be un-imaginable. I hope you understand?'

'Bloody hell,' Phil said angrily. 'You can't mean that, officer, surely?'

'I'm truly sorry sir,' he replied firmly but kindly. 'I do mean it.'

What could we do? With heavy hearts we returned our protest-ing dogs to the cars, as if they somehow were less important than we were – as if they had no part in the memorial ceremony we had been invited to attend. The truth was though, that without them, we would not have had a role to play in the whole dreadful event that was Lockerbie. Further, it is very likely that the many human remains we did successfully locate would have remained hidden forever beneath the fuel-laced mire that was once Sherwood Crescent. Therefore, instead of laying ghosts to rest that day, the memorial service left us all feeling somewhat robbed of closure.

Chapter 12

In 1989, I received a letter from the Irish Mountain Rescue Association, inviting me to attend a seminar they were hosting in Waterford city. One of the topics to be discussed at the event was 'The effects of psychological trauma on volunteer helpers engaged in recue work', or post-traumatic stress disorder (PTSD) as it is now widely known. The letter also stated that they had invited a professor of psychiatry from Cork University who specialised in the condition. He was going to give a presentation outlining the symptoms a sufferer could expect, and also some suggestions on how to cope with them. My part in the conference was to recount what I had done in the recovery operation at Lockerbie and to touch on how, if at all, I had been affected. I saw no problem in that, and readily agreed to attend.

I went down to Waterford, taking Pepper with me and, out of force of habit, all my hill gear, just in case there was a callout. 'It was better to be looking at my gear than looking for it', as the saying goes.

As the good professor outlined in great detail the psychological and emotional symptoms one might expect to experience after an event like Lockerbie, I realised that I still had a big, big problem. Whilst the leaflet I had been given by Strathclyde and Galloway Social Services when we were leaving Lockerbie had given me some help, I now I realised that I was far worse than I had first thought. In fact, I had all the symptoms the professor was outlining. It wasn't until the early nineties, when I was studying for a Master's degree in guidance and counselling at Queen's University Belfast, that I was able to begin to confront the difficulties I had been facing.

But back in 1989 in Waterford, when it was my turn to speak, I tried to minimise the effects I was suffering. At that time I didn't want to admit any perceived weakness to these rescue peers of mine. I therefore emphasised the part played by the dogs and, in doing that, tried to deflect attention away from my psychological turmoil.

With unbelievably good timing, I was rescued from further discussion when a Garda officer poked his head into the room, excused the interruption and said that the Kerry mountain rescue team urgently needed a search dog. I left the room in relief. I could not believe my good luck, not that I wanted any ill to befall whoever the subject of the callout was.

In the hallway outside the lecture room, the Garda officer told me that a hillwalker had gone missing on Carrauntoohil and that the Kerry team were having no luck finding him. They had done what they could, but without success. They felt that a search dog was the only hope of finding him and, to speed things up, they had arranged for the Irish Air Corps to send a plane to collect me. He advised that I should get myself out to the airfield on the edge of Waterford city as quickly as I could.

I went outside to scrounge a lift from somebody and there I found my mum and dad who had just arrived, having travelled all the way from Cobh in County Cork to see me. I had no idea that they were coming to Waterford and, while I was thrilled to bits to see them, I had to leave. When I explained what had happened they insisted on driving Pepper and me to the airfield, like the great parents they had always been.

When we got there I was surprised at how small the place was – just a single runway in the middle of a very big field. The gates were closed and we were asked to wait outside. There were some Irish Air Corps people standing around and one of them came over to speak to me.

'Are you the lad who's going to Kerry?' he asked.

'Yes. Me and my dog here,' I replied, my throat dry because of my all-consuming dread of flying. Big civilian passenger jets were bad enough, but I guessed a much smaller one was going to take me to Kerry.

'A bit nervous of flying, are you?' the bloke asked innocently.

'Nervous, did you say?' I croaked. 'I'm shitting myself.'

'You'll be grand – as long as it isn't one of them vomit comets they're sending.'

'Them what?' I croaked. My anxiety meter had by then gone off the scale. He had mentioned the word vomiting. Now, in addition to my paralysing fear of flying, I also have a mortal dread of vomiting. That first came to light at age five, when I was laid low by a viral infection causing me to vomit for days.

'Excuse me,' I said, 'but what do you mean, vomit comet?'

Now I knew as soon as I had said it that I would have been better remaining in ignorance, but it was too late. My informative new friend turned, smiled and said, 'Well, let me explain it this way. The vomit comet is a small two-seater plane. It's fairly light, so it tends to go up and down a lot as it flies along like a big dipper thing at the fairground. Have you ever been on one of them?'

'No,' I replied. 'I hate the things.'

At that moment, there was a bit of a stir among the more alert spectators, then in the distance, we could all hear the very faint sound of an approaching aircraft.

'There you are,' my Job's comforter exclaimed. 'Here it comes now …' His voice tailed off in silence a second time.

'What? What?' I asked, dreading to hear what I was certain would be coming next.

'I'm afraid this is not your day. It is the vomit comet!!'

'Oh sweet Mother of God!'

I stood transfixed, mesmerised as a tiny single-engine aircraft, coloured military green, pitched and wobbled its way over the boundary fence to land with a resounding thump on the tarmac. My friend turned away and I could hear him speaking into a radio but I had no idea who he was talking to. I later found out it was to the pilot.

I lifted my gear, said goodbye to my folks and then, with Pepper bouncing along beside me, walked the very long walk to the burbling little plane. It seemed far too small to take off with two people, a dog and a large heavy rucksack. Pepper and I got in and we were soon bouncing down the runway going faster and faster, the noise deafening.

'Oh! Have you closed that door tightly?' the pilot suddenly shouted at me.

'What the hell do you mean "tightly"?' I quavered.

'You need to give that bloody thing a damn good bang otherwise it might burst open up there and we don't want that now, do we?'

'Oh my God! How do I know I've shut it tightly enough?' I asked him, beside myself with panic.

'Well just open it and wallop it shut. I'll slow down a bit to let you do it. Okay. Go on. Do it now!' he shouted, as the engine noise died a little.

So there we were, hurtling along a rural airstrip in a very small, noisy, bucking, vibrating plane, with me trying to prevent myself from falling out, opening and hauling a door shut and knowing that the pilot was about to take off. The end of the runway was getting closer at an enormous rate of knots, when suddenly the pilot pulled the joystick back hard and we swooped into the sky. We bucked and rocked and rose and sank and climbed away from the ground.

Meanwhile in the space behind me, I could see Pepper throwing himself from one side of the plane to the other trying to take in as much of the view as he could. He was really into flying, the little shit, ever since his first helicopter flight a few years before. He's just too frigging stupid to be scared, I thought to myself. The voice of the pilot came on the earphones again.

'Where are we off to then?' he asked innocently.

'Kerry,' I replied.

'Kerry. Okay. That's to the south-west somewhere, isn't it?'

I told myself that he must be taking the piss so I said, 'Yes. South-west!'

'That's over that way, isn't it?' he said, pointing to the right. I stared at him, not knowing whether to laugh or cry, looking for a smile or anything to tell me he was joking. There was nothing – just the sincere look of someone trying to get the right answer.

He nodded to himself, seemingly having reached a decision.

'Well, let's try it then,' he said, glancing at the compass. The plane banked around and seemed to slip sideways. I gripped the dashboard, or whatever it's called, with white knuckles.

'South-west it is! Here we go. How far would you say Kerry is from here ... Neil, isn't it?'

'Yes – I have no idea how far it is.'

Staring intently ahead he muttered, 'Will we get there before dark, do you think?'

'What? Listen, I haven't a bloody clue, mate.' I was nearly sick.

'Well, it's just that I am not rated for night flying, so if it gets dark before we arrive there might be a bit of a problem!'

'Oh Sweet Jesus,' I said.

'Not to worry! We'll give it a go.'

Talk about crapping the togs – I was in a bog of sweat, a sea of blind fear and just for good measure, Pepper was barking like something possessed. He was nearly deranged with excitement. What a bloody noise!

'Do you recognise any of these towns?' the pilot asked me after a few more minutes of bedlam.

'No,' I croaked.

'That one over there, look, that might be Limerick, then again it could be Cork. I'm not really sure. Oh well, let's go for Limerick!'

The thoughts whirling around my head included questions like 'Is this real? Is this happening? What sort of twits do they let fly these things?' and so on. His voice came over the headphones again, in a tone that sounded very much like relief.

'Oh yes! I think I know where we are now.'

I found myself looking desperately at him for some sign of confidence. Anything. Then reassuringly he added, 'Yes, I'm right. I'm sure that's my girlfriend's house down there. Do you see it? The one to the left with a big red shed beside it. See?' He was pointing forward and down. I didn't want to look down. I didn't give a shit about his girlfriend's bloody house, to be perfectly honest, but I heard myself answer weakly, 'Oh yes. I see it.'

'Yes, that's the one all right,' he said nodding. 'Would you mind if we sort of flew over her house just to say hello?'

Me, my wife Kate and our two daughters Clair (left) and Emma

My early mountaineering days

Me and Kim, my first search dog

Pepper on Thomas's Mountain in the Mournes

Me and Pepper on the day we returned from Lockerbie

Neill Powell with his rescue dog Pepper after their return from Scotland.

Newcastle man back after Lockerbie search

A Newcastle mountain rescue leader has just returned home after taking part in the search operation after the plane crash at Lockerbie in Scotland.

Neil Powell and his rescue dog Pepper are part of the Search and Rescue Dog Association of Ireland and were flown to Lockerbie shortly after the Pan Am 747 crashed into the town, and spent four days looking for bodies and pieces of wreckage.

Neil and Pepper, along with Andrew Mitchell and Vicki Cameron from Bushmills and their dogs Duffy and Megan, were put on standby as soon as news of the Lockerbie disaster was released.

They were called to the scene on Boxing Day when they were flown by RAF helicopter to the scene of the carnage.

The Irish team were stationed right at the heart of the crash, in the huge 20ft deep crater which was at the centre of news reports of the crash.

Neil, who is the leader of the Mourne Mountain Rescue Team, was stationed right inside the crater with instructions to look for bodies and significant pieces of wreckage.

"The dogs took about an hour to settle down, but after that they were fantastic," he said.

"Pepper even managed to find one of the victims that was buried four-and-a-half feet deep," he added.

"We also spent some time outside the crash site looking for important pieces of wreckage or personal effects which could be returned to relatives," said Neil.

Neil and Pepper have recently been selected for a new Disaster Search Unit, set up in the wake of the Armenian earthquake tragedy.

They are the only Irish pairing in the new unit which includes five other pairings from England.

It will mean that Neil and Pepper could be called on to travel to a major disaster anywhere in the world to assist in the search for survivors or look for bodies.

January 1989

My friend Phil Haigh and his dog Scherne in Glencoe, Scotland

Me and Cuisle

Cuisle searching the Glenties River, County Donegal

Cuisle helping to search Castlewellan Lake,
County Down

Cuisle training in Wales

Cuisle and Cracker

Cracker in training

Cracker off-duty

NEWCASTLE SEARCH DOG IS A REAL CRACKER!

TWO weeks after being released from six months in quarantine, Newcastle-based search and rescue dog Cracker has been shortlisted in the National Golden Bonio Dog Awards.

The life-saving five-and-a-half year-old Golden Retriever, who is owned by Neill Powell, was nominated for his work with the United Kingdom Fire Search and Rescue Team.

In the past year Cracker's involvement with the team led him to travel with Neill to the scene of the horrific Turkish earthquake last August.

During his four-day trip the hard-working dog endured searing temperatures while searching among rubble, ruins and unstable buildings for survivors.

Although the rescue attempts by Neill and his faithful companion proved to be in vain, Cracker and fellow search and rescue dog Denke were instrumental in locating around 170 bodies.

Cracker, who is one of 30 short-listed finalists for the nine different categories, was nominated for the award by Neill.

If successful Neil will collect a trophy and £250 in recognition of Cracker's work in the field of search and rescue.

And if Cracker is se-lected as the overall winner, Neil will collect a cheque for £1,000 on behalf of the hard-working Canis Specialist Dog Team member at a glittering awards ceremony in London in April.

January 1989

Cracker and his brother Dylan

With Phil Haigh and the search and rescue team
in the Hercules on our way to Turkey

Me and Cracker searching for survivors in Turkey

Visiting Cracker in quarantine after our return from Turkey

'No. Not at all,' I gasped back. I hadn't the slightest idea what he was talking about and was very close to the limit of my sanity.

'Great stuff!' he said joyfully.

In an instant, we were plunging towards the earth at a mind-numbing speed, the little plane shrieking and vibrating. In the back, bloody Pepper was yelping and woofing in a frenzy of support for what this lunatic was doing. He was almost berserk now, flinging himself from window to window, totally unaffected by the massive G-force which was driving me backwards into my seat and threatening to take my face off. It was horrific – the stuff of nightmares.

The plane was nearly on the ground, and the house threatening to come through the windscreen, when suddenly we were swooping upwards again. Now all I could see was the sky, the ever-so-slightly darkening sky. Oh God, this bastard can't fly in the dark, I remembered. Up and up we roared, 'bark, bark, bark' went Pepper. Suddenly we levelled off and everything went quiet and peaceful. Then I heard the pilot saying, 'Oh shit. I forgot! She'll be at Mass now. She's not at home at all. I'm a silly prick! Look – that's her chapel over there. Would you mind if we just say hello to her again? I know she'd love that.'

There was no time to answer as suddenly we were at it again, diving straight for the ground!

'Oh, fuck me pink, I'm going to puke!' I roared over the horrendous noise of the engine and the insane barking of Pepper. Then in a voice of whining supplication, 'Not again!! Oh dear sweet Jesus! I'll never sin again. Please let this stop!! Please!!!'

The downward plunge came to an abrupt end as we violently changed direction and rollercoasted heavenwards again. I was a gibbering wreck.

'That'll please her for sure,' he shouted in triumph, and then, 'Now where the fuck do we go from here?' He looked this way and that and announced, 'That's the way. Yes. That's it, I'm sure,' pointing somewhere into the gathering darkness.

The darkness. Oh my God! As if reading my mind he chirped up, 'How much daylight do you think we have left, young Neil?'

'I– I– I– I– I don't know. Maybe twenty minutes or so.'

'That might just about do it.' He seemed relieved again. 'I

wonder how much further Kerry is? Ah well. Can't stay up here all night wondering about shit like that, now can we?'

'No,' I heard myself say. 'No! You're right.'

He let out a roar and shouted, 'There!! Do you see it? Over there! I'm sure that's Kerry airfield. Will we give it a lash?' he asked, a big stupid smile all over his face.

'Yes please! Let's do that,' I said, praying for the nightmare to end.

And then we were landing.

As we taxied to the control tower, I read the sign announcing 'Kerry airport'. 'We made it then, Neil,' says he. 'Now all I have to do is find my way back to Dublin ... any suggestions?' I had been well and truly stitched up. What's more, he knew I knew. I staggered from the plane, Pepper leaping reluctantly after me. I shut the door and, as suddenly as we had arrived, the little vomit comet was off, lifting into the darkening sky. No night-flying rating indeed.

Chapter 13

Mountaineering and hillwalking are high-risk sports in which participants confront many challenges, such as sudden and dramatic weather changes and terrifyingly steep slopes. Climbers offset such risks against the sweet sensation of isolation and peace that they feel at the top of the highest summit, and the unique sounds and scents of the upland wild places that they experience.

However, when things do go awry for a mountaineer, particularly one who is climbing alone, disastrous consequences may follow. A simple slip on exposed ground can cause him or her to fall many hundreds of feet. A twisted ankle or, worse, a broken leg can render the descent from the mountain a truly daunting prospect, if not an impossible one. Low cloud or darkness and driving rain or snow can disorientate even the most experienced climber and lead to calamity. Therefore, on Carrauntoohil, the highest mountain in Ireland, the solo mountaineer is tested to the limit and runs a very high risk of serious injury or death.

However, when I walked towards the lights of the terminal building that night, as well as being overwhelmed by relief at having arrived in one piece, I was full of optimism about the possible outcome of this latest search. My optimism only increased when I was met just outside the doors by the Kerry mountain rescue team leader, in the form of a six-foot-something, long-haired, bearded, loud and cheery giant of a man called Con Moriarty.

'Young Powell!' he boomed.

'Con Moriarty!' I shouted back, delighted to see him.

'Did you enjoy your flight?' he asked, almost too casually. I wondered just how much he actually knew. He led me through the terminal to the outside car park.

'Jump in, jump in,' he said, pointing to the four-wheel-drive vehicle, emblazoned with the legend, 'Kerry mountain rescue team'. We drove directly to their base, where a cup of tea (with something else added) helped soothe my shattered nerves.

'Well now,' Con said pointing to a map of the area, 'what we've got is a German walker who is missing, about twelve hours. It's believed he was going to the summit of Carrauntoohil but there's been no sign of him since. We've had search teams out, but they've all drawn a blank. It's probably a job for the dog.'

We worked out a search plan for first light and I was assigned Pat Falvey – a very experienced team member – as my guide. Pat was a Mount Everest summit hopeful, an ambition he was to realise years later in 1995, when he completed a successful ascent.

Early next morning, we drove to Cronin's Yard, the car park everyone uses when going up the Hag's Glen, the gateway to Carrauntoohil. We had hardly locked the vehicle when Pat marched off at a blistering speed, one which until now I thought could only have been achieved on a bike.

Desperately I shouted at him, 'For God's sake, Pat, would you ever slow down? I'm dying here and you're getting in Pepper's way!'

He dropped back, smiling and apologising, and matched his pace to mine. He had never worked with a search dog before so I explained to him that Pepper, and all mountain search dogs for that matter, were trained to search for human scent upwind, and today I wanted that person to be the missing man, not Pat Falvey. He had to stay downwind of the dog if Pep was to have any chance of success.

It wasn't long before we had slipped into a much more efficient search routine, with Pepper staying out in front while Pat walked to my right and slightly behind. We made good time to the base of the Devil's Ladder, a steep gully filled with loose scree and boulders, which led to the summit of the mountain. Pushing Pepper ahead, we made our way up the gully and after what seemed an age, we arrived at the top, shrouded in mist.

Pat, who knew the area like the back of his hand, led upwards towards Carrauntoohil's summit, while I sent Pepper over the steep ground to one side, to search the ledges and fissures we could not reach. Being light and agile, he had no difficulty in the work, but in the taxing wind conditions it was futile. He was unable to find any trace of the man.

We spent a couple of hours searching the steep ground, but still without success. It was time to go back. Pat radioed to Con and told him that we were returning to base and had as yet found no trace of the missing man. Seemingly, everyone else had also drawn a blank.

Back at base I was amazed to hear how much ground the rest of the team had covered, but it was like looking for a needle in a haystack. I suggested asking for help from the search dog handlers in north Wales. Con rang them but was told that as no helicopter was available, they were going to have to travel by road and ferry, and that was going to take a day and a half. Things were not looking good for the overdue mountaineer and a growing sense of unease was starting to prevail. Everyone was feeling a bit down, never a good thing in this sort of work. There has to be clear thinking and, wherever possible, a bit of humour lightens the load. As it happened, that was provided by Con the next day, with me as the butt.

Early in the morning, he, Pepper and I were directed to search on the right-hand side of the Hag's Glen. This is a steep area well above the approach path which Pat and I had searched the day before. For a while we climbed higher and higher and all was well. Finally we reached the narrow pinnacle so quaintly named the Hag's Tooth. From there, a narrow jagged spur curves around to join Carrauntoohil itself.

As we got ready to traverse this very steep ridge, my good friend Con said, 'Now Powell, for fuck's sake watch your step up here! If you slip you're dead. Got it?'

'Pardon?' I said. 'Here, Moriarty, wait a minute! What did you just say?'

But Con was already striding away in front and tossing some other gems carelessly over his shoulder. 'We are going to circle round and onto the upper slopes of Carrauntoohil and, from there, we'll make our way over to the mountain rescue shelter.'

'Here Con … hang on a second …' I said but, ignoring me completely, he launched into a lengthy description of the mountain refuge we were heading for.

'The shelter is actually a water tank which was airlifted into position a few years ago by helicopter. It's hidden under sods of turf, so you would hardly know it was there. Some of the 'tree huggers' objected to it, but what do they know,' he spat disdainfully.

As he was prattling away, I noticed that we were getting on to some very, very, very steep ground. In fact it was so steep that when I stopped to have a good look, the sight made me freeze solid, petrified with fear. The path we were on, which had started as fairly steep section of grass-covered mountain, had become an almost vertical wall. So between my feet was a vertical slope of grass and heather, dropping straight down to the valley floor, a thousand feet below. Suddenly, my legs refused to work and my stomach started turning somersaults. I had very quickly come to the verge of a complete nervous breakdown.

'Con!' I quavered. 'Con – I'm stuck!'

He looked back. 'What the fuck do you mean you're stuck?'

'I can't move! Can't you bloody see, you crazy bastard?'

'What the hell's the matter with you? Come on, man. We haven't got all bloody day.'

'Stop, for fuck's sake. Haven't you noticed that bloody great drop down there?' I shrieked.

'Oh that – don't worry about it. Come on, follow where I walk. Just don't fucking trip or you won't stop till you get to the bottom!'

'Oh my sweet Jesus! That is just what I need to hear,' I whispered.

With growing exasperation he said through clenched teeth, 'Look, Powell, will you get a bloody move on? We can't bloody stand here all day! Look at bloody Pepper. He's all right.'

'He doesn't have any imagination. I fucking do! For fuck's sake! I can't move my legs!' I said.

'Bloody amateurs!' he grunted, making his way back towards me.

'Look, Powell, you bastard! I'm now going to walk directly below you, right? I'll keep pace with you here, so, if you fall you're

96

going to take me with you. Now let's fucking walk along the path or I'll get on the radio and let them all know that Powell, the great mountain rescue dog guy from the north, is shitting a brick and can't move!'

Oh God, what a choice – to die by falling off, or to die of shame. I took one faltering step forward, my eyes tightly shut. I opened them and took another step and then another, inching across the yawning chasm, with Con keeping pace right below me. Pepper, meanwhile, carried on searching as though he was on a football pitch. Lack of imagination – that was his bloody trouble.

An eternity passed and we finally made it to the mountain rescue hut, where some of the team were already waiting for us. I collapsed in a heap beside Pat, my guardian from the night before.

'Pat,' I gasped, 'that Moriarty is a raving lunatic!'

'Yes. We all know that,' he said proudly.

'Have you any idea what the bastard just took me across?'

'My God, Neil, if you thought that was bad, wait till you see the next bit. You're going to love it.'

'What?' I whimpered.

'Well, let me put it this way – the escape route from here to the valley floor is not exactly flat!'

How right he was, and while we did eventually make it down without any mishap, I can safely say that that day was truly one of the most horrendous mountaineering experiences of my life.

As for the missing walker, he was found seven weeks later in a gully on the east face of Carrauntoohil. It was thought that he had fallen during his descent, due to a bad choice of route, and died where he landed. Only his skeleton remained, the poor man.

While all mountain rescuers and search dog handlers know that, on occasion, they will fail to reach a casualty in time, it is still difficult to deal with an unsuccessful search when it happens. Questions abound. Were we searching in the wrong place at the wrong time? Could we have got there sooner? Was the weather really that bad?

Chapter 14

On 12 April 1989, on a typical humdrum day in Warrenpoint, a bomb exploded in the town. I was teaching at St Mark's as usual, and we heard the explosion in the school as a dull thump. A few minutes later, the phone outside my classroom door started ringing urgently. When I answered it, one of the secretaries in the office said the police in Newcastle wanted to speak to me urgently. It was Willy Brown, a sergeant who worked a lot with the mountain rescue team as a liaison officer. He was a very good man who we all liked. He said, 'Neil, you've probably heard the explosion. There's been a bomb in Warrenpoint. Can you get your dog and go and help please? We believe there might be some people missing after the blast. An elderly lady was seen going into the hardware shop but has not been seen since.' He went on to tell me that the bomb had been intended for the police station in Warrenpoint but that the bombers couldn't get any closer than the hardware shop next door. They planted the bomb but didn't give enough warning for people to evacuate in time.

I told him I'd be there as quickly as I could. My problem then was how to get Pepper from home – twenty miles away in Newcastle – to Warrenpoint. I rang Michael Curran, a friend of mine who worked and lived in Newcastle. He was in the mountain rescue team and was quite familiar with getting unexpected phone calls, asking him to 'drop everything and run'. He hadn't heard about the bomb, so I filled him in and, as ever, he was only too willing to help. Pepper knew Michael well so I knew that Pepper would be willing to go with him.

Next I had to get permission from the school principal, Hugh MacNamara, to leave my classes. When I got to his office, he was staring out of his window in shock as the huge plume of black smoke rose slowly above the town. Hugh was well known for the quiet work he did within the community and this was an attack on those very people he had grown to love.

'Boss, that was the police asking me to go to the bombsite with my dog. They're afraid some people might have been buried in the rubble. Can you let me go?'

'Sure, Neil. I'll get your classes covered for you,' he said without hesitation and reached for the phone.

As I turned to go, one of the secretaries came into the office, a look of distress on her face.

'Mr MacNamara, it's about Paul Reilly. It's his daughter Joanne. She works in the hardware shop's office in the town. He's worried sick and wants to go down to look for her,' she sobbed. Paul was our much loved and valued school caretaker and Joanne had been a pupil at the school until a couple of years ago. She was a quiet, well-behaved girl, loved by all. 'Oh my God. Bring him in,' he said. I turned to go, thinking, 'I can't be here when Paul comes in.' The boss wished me luck and I left.

When I got downtown, there were police and fire personnel everywhere. Smoke and dust filled the air and partly obscured the shattered remains of a once-thriving family business. Sirens of approaching ambulances added to the sense of devastation and the blue flashing lights of the fire engines focused everyone's attention on the horror of what had been done in the name of Ireland. I watched as the fire brigade tried dousing the flames.

A police inspector who I knew waved me over to where he was talking to Jacky Kennedy, the area fire brigade commander. He asked where my dog was. 'He'll be here shortly, Inspector. Michael Curran is bringing him for me.' The inspector knew Michael well from his association with the mountain rescue team as another police liaison officer. 'Good. As soon as he arrives bring him over. We have at least one person unaccounted for. She's an elderly lady who was supposed to have been there when it went off. She may well have got out but we don't know.'

'What about the wee girl in the office?' I asked, knowing in my heart what the answer was going to be.

'I'm sorry to say that she was killed outright. She was in the office right beside the explosion. She never knew what hit her, poor kid. Did you know her?'

'Yes, I used to teach her. Her dad is our school caretaker. This'll kill him.'

Just then a policeman excused himself to the inspector and said that Michael had arrived with Pepper. Michael, gracious as ever, said he would hang around in case we needed anything else and then moved away to stand outside the cordon.

As I was getting ready to search the building, or what was left of it, Jacky said, 'Right, Neil, here's what I want you to do. You'll need to crawl through that hole under the rubble right over there. See it?'

I nodded. I found myself staring at the place. I have always had a real fear of small confined spaces but how could I admit that now?

'Now, when you get inside, have a good hunt about. Hang on … are you not happy about this?' he asked, immediately sensing my anxiety.

'Well, I suffer a bit from claustrophobia, Jacky,' I replied weakly.

'No problem. I'll go in first and you come in after me. Okay?'

'Okay,' I agreed, feeling thoroughly ashamed. Jacky Kennedy, the boss of the local fire brigade, was going to crawl in under the rubble with me.

The firemen were playing water on the smouldering ruins. I waited as Jacky pushed himself into the dark recess of what was left of the hardware store. Above him hung all this loose building material, teetering on the verge of crashing to the ground. I squeezed in behind him.

We were in a small space about ten feet wide and about four feet high. It was hot and very smoky. In the far corner was another opening and what looked like a plank of wood disappearing deeper under the rubble. Water from the firemen's hoses was dripping down and soaking us. Pepper was not too happy.

'Can you ask them to stop spraying the water for a while?' I asked.

'Turn off the water, lads,' he shouted, 'but keep a close eye on things until we come out.'

Pepper began to nose about the small space, checking for signs of life. I sent him to the other opening I'd noticed when we came in. 'Find him, Pep,' I said. In he went and we could hear him searching around deep inside the rubble. After a minute or two, he emerged and just stared at me as though saying, 'Nothing there.'

'Right, Neil. Let's get out of here then.'

We were both covered in dust, pouring with sweat and soaking wet from the water as we came out. 'Can you now check over the far side, Neil,' Jacky asked. 'Just make sure it's clear will you?'

I found a plank of wood to let Pepper cross the rubble which was full of glass and jagged edges. Two of the fire brigade members held it steady as Pepper walked across. He went all the way to the end, checking as he went, then turned and came back again, still sniffing to left and right. I knew from his behaviour that there were no other bodies buried. 'That's clear, lads,' I was able to tell them.

We then turned our attention towards the Portakabin which had been the office where Joanne had been working. I sent Pepper to search for … well, just to search for whatever he could find. Pepper had been in a similar situation in Lockerbie so he would know what he was looking for when he found it.

He worked slowly through the debris, inch by inch. He stopped, stared at the ground, looked up at me and back again to whatever he had found. I made my way over to him and when I saw what it was, I knew that the body of Joanne would now be complete. I called quietly to one of the fire brigade men. Our job was over.

I went back to the school in an awful state. I found the boss and told him what I had seen and what we had found. Hugh knew all the kids in school by name, including those who had long since left school. He knew Joanne well and was badly shaken by the completely pointless loss of her innocent life.

Paul came in to the office and quietly and with great dignity asked, 'Did you find our Joanne, Mr Powell?'

'Yes Paul, we found her,' I answered.

'Was she all there?' he said. What a dreadful question for any father to have to ask.

'Yes, Paul,' I answered him truthfully. 'She was all there.'

'Thanks, Mr Powell,' he said and turned away, broken and totally devastated.

Chapter 15

Mick McCarthy – a dog handler friend from Cork – had a cracking German shepherd bitch. When she finally produced puppies, one of them was kept for me. I decided to call him Cuisle (which means 'loved one' in Irish) because I had long wanted a sort of reminder of Kim, and harboured a longing to train another German shepherd in search and rescue – they are such proud, regal dogs and a very challenging breed, as I had already discovered with Mac.

Now Pepper, you will remember, hated all other dogs and so bringing little Cuisle home was going to be challenging at the very least. I decided the only way to deal with the situation was to plonk the pup down in front of Pepper and see what happened. Pepper was astonished to see me do such a thing and stood back in shock, staring at Cuisle in disbelief, every fibre demanding, 'Who the *hell* are you?' Recognising a fellow member of the dog world, Cuisle made a playful charge at Pepper. That was way too much and an outraged Pepper scarpered behind the settee. Cuisle lost interest at that point and busied himself in making fake charges at more interesting things.

Slowly, Pepper reappeared, nose first, cautiously eyeing the intruder from a safe distance. Very slowly, he advanced from his hiding place, fixing the little pup with a glassy stare. Quivering and quite rigid, he allowed Cuisle to move closer, all the while glaring haughtily at him, his tail arched menacingly. He sniffed a little more, strutted a little more, circled a little more and then went into a play bow. Young Cuisle, reading the signs perfectly, yelped with excitement and charged, launching himself at the waiting Pepper. He had passed the test. Pepper seemed satisfied that Cuisle was no immediate danger to him or to us.

From that moment, they never looked back and the bond between them grew, as indeed did Cuisle. He was soon towering over Pepper. It was my firm ambition to train him as a mountain search dog like Kim and for a while all went well. But then one fateful day on the mountain, he met his first sheep and it all went tits up. Cuisle squared himself, stared at the sheep and started to creep forward, body slung low to the ground as he prepared to charge. I stepped in and bellowed, 'Leave it!' The sheep bolted and Cuisle hesitated for a fraction, uncertain whether to ignore or to obey. He stared at the retreating figure of the surprisingly nimble ewe and then, most reluctantly, turned and came back.

Having been in that position before with Mac, I just gave up. And so Cuisle's mountain rescue career ended that day. I was devastated. What was I going to do with him now? As if the sheep thing were not bad enough, he had also begun to display another character flaw. He had a tendency to intensely dislike certain people. Not all people, just certain people. He could even suddenly turn against people whom he had accepted before.

Despite my best efforts at socialisation and good leadership, he seemed to get worse. Trying to rationalise this behaviour, I wondered if it had anything to do with his having been taken away from his mum and litter mates at the very early age of six weeks. I wasn't sure then, although today I am certain that such early separation is not a healthy thing. My new priority therefore was to find some way of getting the best from Cuisle as a search dog while not putting the general public or any sheep at risk – a seemingly impossible task.

The answer eventually came from a most unexpected quarter. In 1991, I was invited to attend the very first international symposium on search and rescue dogs. It was hosted by the Swedish working dog club in Stockholm. Delegates attended from all over the world and part of the organisers' remit was to create the very first international search and rescue dog committee, known as the IRO (International Rescue Dog Organisation). The new committee invited me to become the UK's representative – much to the chagrin of some members of SARDA (England) when they heard about my appointment weeks later. I was then chucked out of my new post. Ah well, it was sweet while it lasted.

Anyway, among many other fascinating items at the symposium was a unique demonstration by a Swedish special forces officer, Lieutenant John Sjoberg, and his Australian kelpie, Sampo. The announcer informed us that John had trained Sampo to search from a boat for unwelcome underwater visitors to Sweden. We were told that Russian military personnel frequently attempted to infiltrate the Swedish archipelago on spying missions. Sampo had been trained to alert John and his colleagues to the underwater presence of these personnel by barking when he picked up their scent, emanating from beneath the water. But everyone knew that scent couldn't come from the water … didn't they? I was hooked.

I watched in astonishment as, with Sampo standing at the front of a flat-bottomed metal boat powered by two large outboard engines, John skimmed across the waters. He was searching for a diver who had previously hidden himself beneath the waves. Staring at the water as the boat zipped along, Sampo suddenly began barking, indicating to John that he had found the diver. The boat stopped and John revved the engine. This, it transpired, was a signal to the underwater swimmer that he had been located. We watched spellbound as bubbles came to the surface, closely followed by the masked face of a diver. He was lurking no more than six feet from where the boat had stopped. It was a stunning demonstration.

Inspired by what I had witnessed, I made up my mind there and then that I would have to meet John to try to learn more about this unique use of a dog's nose. Perhaps it was something that I could train Cuisle to do. I spoke to one of the symposium leaders who kindly contacted John for me and arranged the meeting. At the appointed time, I found him sitting outside a military tent, cleaning stainless steel containers which were used to hold dead piglets. Piglets, he explained, were the scent source used to train Sampo because pig tissue is biologically very close to human tissue.

John was a very softly spoken, gentle man, completely at odds with what one might have expected from a special forces officer. We exchanged phone numbers and addresses with a view to keeping in close touch so that I could learn more about his methods, of which more later.

Chapter 16

In the summer of 1992 I was in Cork with Pepper, staying with my parents and doing some training with Mick McCarthy, when Sean Rodgers from Donegal contacted me – he had tried me at home and Kate had given him my parents' number. Sean was the leader of Killybegs cliff and coastal rescue team and was firmly behind the use of search dogs when necessary. He asked if I could help in a search for an eleven-year-old child who had been missing for over thirty-six hours.

Apparently, the child had been part of a scout group from Germany. They had been hiking on a mountain called Slieve League on the coast of Donegal, the first stop for any Atlantic storm sweeping in from the west. The area has the biggest sea cliffs in Europe and is notorious for its bad weather. Somehow the eleven-year-old had become separated from his group when heavy rain started falling. The search teams had been out since lunchtime the day before, including Sean's Killybegs-based team, the Air Corps, the Civil Defence, mountain rescue teams and dozens of local people. 'Bloody brilliant,' I thought. 'Call for the dogs when all else has failed.' But what I said was, 'I'll be there, Sean, but it'll take hours by road from here. I'm down in Cobh.'

'I know,' he said. 'Look, I'll get on to the Air Corps and try to get them to fly you up. Hold on and I'll ring you back.'

'Sean, can I bring another dog and handler up with me as well?' I asked.

'Who is he?' he asked cautiously.

'He's called Mick McCarthy and his dog's called Dex. I trained them a couple of years ago, so they are part of SARDA.'

'If you say they're all right. Bring them along. I'll get back to you in a while.'

While I was waiting, I called Mick, gave him the brief and asked if he wanted to go. 'When and where?' he asked.

I explained that I was waiting for Sean to pull some stunt with the Air Corps and I suggested he get his gear together and wait for my next call.

About thirty minutes later, Sean rang back and asked me to get to Cork airport as quick as I could. He had managed to get us a lift in a very posh aircraft owned by the Irish Air Corps. He said I'd like this one because it was normally used for ferrying big shots from the Irish government to meetings in Europe. 'My God, Sean, we're not that important,' I said.

'Quick as you can, Neil … ' Click. He had hung up.

I got my gear, loaded Pep into the car and my dad drove us to the airport. Mick, who lived in Cork city, was waiting for me with Dex, his big gentle German shepherd. Pepper disliked Dex just as much as he hated all the other dogs in the world. He grumbled and stared daggers at him as we were taken out to the aircraft in a van. Thank God, Dex remained aloof, towering head and shoulders over Pepper and avoiding eye contact. Pep, of course, was livid but must have realised he would have no hope against this battle-scarred monster. He didn't push it but I had no doubt that the little shit was just biding his time.

Apart from the crew, we were the only passengers. We were politely shown to our seats by a smiling Air Corps sergeant who said, 'Well now, lads, you must be nearly as important as the president of Ireland herself to get this sort of treatment.' The pilot must have been given immediate clearance because in seconds we were hurtling down the runway and soaring skywards. We left the bright lights of Cork behind and turned north.

In what felt like an instant, we were descending again and we landed in the dark in an airfield somewhere up in north-west Donegal. A helicopter was waiting to fly us direct to the search area at the base of Slieve League. In ten minutes we had landed again and were met by the Garda. They drove us to a remote farmhouse which had become the operational base. A crowd of locals and members of rescue teams from all over Ireland were standing around expectantly. Those at the front moved aside and Sean Rodgers materialised from the dark. We shook hands and I introduced him to Mick and Dex. 'Good of you to come, lads. Welcome. C'mon with me to the ops room.'

Formalities over, he then took us to the room from which the whole search operation was being controlled. It was abuzz with activity, with maps spread out on the table or pinned to the walls, radio messages coming and going and, on a side table, a huge pile of sandwiches. We met the senior Garda officer and then Mrs Byrne, the lovely lady who owned the farmhouse. With typical Donegal hospitality, she had thrown her doors open to the teams and everyone else involved in the search. She sat and listened as Sean told us everything they had done to date. On the map we were shown the place where the young boy had disappeared. Sean said that since then there had been low clouds and heavy rain, driven in from the Atlantic by the strong south-westerly gales. His briefing went into great depth, detailing all the areas his team and the others had been searching. The Air Corps helicopter had been flown to its limits all over the area. Unfortunately the crew was unable to do as much as they would have liked because of the very poor weather.

Sean said that everyone was now extremely anxious about the child and that his survival was dependent on his being found over the next three or four hours. There was a hint of pessimism creeping into Sean's voice. Nevertheless, ever the professional, he suggested that the best use of the dogs would be to work them over the same ground as the teams had searched. That was where he was convinced the boy would be found.

Mick and I studied the map for a while and decided to split the search into an upper and lower section, with me and Pepper covering the low part and Mick and Dex covering the upper area. The rationale for this was that Pepper, being a Border Collie and younger than Dex, would be much quicker at clearing the extensive lower slopes. Dex would be better at searching the more confined gullies and steep ground. I suggested making Pepper overlap the top of his section with the bottom of Dex's area, which would mean we could then be fairly sure that the whole area had been thoroughly gone over.

When we set off it was close to midnight and the weather had improved significantly – the wind had dropped and the rain had subsided to a steady drizzle. Night-time is always the best time for getting the most from air-scenting dogs. The conditions seem to favour the transmission of scent and the dogs themselves always appear more alert and keen to work, at least in my experience.

Over the next couple of hours, both dogs worked hard and the overlap system made us feel confident that they had missed nothing. One more hour of hard slog over the heather-clad hillside and we decided to make our way back to the farmhouse for a break and a re-think of the search plan. We got back at around 4 a.m. and found that Sean was still out with his team. Mrs Byrne, however, was there to welcome us again. I could not help marvelling at her goodness. By then, she must have been on the go for more than forty hours …

We sat in the kitchen and, as she plied us with more tea and sandwiches, we described where we had searched. Obviously she knew the mountain like the back of her hand, so she was able to visualise what we described. She listened closely and then, having been deep in thought, said, 'I think, if you go about half a mile further over, that's where he'll be.'

'What makes you think that?' I asked.

'I just have a feeling that's where he is. I don't know why,' she said shrugging her shoulders.

We only had about an hour of darkness left and Mick and I were well aware that once first light came the mountain would be teeming with searchers. That was good in one sense but, as far as Pepper and Dex were concerned, it would render their unique scenting ability redundant: the air would be full of human scent and the dogs would be confused. Mountain search dogs are trained to search for human scent upwind of them and are unable to discriminate one person from another. Thus, other human searchers and the missing person are indistinguishable. For any chance of success, we had to get back out on the hill right away. Thanking our wonderful host yet again, we steamed off to search the area she had suggested.

Thirty minutes later, we had made our way to the start of the new search area, where we split up and sent the dogs off. Dawn was breaking. I sent Pepper a long way down slope from where I was standing, and I could see from his behaviour that the youngster was definitely not down there. Looking up slope, I watched as Dex carefully crossed a gully and, when he had reached the far side, turned and made his way back. On the radio, Mick suggested I put Pepper up to the same place, because he was not happy about what Dex had done. I whistled to Pepper, pointing upwards and, quick as ever to obey, he climbed to where Dex had been.

He carried on going across the slope for about another hundred metres, then, suddenly, he stopped. He was looking at something on the ground. He looked back towards me, gave a bark and then began running down the slope.

'Fuck me! That looks like a find,' I shouted to Mick, who was much closer now.

Pepper arrived and started dancing and barking with excitement.

'Show me, Pep,' I shouted, feeling just as elated as Pepper. He turned, ran straight back up to the high point and then stopped beside what looked like a narrow trench cut into the side of the hill. Gasping from the exertion of running after him, I stopped, my chest heaving as I gulped in air. Pepper was staring into the narrow slit in the hillside. Then he began barking again and spinning in circles.

I ran over, hoping to God that we had found the kid, but when I arrived and looked down, all I could see was a sheet of green tarpaulin stretched across the length of the narrow trench. I was devastated. I had been sure that Pepper had made a find. The tarpaulin looked as though it might have been blown there or possibly dumped by somebody. However, training takes over at a time like that and, just to be sure, I lifted a corner of the tarpaulin to check beneath it. There inside was a little blonde-haired boy, and he was still alive!

White-faced, he peered up at me as if he were seeing a ghost. He said something in German, which I didn't understand, but there was no doubting his elation at seeing us. 'Good lad, Pep! Good lad!'

I shouted at Pepper and then asked the youngster if he was okay.

'Yes, thank you,' he said weakly. 'Thank you for coming. I have been here a long time. I heard a helicopter yesterday and I waved but it didn't see me. I heard people walking by and I called, but they didn't hear me either,' he whimpered.

'Well you're going home now,' I said.

'Mick! We have him!' I shouted. 'He's here! He's alive!'

'Yesssss!' he shouted back. 'Oh yes!'

Mick climbed up to where we were, fished in his pack and brought out a flask of tea. The youngster drank it eagerly and fairly wolfed down the bar of chocolate we offered him.

Given that all he had been wearing were those lederhosen things and a light summer top, it was a miracle that he had survived at all. The piece of green tarpaulin – an emergency shelter he had carried in his rucksack – had undoubtedly saved his life. That and the fact that he had had the wit to get into the trench out of the wind.

We radioed base, told them the good news and gave them our position. All we had to do then was keep the youngster warm and wait for the teams to arrive to carry him down, but he seemed embarrassed and wanted to walk out himself. We advised him not to, but he was adamant. He struggled to a standing position, took a couple of steps, stumbled and nearly fell over. We persuaded him to wait for the stretcher.

In about an hour, the Killybegs team members arrived and wrapped the protesting eleven-year-old in a casualty blanket. They secured him, still protesting, to the stretcher, ready to be evacuated to the roadside below. In all, he was about three-quarters of a mile from the road and when we arrived there, he was greeted by a waiting crowd of locals and rescue team members. His mates were there too and they crowded around, clearly overjoyed to have him back safe and well. They clapped and cheered him for his bravery, which may have helped soften the poor kid's obvious mortification. The cheers continued long after he was driven off to hospital where his parents, recently arrived from Germany, were waiting. It was a brilliant result and I was so proud of our two dogs and especially of Pepper.

We got a lift back to the farmhouse-cum-operations base with Sean and, true to form, there again was Mrs Byrne, the good lady of the house, as welcoming as ever. It was her unwavering conviction that directed our search efforts to the place where we finally located the child. She was ecstatic and the help she gave us is something she should be proud of for the rest of her life. The only thing left to do, then, was for Mick and me to find a way to get back to Cork. We spoke to Sean who arranged to have us driven by the Garda to Dublin airport. He also arranged for us to join a scheduled flight back to Cork.

Chapter 17

1994 was a significant year for me and for my work with search dogs for three reasons. I had been ferreting around for some time trying to locate a really good working strain golden retriever pup, but without success. Then in April, completely out of the blue, Nikki Reece, an English breeder of top-class, working-strain golden retrievers rang to offer me just such a pup. Her champion bitch, she said, had produced a litter. 'Two of them are really classy males, Neil. One's darker than the other, always poking into things, whereas his brother just wants to be cuddled. I think you should have the dark one. But you make your own mind up when you see them.'

Now Pete Brown – a friend whom I had first met through climbing, and who had become a trainee search dog handler in the early nineties – and I had been talking for ages about getting a retriever pup each because they seemed to have lovely temperaments. I was straight on the phone to him and we arranged to go over to collect the two brothers as soon as it suited Nikki. When we met her near Stranraer, she pointed to the two tiny golden bodies, curled up together on the back seat of her car, fast asleep. For all of us, it was love at first sight and straight away Kate, who had also come, decided to call mine, the darker of the two, Cracker. Pete chose the name Dylan for his little chap.

We became so wrapped up in the two pups, yawning and stretching and shooting out tiny pink tongues, that I hardly remember saying goodbye to Nikki. The journey back home was euphoric and the future seemed to be golden retrievers. Indeed, little did I know just how magnificent those two little pups would prove to be.

But 1994 was also the year which marked the opening of a totally new chapter in my own work with search dogs. In May, John Sjoberg came to Ireland and spent a week here, refining the training I had been doing for the previous two years with Cuisle. On the last day, he set up a formal assessment to test our ability to locate drowned victims. We passed, so Cuisle became the first drowned victim search dog in the UK and Ireland. Though I would later realise that the difficulties and prejudice I had experienced as a mountain rescue dog handler would be equalled if not surpassed by the opposition I encountered to the concept of a drowned victim search dog.

On 29 December 1994, only months after Cuisle had qualified as a drowned victim search dog, the coastguard asked for his help in a search for two men whose boat had sunk in Strangford Lough. Six friends had been visiting a bar to celebrate the end of the holidays and, while they were returning to Kircubbin on the other side of the lough, their boat's engine cut out. They tried to throw out an anchor but the boat capsized and sank. One of the men managed to use his mobile phone to alert his family to what had happened.

They began swimming towards Trasnagh island which was about a mile away but only one of them managed to make it – he was later picked up by helicopter. Later still, three other bodies were located but at the time we were contacted two of the party were still missing. I asked my friend and SARDA colleague Martin Bell to bring Judy, his new mountain search dog, to help with the search.

When we arrived at Strangford Yacht Club in Killinchy, Martin and I were taken straight down to the new Portaferry in-shore lifeboat, which was waiting at the slip. The plan was that the lifeboat would first ferry him and Judy out to Trasnagh island, where he was to check the whole island and its shoreline for any sign of the two missing men. The boat would then be used to let Cuisle search the waters between the point where the boat had sunk and the shoreline at Killinchy. Assuming the men had indeed drowned, then it was hoped that Cuisle would be able to locate their bodies.

Having put Martin and Judy ashore, the coxswain navigated out over the dark waters of the lough, criss-crossing the area slowly.

Cuisle perched himself on the bow, twisting his head from one side to the other as he scanned the waters for traces of scent from the men.

An hour passed when, suddenly, Cuisle began to bark. Then just as quickly, he stopped and silently hung most of his body out over the front of the boat, staring intently at the water. He seemed to want to satisfy himself that he had made a find. He began to bark again. We were close inshore by that time. 'What do you think?' the cox asked me.

'Well it looks like he's found one of them,' I said. The coxswain reported our position to base, giving the longitude and latitude where Cuisle had made a positive indication.

At dawn, we returned to the island to pick up Martin and Judy. Unfortunately, they had had no success, but there was still hope that one or even both of the men might still be found drifting alive somewhere. The wind was blowing on-shore, so Martin offered to keep searching from the beach with Judy. The boat brought them to the slipway and they were dropped off to carry on while we collected a waiting civilian diver and went back to the place where Cuisle had been barking.

As we nosed slowly into the area, the diver, looked over the side and muttered glumly, 'How the hell am I going to find anybody in this shit? It's full of seaweed.'

The boat stopped, the coxswain cut the engines and the diver slipped over the side. After a brief thumbs up, he sank beneath the surface in a welter of bubbles and disappeared into the waving kelp. It seemed an age before he reappeared. He took out his mouthpiece and called up, 'It's far worse than I thought. Even if he was down there, it's impossible to see more than a foot in front!' He was hauled back into the boat and the coxswain reported a negative result.

Later that morning, when Cuisle, Martin, Judy and I had gone home, a member of the public, walking along the shore, saw a body floating in the seaweed very close to the point where Cuisle had been barking. One of the missing men had been located. Eventually the other body was found too, and a very sad chapter in Strangford Lough's history was closed.

Weeks later, relatives of the drowned men and all the people who live in villages around the lough held a massive fund-raising drive for our search dogs. From the proceeds we were able to buy a brand new 5.8-metre rigid inflatable boat. (Up to then we had been using a loaned rubber dinghy of indeterminate age and many leaks.) To add to this great act of kindness, Lough Neagh Rescue, a privately funded lifeboat group based on the shores of Lough Neagh, also helped us. They provided the new boat with an outboard engine, radio and echo sounder, and gave us free RYA training in powerboat handling.

However, completely overshadowing Cracker's arrival and Cuisle's new career was the very rapid decline in health of Pepper, my little black-and-white warrior. I had retired him from mountain rescue, much to his annoyance, because he just couldn't cope with it any more. Whilst he still had the heart of a lion, Pepper's health had, unknown to me, deteriorated rapidly. I had absolutely no idea just how ill he had become until we made a visit to the vet to get to the bottom of a persistent cough he had developed.

Gilbert McKnight was Pepper's favourite vet. And so it fell to Gilbert to conduct a series of tests on Pepper before being able to confirm the diagnosis he had suspected. Pepper had developed respiratory cancer and it was just a matter of time before we lost him. It was a bombshell and my world crumbled. I rang Phil to tell him, only to be told that his dog and some of the others who had been to Lockerbie had been diagnosed with exactly the same illness. It transpired that four of the dogs who had been working in the main crater at the Lockerbie crash site had died from similar tumours, all of a most unusual formation.

Meanwhile, my poor old Pep was getting worse and worse as the disease took hold of him. My daughter Clair, now a trainee nurse, took upon herself the full responsibility for his care. She left care plans for him when she was away from home – she pinned detailed instructions for feeding him and administering his medication to the wall in the kitchen. Eventually, however, he began to have great difficulty in swallowing his food, even when we softened it and fed it to him by hand. We made constant visits to the vets in Belfast who did everything they could, but to no avail.

The day finally came when we all knew that enough was enough. Poor Pep had suffered too much and was continuing to suffer because none of us could bear to part with him. The time had come. It was the most heartbreaking decision I have ever had to take. We were all drained by the thought of parting with him. I asked Kate to drive us to Belfast so that I could sit in the back of the van with him. I wanted to treasure as much of his remaining time with us as I could. Clair was in the passenger seat. I cradled Pepper and talked to him and cried my eyes out all the way to Belfast.

When we got to the vet, Kate carried him inside, while I — coward that I am — stayed where I was, in floods of tears. Pepper died on 19 January 1995 and he broke all of our hearts. Even today, many years afterwards, I miss him so much and still cry when I think about him.

We drove home from Belfast in stunned silence to a very lonely house. Pepper was a truly special little dog and, in his ten short years, had found something like sixteen lost people in the mountains of Ireland. He had worked tirelessly in the huge crater and in the surrounding countryside of Lockerbie, where he found many body parts and gave a small measure of dignity back to those poor people whose lives had been shattered by the bombers from Libya.

Cracker missed him too and, in the days that followed, kept searching the house and the garden for him. He moped around and went off his food for a while. I kept thinking that Pepper was somehow going to burst through our living room door any minute and drop something at my feet for me to throw for him.

Now today, more than fifteen years later, I still have his collar and search jacket, and a little bit of his fur. Not one day passes when I don't think of him and, even now, I am looking at his portrait, done by Muriel, my sister-in-law. She perfectly captured the cheeky expression that was so much the character of this larger-than-life little hero of the Mournes.

And Pepper is remembered in Angela Locke's wonderful book, *Search Dog*, where she gives him special mention and has included a photograph of him wearing his green search dog coat. And in the operations room of the Killybegs cliff and coastal rescue team, a photograph of Pepper hangs as a lasting tribute to the little black-and-white collie who found the eleven-year-old German boy scout. There were even cards and letters of sympathy from people who, over the years, had become part of a small but devoted Pepper fan club. One card and enclosed letter from Brendan O'Donnell of County Clare said, 'Pepper will be remembered long after other mountain rescue dogs have been forgotten.'

So, for now, farewell Pepper ... rest easy, wee man. We are all very proud that you did so much to help humanity in your few short years on this earth. Good boy.

Chapter 18

By the time the two boys, Cracker and Dylan, were a year old, they had started their training as mountain rescue dogs. Dylan was steady and meticulous in the way he went about things – he could probably best be described as a very chilled dog who would condescend to do things. Cracker, on the other hand, was full on, keen to please and hyperactive – always in your face.

One of Cracker's weaknesses was his addiction to potato peelings. Whenever Kate was peeling spuds (which was not that often because she hates cooking), Cracker would sit behind her staring at her with such intensity that she could almost feel his gaze burning a hole in her back. If he got no reaction from that approach, he would make small moaning sounds which started off as a suppressed bark and ended in a sort of 'mmm' sound. That was level two on the attention-seeking scale. For level three he would drum his front feet and shuffle his back feet. That would eventually get him the result he was looking for: Kate would turn round and toss some peelings for him and the rest of the dogs, who only had to sit and wait, knowing that Cracker, the boss, would sort things out for them.

I was committed to making Cracker a mountain search dog until one lovely Saturday afternoon when we were on the hill for some training. I decided that this would be the day that I would check Cracker out with sheep. You will remember the experiences I had already had with Mac and Cuisle, and so I just had to know if I could trust Cracker sooner rather than later.

We were in the Glen River valley, where all the sheep were owned by John Magin. A small group of ewes was grazing peacefully a few hundred yards from where we were standing, so Mike Starrett volunteered to be 'body.' He went, SAS-style, on a wide sweep to the other side of the sheep and hid. The breeze was blowing through the sheep, towards Cracker and me. Perfect!

The plan was then to ask Cracker to 'find' Mike. If all went well, he should follow Mike's scent right to where he was hiding but ignore the sheep completely.

'Right then,' I thought, 'here goes.'

I shouted, 'Find him, Crack.'

Cracker looked at me as though to say 'who me?', then shot off across the heather like a real mountain search dog. For a while, as he ran into the invisible scent plume which was drifting towards him from Mike, things looked really good. But unfortunately, as he got closer to the sheep, they all scattered, except one. She stood her ground and defied Cracker, who unashamedly rose to the challenge and ran straight at her.

'Cracker! You bastard!' I roared.

Mike saw it all unfolding before him. He jumped up and shouted at the top of his voice, 'Cracker, no!'

The noise of me shouting and Mike thundering towards him was enough to distract Cracker from his evil intent and he stopped in his tracks. Mike arrived first and held him tightly by the collar until I could get a lead on him. That was that. Cracker had committed a mortal sin and his days as a mountain search dog were over. He could never be trusted to work safely on the hill again. What a blow. I went home in deep depression, my high hopes for Cracker gone in seconds. 'What is it about my bloody mountain search dog hopefuls and sheep?' I asked myself.

It's funny how things sometimes work out though – one door shutting and another one opening. A few months prior to the Lockerbie disaster, a few of us had been talking about forming an international search dog team. Television coverage of the Armenian earthquake which struck on 7 December 1988, just before Lockerbie, and killed twenty-five thousand people, had been the initial catalyst and Lockerbie confirmed our belief that a specially trained team for major disasters was needed. Therefore in the mid-nineties a preliminary meeting was held at Davey Jones's place in

Penmaenmawr, north Wales, to discuss the idea. Davey had been a stalwart of SARDA for years and was the main instigator of this new venture, following his own experiences at an earthquake in El Salvador in 1986.

The founder members were all active mountain rescue people and brought a wealth of experience: Phil Haigh, Neville Sharpe, Jim Greenwood, Uncle Ray Jones, Dave Reilly, Rodney Murray and Bob James, who could not be present but who was still a founder member. He is one of the kindest and most generous men I have ever met but he appears to be brusque and blunt. With Bob, there are no back doors – no hidden agenda, so to speak. What you see is what you get.

Once we had agreed such issues as the membership of the team, our objectives and the right kind of training and assessment for us and the dogs, the next focus of our attention was the medical equipment and medical cover that the team would need abroad. Rodney Murray, who was (and still is), one of my best friends, a committed lover of dogs in general (although he never had one of his own), and a great supporter of SARDA, was a senior registrar anaesthetist and became our medical officer. He wanted to make sure that when we were away we would have the best medical support he could provide. Dedicated and unselfish, he is the ideal medic to have on an international deployment.

To help him with the medical cover, Rodders enlisted the help of Charlie Cooper, another anaesthetist and a good friend who had a similar outlook on life. Together, they built up the most amazing medical kit. It was filled with all manner of drugs, splints, bandages and metallic shiny things, only to be used when the team was officially on deployments. It was kept at a central location and accessed only in the event of a major incident. Each team member had to have the appropriate vaccinations – to protect us against rabies, hepatitis B, typhoid, diptheria, tetanus and polio, among others – which were recorded and had to be regularly updated. The doctors had also collected the information about our blood groups and had arranged for a supply of blood bags to be held at Sheffield Northern General for us to be collected in the event of deployment, which meant we could have blood transfusions in the field, if necessary. The two doctors were on permanent call and would arrange who would accompany us to a disaster between themselves when the time came.

In addition to all these preparations, we also had to talk to our employers about getting time off from our work to go overseas in the event of being deployed after a disaster. In my case, the Department of Education gave the principal of St Mark's School permission to employ a substitute teacher if I was needed abroad.

We had several more meetings and then, finally, the new search dog group was formed. It was the first of its kind in the UK or Ireland and was known as British International Rescue Dogs (BIRD). Training the dogs was our next job. Because we were preparing them to work in the aftermath of earthquakes, they had to learn to work on top of and beneath rubble. Throughout the training we placed strong emphasis on the dogs' natural agility, and we developed a system of crawl training for them so that they would be happy working in confined spaces. The dogs needed to learn to search only for a person beneath the rubble – someone they could not see – and so we trained them to ignore people they saw standing around the site, or those engaged in clearing away rubble.

The way of indicating a find was different too – the dogs were trained to stand and bark at the casualty, or rather at the place where scent from the person was rising out of the rubble (in contrast to mountain rescue dogs who return to their handlers to tell them of a find).

Cracker and Cuisle both loved this new search game and soon Pete Brown and Dylan joined the team. British International Rescue Dogs was becoming a viable entity. Finally, in 1997, eleven long years after Lockerbie, the UK's very first 'collapsed structure search dog assessment' was held. I know Cuisle had certain issues about people but I was convinced that he would so excel at this kind of search work that his occasional bellicose lapses would be manageable.

On the way to the assessment, Pete and I flew into Heathrow with Cuisle, Cracker and Dylan in their sky kennels. Naturally passers-by, seeing crates marked 'Search Dogs', were curious and wanted to say hello to the dogs. Unfortunately, that was the bit

Cuisle hated – he could not accept people looking at him directly, let alone approaching his crate. His belligerence knew no bounds as he tested the locking mechanism of his sky-kennel gate to breaking point. He was an embarrassment, and so in the end I had to resort to covering the gate with a coat so he could not see out. Yet when Cuisle was working he had no such problem. He loved it and thought all the bodies he found were very nice people because, of course, they all played with him when he found them. Cuisle was in effect an oddball, but I loved him dearly.

Assessors for the test had been selected from experts outside BIRD and included a police dog handler, an arson investigation dog handler from the fire service and a search dog handler from SARDA. Happily, Cracker, Cuisle and Dylan all passed with no problems and BIRD became an operational entity. A year or so later, however, I decided to drop Cuisle from the work so as to let him concentrate on drowned victim search work. He was brilliant at it and the work was better suited to his temperament. In 1998 John Sjoberg came back to Northern Ireland and formally assessed Cracker as a drowned victim search dog and awarded Cuisle the advanced drowned victim search dog grade.

After the collapsed structure search dog assessment, there followed a steep learning curve for everybody. Lockerbie had been our only benchmark against which to measure a disaster, but we had no experience of an earthquake. What kind of food would we take with us if deployed? What sort of tents and sleeping bag would we need? Should we include tools for digging? How would we travel out to an earthquake-hit country and how would we get around once we got there? None of us had a clue about any of these things. We appointed Rodders to research the equipment side of things because, in his spare time, he worked in an outdoors pursuit shop, and had done for years. Another team member was tasked with the transport and deployment side, while Phil and I focused on another major headache – the issue of quarantine for dogs returning to the UK following trips abroad.

We did a lot of research into rabies and its preventative vaccination regime. We also lobbied MPs about the possibility of giving our dogs a special exemption from quarantine. At a meeting with representatives from the Department for Environment, Food and Rural Affairs (DEFRA), we presented a case which we hoped would sway them. We proposed that dogs going abroad would only do so on the following conditions:

- They were sent by the UK Government to assist in humanitarian work in natural disasters.
- They would only be out of the country for between five and seven days.
- They would be under continuous and close control.
- They would be within the pet passport scheme protocols.

We also assured DEFRA that it would be most unlikely we would be deployed to such events on a regular basis given their relative infrequency.

However, despite our very best efforts, the principal veterinary officer present made the following objections:

(a) We could not guarantee dogs would not ingest saliva from a rabid host dog.

(b) We could not guarantee a dog would not be bitten.

(c) A dog working out of sight would be at high risk of infection.

(d) The anti-rabies injection was not one hundred per cent reliable.

(e) The scheme would not meet the requirements of safety.

(f) Our proposal was not one hundred per cent safe and was consequently unacceptable.

We were very disappointed as we returned home but we resolved to examine every one of these issues very carefully. After a lot of hard work and further research, we felt that we were in a position to refute all of the Chief Veterinary Officer's objections on the following grounds:

(a) We learned from an eminent virologist at Glasgow Veterinary College that 'the virus in the saliva of a rabid animal has a limited lifespan of only a few minutes in the open air, therefore there is only a very remote possibility that another dog would ingest it as a live virus. In any event, where a dog had been properly injected against rabies, the chances of it contracting the disease under any circumstances would be very remote.'

(b) We gave an undertaking that when searching a collapsed structure site abroad, we would only work our dogs on a leash to protect them from contact with other dogs. In the unlikely event that a dog was thought to have been bitten, it would immediately be isolated from other dogs and on return to the UK, enter quarantine, remaining there until a blood test proved it to be free from rabies.

(c) We gave a further undertaking that a dog working on a leash would not be able to work out of sight. In practice, dogs are never more than a few feet from their handler anyway, because of the inherent dangers in this kind of search work.

(d) According to the same virologist referred to above, 'in all studies so far undertaken, 96/7% of the population of dogs vaccinated against rabies develop antibody levels sufficient to give them 100% protection against rabies. The remaining group when re-inoculated will usually achieve the desired titre levels. There remains, however, a very small percentage which may still not fully meet the optimum antibody level, but even they would be deemed safe within the current guidelines.' This viewpoint was substantiated by an eminent risk analyst for the World Health Organization in Geneva: 'It is easy to make your case quantitatively. Let's say your dogs are typically exposed to rabies incidence rates of 100/million/year – which was our best estimate for high-incidence countries (though locally it can be higher). Assume also (as we did in the MAFF exercise) that a dog born in the UK, kept fully vaccinated, with antibody titre always above the defined threshold, is 99% protected against a rabies bite. I don't know how much time your dogs spend in the field. However, if they spend 100 dog-days/year (made up from any number and combination of animals) at work outside the UK, the risk would be 1 in 3.65 million/year. This risk is about 100,000 times lower than the expected risk under PETS (which in itself is low). If they spend as much as 1000 days/year in the field, then the risk would only be 10,000 times less than under PETS. In any event, the risk is – relatively and absolutely – very low indeed.'

(e) Another senior scientist at the World Health Organization stated, 'WHO has been trying to facilitate the movement of pet animals particularly cats and dogs in between countries which have differing rabies situations. In the early 90s the Expert Committee on Rabies, proposed special exemption for guide dogs for the blind. OIE proposed different modalities from those of WHO, these modalities have been adopted by many countries including the UK. WHO is supportive of your opinions re "sniffer" dogs and the same conditions could apply for them as for guide dogs.'

We submitted these arguments to DEFRA and some months later got a response which said that, while our arguments were sound, 'nevertheless, dogs entering the UK from countries outside the Pet Passport Scheme, would still be required by law to spend six months in quarantine.'

It was painfully obvious that we were beating our heads against the proverbial brick wall – despite all our best efforts, DEFRA was not going to budge. As a team, we came to the decision that if, in the event of some major human catastrophe abroad, our team was asked to help, then we would go and we would be taking the dogs with us. The consequence of that decision, of course, would be that on returning to the UK, our faithful dogs would be scooped by the quarantine enforcers. We just had to prepare ourselves emotionally and practically for that eventuality. Therefore, one of the team was tasked with checking out various quarantine kennels around the country and asked to recommend the most suitable one.

Furthermore, the details of each dog were placed on a database and the protocols for their subsequent incarceration following any international deployment agreed with the authorities. While none of us wanted those circumstances to arise, the reality was that someday soon another big earthquake would occur somewhere in the world and we would be going to assist at it.

Chapter 19

My search and rescue work closer to home continued. On a Friday evening in April 1998, Sean Rodgers rang me saying, 'Young Powell. Guess who?'

'Hi, Sean. Who's gone missing now?'

It transpired that there had been a tragedy in Mayo – two lads from Enniskillen had been fishing for eels on Lough Conn when their boat went down without trace. Both were now missing, and Sean wanted me to come with the dogs. Alan Black and Pete Brown (of the Mourne mountain rescue team) and Adrian Mussen (a member of SARDA, who would act as coxswain on the boat) agreed to go with me and within the hour we were driving out of Newcastle.

It was a seven-hour journey, but with the usual banter and craic, it passed quickly. We drove to Ballina where, as arranged with Sean, we reported to the Garda station. The duty sergeant led us into his office where he gave us a full run-down on the fishing tragedy. The Garda were working on the basis that the two men had been fishing at the north-eastern end of Lough Conn when their boat mysteriously sank. The sergeant said that the men simply disappeared and that, as far as they could tell, neither of them had been wearing a life jacket. Locals had been scouring the waters since, but without success. Next the sergeant turned his attention to the dogs I had brought and wanted to know what exactly they could do. I told him that Cuisle had been trained to scent bodies below the water. Clearly, that information stretched his credulity to breaking point.

In contrast to our recovery operation on Strangford Lough,

when we had searched at night because there was a hope of finding survivors, and because we had the expertise of a local lifeboat crew to navigate the area for us, here there was nothing more we could do until morning. The sergeant very kindly offered to buy us our dinner in the hotel next door. We happily followed as he breezed past the young lady receptionist and announced that he would like 'the works for these lads from the north and we'll pick up the tab at the Garda station'. What a meal we were given! We were full as ticks. Now we needed to find out where were we going to spend the night and yet again, our benevolent sergeant came to the rescue: 'Well, lads, do you want me to see if I can get rooms for you in the hotel?'

'Not at all, Sergeant,' said Pete, trying to be so macho, 'we're used to roughing it. Have you anywhere in the station we could doss down?'

'Well, of course we have,' he beamed, visibly relieved that the price of our visit would be slashed to the cost of one dinner and one breakfast each. 'You're more than welcome to stay in the station if you want.'

He led us into the recesses of the Garda station and down the stairs, past a sign reading 'to the cells'.

'To the cells.' Pete chortled. 'Look at that, lads. That's somewhere I hope we never see the inside of!'

The sergeant stopped outside the door to the detention suite and, smiling broadly, waved us inside with a sweeping bow.

'Here we are then, lads. I hope you'll be comfortable. There's beds and blankets and pillows … ah sure, you'll be grand! Good-night. See you in the morning about eight. Okay?'

Out he went, pulling the heavy steel door behind him. Force of habit, I suppose.

'Pete, you bollocks!' hissed Adrian. 'Look what you've dropped us in now, for fuck's sake!'

The cell, for that's what it was, was all you might expect it to have been in days gone by. The beds or bunks, or whatever they were called, were heavily stained and reeked of very old urine. We were stunned, everyone looking at everybody else in silence. Pete, feeling responsible, had begun to shift nervously from foot to foot and then directed all his attention to the graffiti on the walls.

We elected to sleep on the floor – it stank of disinfectant but that was preferable to the stench of stale pee on the bunks. Everyone hauled out Karrimats and sleeping bags, engrossed in what they were doing. Everyone, that is, except Pete. Suddenly he announced, 'Right men! This spot here will do nicely for me, I think.' He pointed to a place between Adrian and me and, with a dramatic flourish, pulled out the tiniest piece of Karrimat I had ever seen. It could only have measured about four inches by four inches. A sample, obviously – a fragment he had picked up somewhere in his wanderings through outdoor-equipment shops. He placed this beer-mat-sized object on the floor and delicately adjusted its position. He lowered himself on to it and, with an exaggerated sigh of contentment, closed his eyes. There was no sleeping bag, just this miniscule piece of mat.

Pete gave another big attention-seeking sigh, turned over and let on he had fallen asleep. There was a moment's shock from us all and then we fell about laughing. It was insane. Tears were running down my face. It was so Pete Brown. He had forgotten everything as usual. Sleep came with great difficulty, given the constant jokes and laughter, and the volcanic breaking of wind. The latter eventually developed into a kind of bizarre competition which went on into the small hours.

We got up shortly after dawn. The sinks were revolting so nobody felt like washing. At eight o'clock, we heard the sound of measured steps, heralding the appearance of our friendly sergeant. He pushed the door open with a cheery, 'Good morning, lads. Hope you were comfy last night?'

Silence. Was he having a poke at us?

'Good,' he carried on, apparently oblivious to our reaction, 'let's get you some breakfast then.'

'Lead on, my man!' chirped Pete. I marvelled at his bright and breezy attitude, given last night's experience and the fact that he was entirely responsible for it.

In the hotel, the staff were waiting, all the tables laid and the air filled with the smell of full Irish breakfasts. Last night was forgotten in an instant. Over his third cup of tea, the sergeant casually said that the Garda dive team, who were also going to be involved in searching for the missing fishermen, had spent the night in the Pontoon Bridge Hotel. It was four or five miles from Ballina and had a three-star rating. 'Bloody hell!' someone said with envy.

Breakfast over, we piled into the Land-Rover and, with the 21-foot boat hooked on behind, nosed out into the busy morning traffic of a newly awakened Ballina. We drove south-west, following the road which winds its way through the rock-strewn heathery hills that are so characteristic of that part of Mayo. At the Pontoon Bridge Hotel, where we turned north for Crossmolina, we noticed the Garda dive boat, bobbing empty and smug beside the hotel jetty. Continuing along the twisty road, we passed the conical mass of Nephin Beg, a perfectly formed, symmetrical mountain towering over Lough Conn. Then, on the outskirts of Crossmolina, we turned right to enter a much narrower road leading to an idyllic small harbour.

This tiny haven for the fishing boats of Lough Conn looked almost magical in the morning sun. It had stout, hand-cut stone walls, which offered safe mooring to the half-dozen colourful, long rowing boats, bobbing patiently, awaiting the return of their fishermen owners. Outside the harbour, a gentle breeze ruffled the peaty water splashing sunlight on the sandy shore. The plan was for Alan and Pete to search along the shoreline for any sign of the two missing men, while Adrian and I searched from the boat. Our intention was to work our way over to the eastern side of the lake which was where the Garda officers thought the boat might have sunk.

Conditions were ideal, the wind being steady from the south and not too strong. Its direction could not have been better either, because it allowed us to drive at right angles to it, giving Cuisle the best possible chance of finding the missing men. He could pick up scent from as much as half a mile upwind. But while we could not have asked for more favourable weather, I couldn't help thinking that the day was too beautiful for us to be doing what we were doing – searching for the dead. To do that, the cloudless blue skies should have been overcast and the water dull and lifeless, but the sun was shining and the sea sparkled. It seemed wrong somehow.

We began a grid search: we drove across wind for approximately a quarter of a mile and then ran upwind for a hundred yards, before turning back across the wind and reversing our course. This pattern kept the boat at right angles to the wind for most of the time. After about twenty minutes Cuisle became very excited, moving position frequently and concentrating hard. He leaned his body way out over the side of the boat, stretching himself into the wind. His head was twisting this way and that as he tried to pinpoint the source of the scent. 'Turn into the wind, Adrian,' I said over my shoulder, but he had already seen Cuisle's alert and was putting the wheel hard over. We slowly crept forward, following the direction dictated by Cuisle's radar-like nose. All I could really see of him now was his counter-balancing tail which was helping him to defy gravity. He was suspended right out over the water at an impossible angle. He gave one or two quick barks to indicate he might have something and then, satisfied that he had, he stood bolt upright and barked continuously.

From a neighbouring boat a Garda sergeant who was based in Crossmolina was watching us. I called to him, 'I think he's found one of them here, Sergeant.'

'I see that. Great stuff. It's bloody amazing. I'll keep out of your way,' he shouted, as his boat moved off.

We drove the boat upwind away from the area and then came around again to slowly make our way, criss-crossing the wind, back towards the place where Cuisle had indicated. As we got closer to it, he began to strain out over the boat's side. Then, at the exact same place as before, he shot bolt upright and began barking. There was no doubt about it – one of the bodies was very close below us. We dropped a marker over the side, a small white buoy, to let the divers have a target to dive from later on.

The sergeant, who had been watching us, must have radioed the Garda divers because they arrived soon afterwards. They glided across the water to where we were waiting, and we described what Cuisle had done and roughly where we believed the body to be. The boss diver was clearly very sceptical and unsure what to say, and looking back now, I can see why – a dog able to smell a body from under the water? Everyone knows a dog just could not do that, don't they?

But, to his credit, he decided to hedge his bets and organised his men to conduct a quick search of the area. A metal bar was attached to their boat by long ropes and two of the divers held on to it. They then went underwater and were towed along while they scanned the bottom. I couldn't understand how they could expect to see anything clearly with the water being so murky brown from the peat particles suspended in it.

Anyway, after a short time, they surfaced and reported that they had found nothing. I was devastated. I couldn't understand how Cuisle could have got it wrong. I was convinced he had found one of the men. Unfortunately, the Garda dive team were not, and their boat powered away leaving us rocking in its wake.

Next day, we went back and searched the same area with Cuisle and got exactly the same result. I was more convinced than ever that at least one of the missing men was somewhere near our white marker, which was bobbing desolately in the waves. We moved further away to begin a search for the second body. After twenty minutes, Cuisle again did his ship's prow routine as he picked up scent from below the surface. He became more positive, shot bolt upright and started barking and staring at the water. Could he have located the second body, I wondered? We double-checked as usual and got exactly the same result so we marked the spot with another white buoy.

The sergeant we met the day before was out in his boat again and drew alongside us. We updated him on the latest result and showed him the other white buoy which marked the new location. He assured us that he would do all he could to persuade one of the dive teams to check the two sites again.

It was time for us to go home and so, feeling somewhat dejected, we went back to the little harbour, packed our gear, hitched on the boat and we went home. Two weeks later, I got a call from the friendly sergeant. He told me that a volunteer search and rescue group had decided to concentrate on the two areas indicated by Cuisle. They dragged the bottom of the lake with nets and, lo and behold, they recovered both men very close to our two markers.

★ ★ ★

On 28 June 1999, Sean Rodgers asked me to bring Cuisle and Cracker to Donegal. He urgently needed our help in searching for a farmer who it was believed might have drowned in the Glenties River. 'This one is a bit of a mystery, Neil,' Sean elaborated. 'The man had been suffering from depression. He was living with his brother and the two of them are quite elderly. Anyhow, the surviving brother said that two days ago, he just vanished. We've been searching around his land but we've found bugger all. But there's this river flowing past the farm. It's been dived already but nothing has been found. Could the dogs help us out, do you think?' We agreed that I would leave first thing the next morning and meet Sean and the rest of the boys at the base in Killybegs to travel on to Glenties together.

Early next morning, I picked up Adrian Mussen and we eventually arrived at Killybegs close to ten o'clock. We were taken straight into the briefing room to be brought up to date on progress so far. Sean said that the Glenties River had again been searched from first light by local divers and Garda divers but there was still no sign of the man.

'All the outbuildings and fields have been cleared as well,' he added, 'so we are pretty well at a loss as to where to search next.'

I felt a knot of anxiety starting to build in my stomach as we made our way to the search site – the river had been dived, the outbuildings and land cleared and still no sign of the man. Our job was to search the river again and, if the man was indeed there, then we had better find him. In all our other searches, the bodies had been found very close to the areas indicated but not close enough in space or time to convince the doubters that Cuisle could in fact locate a drowned victim. It felt to me as though this search had become a sort of watershed for using drowned victim search dogs and it would be very public. Failure was unthinkable.

It wasn't long before the twisting winding roads brought us to the village of Glenties, a picturesque and peaceful place, with an atmosphere completely at odds with the sombre task we were about to undertake. Sean introduced us to the sergeant in charge of the search and told him that Cuisle was a specialist drowned victim search dog. The sergeant didn't say much to that, but his face and general demeanour conveyed a very clear message – 'Oh yeah?'

We launched the boat and, with Adrian driving and Cuisle in the bow as usual, we started searching the slow meandering river. Meanwhile, on the bank and keeping pace with us, walked our cynical Garda sergeant, watching and waiting. We drifted slowly along, Cuisle completely focussed on what he was doing, ignoring the sergeant. By contrast, I found his presence very intimidating.

Adrian, unmoved, guided us from one side of the river to the other in gentle sweeps, until at last we reached a point where the missing man's garden stretched down to the water's edge. At that point Cuisle got very excited and began barking. Could it be? Had we found the missing man already? From the sergeant on the bank came, 'Don't worry about this part – it's already been dived. He's definitely not there. You may carry on.'

'Thanks for that,' I shouted to him, trying to make myself heard over Cuisle's barking. 'We'll carry on downstream for a bit then.'

'Here we go again, for God's sake,' muttered Adrian.

As we turned the boat to go downstream, Cuisle ran to the back of it in frustration, still barking and twisting his head around from the river to me and back to the river again. I knew exactly what he was saying. He was virtually screaming, 'What the bloody hell is wrong with you? Are you stupid? Can't you see that I'm telling you the bloke is right here?'

'I know, Cuisle,' I said quietly as we carried on downstream and rounded a sweeping right hand bend. Fifty yards later I said to Adrian, 'I don't give a shit what that bloody cop says – I know the body is there.'

He nodded and said, 'Look, what we'll do is keep downstream for a bit, then we'll come back up and see if Cuisle barks at the same place.'

So that was what we did. We worked slowly downstream for about another half a mile, going through the motions of searching, while Cuisle, true professional that he was, forgot his earlier irritation and worked away as if nothing had happened.

'I think this is far enough, Adrian,' I said. 'No point in going on.'

Adrian nodded. 'Let's head back up.'

He brought the boat neatly round and began steering us back upstream towards the place where we were both convinced the body was lying. As we eased around the bend in the river, we saw our stalwart sergeant again, leaning against a tree and looking in our general direction uninterestedly.

Cuisle, still in the bow, had his nose as close to the water surface as possible, his bum in the air and his tail clamped to the sponson, giving him the counterbalance he needed. In the same place as before, he turned his head to look at me and began barking excitedly. The message was clear – 'I bloody told you, didn't I?'

'That's it, Adrian. Our man is definitely below us somewhere here,' I said just loudly enough to carry to our cynical overseer on the bank.

'What's that?' the sergeant asked. 'What did you say?'

'I said that I'm certain the body is somewhere very close here, Sergeant,' I repeated.

'Impossible!' he snorted. 'It's been thoroughly searched. Your dog's wrong, lad!'

'Well I'm going to check it now with my other dog, Sergeant,' I said, convinced Cuisle was right.

'Go ahead, but you're wasting your time,' he grunted.

When we brought Cracker to the same place, he barked exactly as Cuisle had done and that was all the proof I needed. 'I am sure the man is here, Sergeant. Do you know if there are any divers still around to give it another quick search?' I asked, as politely as possible.

'I don't know,' answered the exasperated police officer.

'Well could you check? I mean, what've we got to lose?'

Sean Rodgers, meanwhile, had been standing on the opposite bank and had witnessed the whole thing. He volunteered to phone the amateur dive team leader, if the sergeant had no objection, and get them to dive the place again. The sergeant reluctantly agreed.

After what seemed like an age, the divers arrived, got their equipment on and re-entered the water. Minutes after submerging, one of them resurfaced and said, 'He's there all right, Sean. We're putting a rope to him now.' The poor man's body was directly below the place where Cuisle and Cracker had been barking.

The diver again slipped below the surface in a welter of bubbles. Sean, who had been watching from the bank, asked if he could join us on the boat. After a few more minutes, the divers came up again and one of them handed the rope to Sean saying, 'Okay, lads – pull him up.'

We hauled and in seconds, gently brought the body of the missing man into the boat.

Later, with the formalities over, the sergeant sought us out and said, 'Look, lads, I have to hand it to you. I really didn't believe it was possible and only for me seeing it with my own two eyes, no one could've convinced me. Who'd have thought it? A dog smelling someone under the water. My God almighty!'

It was a brilliant result and should have made the authorities aware that in Cuisle and Cracker they had a very valuable search asset, but unfortunately it didn't. Months later I happened to be talking to a search and rescue team member from Sligo. In the course of the conversation, he asked if I had ever heard about these new police dogs the Garda had – apparently they could smell people underwater and had recently found a body in the river near Glenties up in Donegal.

Chapter 20

A month or two later, I received a phone call from John O'Donnell, a civilian diver I'd worked with on a couple of searches. He said there had been another possible drowning in a lake near Athlone and he wanted me to bring Cuisle to help in the search. Apparently the missing man had been suffering from depression and some of the local people who knew him well were afraid that he might have ended his life in the lake.

'How soon do you think you can be here?' he asked.

'Well, I'll see if Adrian can come to handle the boat and if he's okay about that it'll probably be later this evening. Anyway it's better for us when it's quiet – there will be fewer people around, less distraction. Is that okay?'

'No problem, Neil,' he said. 'Hang on there a second and I'll put you on to the sergeant in charge.'

There was a brief exchange off the phone and then the sergeant came on saying, 'You'll be down later on this evening then, John tells me?'

'I will, Sergeant,' I replied. 'We'd be there sooner but I'd prefer to let the dog work with as few people around as possible.'

'Oh sure. Not a bother. I'll make sure you have the place to yourselves then.'

'That's great, Sergeant. I'll see you later.'

'Right. Good luck now,' and the phone went dead.

The journey to the lake took about four hours, pulling the 20-foot RIB behind, and eventually we were on the road leading to the lake. 'I'd say we timed that just right,' Adrian said. 'They should all have gone home by now.' As he was speaking, we were inching our way slowly between two rows of parked cars on each side of the road.

'Look at these ignoramuses,' said Adrian. 'They don't give a frig about who wants to get past. What the hell are they all doing here anyway?' This sort of giant car park – of hundreds of vehicles, vans, tractors, cars and even the odd minibus – went on for about a mile.

'You don't think they could have anything to do with this search, do you?' Adrian asked.

'I bloody well hope not,' I answered. 'That cop promised me there'd be nobody here at all. Maybe there's a match on.'

Eventually, we were able to make out the waters of the lake as they drifted in and out of a haze of mist. No, not mist – smoke! We could soon plainly see that the source of this smoke was in fact the mother of all bonfires which was burning furiously on the shore of the lake. Through this shifting swirling pall, we next glimpsed what looked like hundreds of people standing around. We ground to a halt and wound down the windows to study this spectacle more closely.

To our astonishment, we could hear what sounded like someone intoning the rosary followed by the rumbling response of a huge congregation. And then Cuisle started to get very wound up in the back of the Land-Rover, whining and giving the odd growl if anybody came too close 'What's going on here?' I asked somebody who was walking past.

'Oh, that's the parish priest,' he replied helpfully. 'He's saying the rosary for the lad that's lost. The bonfire's to keep the people warm and to drive away the bloody midges.'

Cuisle, meanwhile, had decided that this was all too much and that he really didn't want any further discussion to continue between me and the local man. His earlier agitated whining had now become a full-blown barking session, accompanied by snots and teeth and lunges at the windows. Then along came a Garda officer who turned out to be the one I'd been talking to on the phone earlier. He gave a big smile and said, 'Hello there. You must be the lads from the north. Great stuff. When can you start?'

'Bark, bark, snarl, bark,' goes Cuisle, rocking the two-ton Land-Rover in his attempts to launch himself at the police officer.

'Start?' I shout over the bedlam inside. 'Start? How can we start with all this lot? We were promised there'd be nobody here, Sergeant, and just look at the place – it's like Croke Park on an All-Ireland Sunday! And look at the smoke. It's blowing all over the lake. The dog will suffocate, never mind be able to use his nose to find anyone.'

'Is that fella safe?' asked the sergeant, nodding in the direction of my highly trained search dog.

'Oh he is, Sergeant, but he's a bit pissed off with the travelling and the crowds and so on. No, he'll settle down later.'

'The fifth sorrowful mystery is the finding of the child Jesus in the temple,' boomed the voice of the priest, intoning the rosary and almost drowning out the cop's reply.

'I suppose it has got a bit out of hand all right,' he said apologetically. 'The Father has done the whole rosary once and this is his second time round … oh, and the folk choir is getting ready to start once he's finished.'

Talk about frustration. No doubt the family of the missing man were getting comfort from the prayers, but the bonfire? Cuisle had absolutely no chance of working with smoke everywhere. I was stumped.

'Sergeant, we'll just have to come back early tomorrow,' I suggested.

'Indeed you won't then. You're here now. Look, hang on there a while lads and I'll clear the whole lot away for you. Give me fifteen minutes,' he said with authority.

We tried to find somewhere to turn the Land-Rover and boat, but it was hopeless. We went another three miles before we could find a place to back into and get turned. After what seemed forever, we drove back towards the lake, agreeing that if the crowds were still there, we would go home.

Amazingly, when we got back to the temporary place of prayer, the fire was out and the crowds of people gone. Our Garda friend met us red-faced and out of breath and said, 'Okay lads? Will you be able to give it a lash now?'

'I can't believe you cleared them so well, Sergeant,' I said in amazement, adding, 'Yes, we'll give it a good lash for you now.'

'Good lads,' he said, rubbing his hands.

As we reversed the boat into the water, an important-looking chap came over to us looking very intense and apologised about the crowds, the bonfire and everything. He introduced himself as the search manager and said, 'Well, anyway, the divers have been searching all round this part of the lake in front of us here, right up to an hour ago. They're certain that it's clear. He's not in that part. So the area I think you need to concentrate on is way over there on the far side of the lake,' he told us, pointing. 'See where I mean?' We turned to see that he was indicating a small bay about two hundred metres away, surrounded by trees.

We launched the boat and headed off with the wind coming across our starboard side. Cuisle was in the bows, content to be working and hanging out over the water as he scanned for scent. I wondered about pulling him in, because, according to what we were told, he was only wasting his time on this part of the lake, but I let him carry on, thinking that it might help to calm him down before we reached our designated search area.

Then, as if a switch has been thrown by some unseen controller of destiny, Cuisle started to bark and stare at the water just to our right.

'Cuisle! No, son! Shut up for God's sake. We haven't started yet,' I hissed at him, conscious that we are being watched by the search manager and all his mates. But Cuisle ignored me and got really into it, lunging towards the stern of the boat as Adrian began to gun us away from the place. As we carried on to the other side of the lake, Cuisle finally shut up. We spent a few hours doing what we were asked to do but with no result. We turned round and headed back to where we had left our launch trolley. As we went through the area where Cuisle had been barking earlier, he started again and was going mental. But, according to the information we were given, Cuisle was wrong so I said, 'Cuisle, will you for God's sake give us a break. You really are being a complete prat!'

But it made not a button of difference. I might as well have been talking to the swans swimming serenely a few hundred yards away. He kept right at it until we were back on dry land. Then the manic barking subsided to frustrated whining as I pushed Cuisle into the Land-Rover and shut the back door behind him.

A small group of people were hanging around, watching the debacle. As we packed up the gear, the search manager came over and I apologised to him for failing to get a result. 'Not to worry, lads. You did your best. Go on up to the house. There's tea and sandwiches waiting for you.'

'You're very kind, but we have to go straight back home,' I lied. How could I face the family after that performance?

'Well all right so,' he said. 'Funny the way he was barking so hard out there … anyway, thanks again, lads.'

What can I say? Cuisle seemed to have made a complete balls of things! End of story, egg on face. We headed for home.

Days afterwards, John O'Donnell rang to tell me that the body had been found. Where? Exactly where Cuisle had been barking – yes, right at the start of the search. Given our success at Glenties, I should have been stronger and had more faith in Cuisle, but it was hard to stay confident when so many people doubted our ability. There's an old saying among the old hands in search dog work, and many's the time I've heard it: 'Trust your dog!' I resolved never to doubt Cuisle again.

Chapter 21

Pete Brown rang one Friday evening in the summer of 1995 and explained that he wasn't able to keep Dylan because of problems at home. He didn't want to elaborate, but explained that he had started asking people he knew whether they would like to take Dylan. 'No you don't, Pete. He has a home here with us,' I said. 'If you give him to anyone else I'll never forgive you.'

So Dylan came to live at our house. Our other dogs had always liked him – he was Cracker's twin brother after all – so they made him as welcome as we did. Dylan quickly settled in and for a while all was well …

At the time I had a routine of bringing the dogs to Donard Forest for a good long walk. We did it twice a day, travelling in my Land-Rover to avoid meeting other people because of Cuisle's general dislike for them. We also needed to avoid other dogs because Cracker didn't care much for them either. On one particular day, about a fortnight after Dylan had arrived to live with us, we arrived back home, and I opened the door of the Land-Rover, saying, 'Right lads – out.' They all duly leaped out and ran round to the back garden. All, that is, except Mr Dylan. He decided he was going to stay right where he was. 'Dylan, out!' I roared. He came out then all right, launching himself from the innermost part of the Land-Rover and straight for me like an Exocet missile. He clearly intended to do some serious damage. His teeth were bared and he was snarling furiously. I jumped to one side as he shot past. He landed with a thump on the driveway and, in a flash, rounded and came straight for me, still beside himself with anger. This time he was aiming for my legs.

As it happened, I was wearing a thick winter jacket so I bent down and pushed my heavily padded arm into his wide-open mouth. He locked on to it and, while he was attempting to rip my arm from my body, I reached into the Land-Rover and got hold of a check chain and extendable training lead. I managed to drop the chain over his head while he took a brief break from his activities. Using the lead and chain, I yanked him very hard and marched off up the driveway, pulling him after me. I turned and marched back again and then fired him unceremoniously back into the Land-Rover, being careful to leave the end of the lead hanging outside the door (it was one of the extendable training leads, like the police use).

I gave him five minutes to cool off and went back to the Land-Rover, opened the door and roared 'Dylan, out!', hauling on the lead and giving him no time to decide whether to obey me or not. As before, I marched off down the drive, turned and walked him back again. I then fired him into the back of the Land-Rover and shut the door. Another five minutes went by and I repeated the process, but by then he was jumping straight out with alacrity. Next, I drove him back to the forest where we went through about ten minutes of hard heel work – left turn, right turn, about turn – then back to the Land-Rover and home. In the driveway I opened the back door, only to discover Dylan standing there, waiting to jump out, nice and polite. Problem solved. In his fourteen years living with us, he never once repeated his retriever rage.

Dylan was going to be my next mountain search dog and, thankfully, Pete had already done much of the basic work with him. He was safe with sheep, he barked on command and he knew the find sequence when searching. I just needed to teach him to work for much longer periods without losing motivation. He also had to learn directional work – to go left, right, up and down and so on, on command.

I had been at a training session when Pete still owned Dylan when we tried to teach Dylan the 'go up' command. Crafty Dylan would run up the hill a little way and then hide behind a boulder, out of sight. Pete, believing that Dylan was still climbing, would shout. 'Good boy, Dylan. Go up! Go up!' But all the while, Mr

Dylan hid behind his rock, laughing his socks off, no doubt. This went on for twenty minutes until I radioed Pete to tell him that he was being conned. When I tried to train Dylan to 'go up' he tried a similar stunt, but I was wise to him. So he changed tactics and would just run so far up the hill, lie down and refuse to go any further. When I walked towards him, he would jump up and run straight off up the hill. It became a game, so I just told him he was a good lad and he got better and better at it. I had found the secret switch to make Dylan work. From then on his 'send-away' was spectacular, and teaching him to move left or right was just as easy. In so many ways he was like Pepper – a little four-legged robot that I could manoeuvre around the hill.

In 1998 we did our novice grade mountain search dog assessment and passed it with flying colours. Dylan was doing what he had been born to do – hunt. In fact, his nose was so good that it almost finished our search dog career at his full search dog grade assessment the following year. Well, it was more my stupidity than his nose really. The weather was terrible, with low cloud and visibility of no more than fifty metres once you got twenty metres above road level. I had been given a search on Slieve Muck, which lies beside the Kilkeel Road in the Mourne Mountains. I sent Dylan off, closely watched by my two assessors from SARDA (England), Ken Sloan and Dave Worden. I decided to grandstand a little bit. You would think I might have learned that this would be a bad idea after my showing off with Pepper during his full search dog assessment, but I was supremely confident that Dylan would shine and so forgot my past mistakes …

Just as I was about to disappear into the mist, I saw Dylan pick up the scent of the first body, but I let on I hadn't. I wanted to act all surprised when he eventually came running back to tell me he had found the body. I thought that would impress the assessors. Why? I have no idea, but at the time it seemed important. So when I had become enveloped by the swirling low cloud cover, instead of frequently shouting, 'Find him, Dylan' (which would have let him know where I was to help him find me) I said nothing. What I didn't know was that way below me and in full view of the assessors, Dylan had found body number one. Then, as he was trying to find me to let me know – that's me the twit who was making no sound because I wanted to impress the assessors – he ran straight into the scent of body number two. In full view of the assessors, he went off to find that body. On the other hand, I was blundering higher and higher up the mountain unable to find any sign of my wonderful dog and wondering where the hell he was. Panic set in.

Meanwhile, away to my left Dylan was coming back to indicate that he had also found body number two. However, while he was still searching for the new silent me, Dylan winded some walkers about one mile upwind from him. They were making their way to the summit of Slieve Muck for a day's exercise, but as far as Dylan was concerned, they needed to be found as well. So off he went. An hour had passed and I still couldn't find him. I was soaked in sweat and, what's more, I knew I'd made a major screw-up. There was nothing left for me to do but keep going uphill until I reached the summit. Once there, I hoped that my scent would swirl downwards over the mountainside and be picked up by Dylan.

In almost zero visibility and following a compass bearing, I was nearing the top of Slieve Muck when I heard voices from somewhere to my left. I made my way over and found five people walking in a line. Beside the lead walker was Dylan, resplendent in his high visibility coat with the words 'Search Dog' emblazoned on each side.

'Hey!' shouted the man. 'Do you know who owns this dog? He came from nowhere and won't leave us.' I was mortified. A search dog and he was lost. I thanked them and tried to explain what had happened. I don't know what they must have thought, but we said goodbye and went our separate ways.

There was no point in prolonging things. I started back down the hill to where the assessors were waiting, wondering what on earth this would all look like to them. On the walk back I noticed a bit of blue baling twine caught in some rocks and – I'm now ashamed to admit – the germ of an idea took root in my frantic mind. I radioed the assessors and told a monstrous lie.

'Dog Ken from Dog Neil. Do you read, over?' I waited for the reply.

'Dog Neil this is Ken. There you are at last. Go ahead, over,' he said, inviting me to spill the beans.

'Ken, this is Neil. I've found Dylan. He was with a group of walkers but they had tied a piece of bailing twine to him to stop him running off.'

'Oh, you've found him then, have you?' he asked with just a hint of sarcasm in his voice.

'Roger that. They said they thought he was lost. They were going to take him to Newcastle police station,' I said, digging a deeper and deeper hole for myself. I hate telling lies because I always get caught out and this was a real whopper.

'Roger that. Just make your way back to this location now then, out,' he said, and the radio link was broken. I knew he knew that I was lying through my teeth.

I eventually got to the road and walked the mile or so back to the car park where the assessors were waiting. Dylan was on the lead then but of course I was still carrying my prop, the piece of blue baling twine. I apologised and volunteered to withdraw from the assessment.

'Don't be so bloody negative,' said Ken. 'Get some lunch and then go round to the next area. That was one search. Your bloody dog found all the bodies but you were too busy showing off to us. Weren't you?'

As his words sank in I said in shock, 'What? You're letting me carry on?'

'Why not? Dylan can search as well as the best I've ever seen. It was you that let him down. Now go on. Get your lunch and fuck off round to the next area. Don't screw up again!'

'No, Ken. Thanks, Ken.' What a let off.

I gobbled down my lunch and drove round to the back of Slieve Muck to where the other assessor, Dave, was waiting. I said nothing about what had happened earlier and he didn't ask. He gave us our area and this time I was fully switched on. Dylan sailed through it and did the same over the rest of the two and a half days – except for the very last search.

It was Sunday morning on the Glen River. I was well used to the place and was working Dylan from fairly high up on the side of the hill. There were lots of small footholds and, although it was a fairly exposed position, I felt completely confident. After thirty minutes or so, the radio hissed.

'Dog Neil. This is Dave.'

I fumbled around for the speaker mic and almost lost my footing.

'Go ahead, Dave,' I replied.

'Dog Neil. Please get off that cliff and make your way down to safer ground,' he ordered.

I wondered what the hell was wrong with him, but answered meekly, 'Roger, Dave.'

Dylan found all his bodies again and we returned to the assessor for his comments. What a bollocking I got for putting myself 'in a hazardous position without due care and attention'. Anyway, the upshot of Dylan's full search dog grade assessment was that we passed and, thanks to the wisdom of Ken Sloan, my first-day assessor, I was allowed to forget the big blunder and show them just how good Dylan was.

Chapter 22

We arranged a training weekend for the international dogs in Leyland, a town in the South Ribble borough of Lancashire, about six miles south of the city of Preston. One of our friends in the fire service was Dave Peplow, an accomplished gun-dog man and one of the leading trainers of arson detection dogs. Dave had important contacts in the demolition business, so he was able to arrange for us to use disused buildings and demolition sites for training – sites to which we would otherwise never have had access.

The direct flights from Belfast to Manchester can't accommodate dogs in the hold of the aircraft, so I had to fly via Heathrow. My good friend Pete had agreed to come with me as I am not good at travelling alone. I arrived at Belfast International Airport with Cracker, Dylan and two very large sky kennels. With difficulty, I loaded everything onto two trolleys and waited for Pete. The time for checking in was getting seriously close and there was still no sign of him, the bastard! Eventually I rang, thinking that he must be very close so I should probably start moving towards the terminal.

'Hey boy. Will you be much longer? I'm standing here at the airport waiting for you.'

'What are you talking about?' he replied. 'I'm not going anywhere. I'm halfway home. I have to get my car fixed.'

'You're not coming? Getting your fucking car fixed? What are you talking about? Fuck me! It's a bit late telling me that now!'

'Sorry mate. I can hardly hear you. I'm losing the signal …'

He was gone and I was on my own with two large sky kennels containing two anxious dogs, all my personal protection gear, sleeping bag, spare clothes and a white-knuckle fear of flying. Great!

I made it to check-in, where the young lady waited expectantly for me to say something, but nothing came out. I knew roughly what to expect when trying to board a plane with just one dog, having done it once before – it is, as they say here in Northern Ireland, 'a handlin', fraught with bureaucratic questions such as the weight of the dog, the weight of the kennel, the size of the kennel, the size of the dog, and whether the dog has water, or if he'll bite, or if the door is properly secured. But two kennels and two dogs was something else entirely. It felt as though the problem was not just doubled but multiplied by ten at least!

For a start, the ordinary kind of checking in isn't a possibility. The lady behind the desk directed me to the outsize baggage section where the dogs' kennels were checked for explosives. Then the dogs came out of the kennels while the crates went through the X-ray machine. Of course, while the dogs were standing around, they became a magnet for the ground staff, who bombarded me with questions about the dogs, their work, our trip and obedience classes in Bangor …

Then a new problem became apparent – the airport staff did not realise that their luggage trolleys are not designed to carry kennels of this size. As the first guy started to push his, it overbalanced and started to fall sideways. Cracker, not knowing what was happening, got into a wild panic and threw himself rapidly from one side of the kennel to another and from front to back, apparently at the same time. His water bowl, attached to the outside of the kennel, emptied its contents all over the freshly cleaned floor. All the staff started slipping and clutching at things for balance which – in the case of one individual – was my other sky kennel. It then fell off the trolley, causing an exponential rise in hysteria in both dogs.

When order was again temporarily restored, lifting the kennels back on to the trolleys became the next major problem. Because the dogs were panicking, the crates were moving so much that it was almost impossible to lift them. Clearly Cracker and Dylan now just wanted to get out and go home. I wanted to go home. Then I heard one of the airport staff gasp, 'Oh my God!' I turned around to see that all the twisting and bending had finally popped one of the sky kennel doors open. Out came the wild-eyed, salivating, highly trained, international mountain search dog Cracker, who made a dash for freedom. I ran after him. Panicking passengers scattered in all directions, some falling over and dropping their own bags.

The loudspeaker announced, 'Unattended baggage may be removed and destroyed.' Well the destroy-the-bags team are going to be busy today, I thought to myself as I legged it across the concourse. There are dozens of the bloody things lying around all over the place. Why oh why did I not just stay at home?

By the time I had caught Cracker and put him back in his kennel and the two dogs were being wheeled through the doors marked 'Do Not Enter' on their way to the plane, I was soaked in sweat, had developed severe stomach cramps and the airline was issuing final calls for Mr Neil Powell.

I urgently needed the toilet. But then my name was called again over the loudspeakers. 'This is the final call for Mr Neil Powell.' The toilet thing was not going to happen. It was unadulterated purgatory. Once on board, I was too embarrassed to use the plane's loo. I couldn't foist that on my fellow passengers. Oh my God – when I think back on it, the palms of my hands still run wet with sweat. Just at that moment, I thought briefly of my mate Pete, travelling comfortably to wherever he was supposed to be going. I made a very sincere wish that his car would develop some serious mechanical defect and that he would become stranded on the motorway for six days before help reached him.

By the time we finally landed in London, my cramps had subsided a little and I was able to walk upright. I knew I had to get to where the bags would appear, or I might lose them and the dogs forever. The toilet would have to wait for the moment. Stress was making me sweat from every pore. No sign of the bags.

A shuddering sound of movement came from the carousel and a warning bell rang out. Luggage appeared from the bowels of Heathrow airport. After an age, my bags were spat out. On checking at an enquiry desk, I was told the dogs would be brought up separately. That made sense, of course, but at the time I would not have blinked an eyelid if I'd found the dogs going round and round with everything else.

Finally they arrived from around the corner, being pushed towards me by two porters. The kennels were damaged: little bogey wheels which had been attached at their four corners were missing, one from each kennel. Needless to say, neither of the two porters knew anything about it and couldn't give two hoots anyway.

Meanwhile, my cramps were back and getting progressively worse. I needed to find a toilet most urgently. But of course I now had the two dogs in sky kennels, a mountain of baggage on top of each, and the whole lot balancing precariously on two trolleys! I devised a method of pulling one and pushing the other and was constantly on edge waiting for a kennel to slide off like it had in Belfast.

At last I spotted a toilet up ahead. In desperation, I left the kennels and all my gear outside. I didn't care if anybody stole the lot! I closed the door. Afterwards, I felt so much better and confident now that things could only improve, I made to leave the cubicle only to find that, to my horror, I couldn't get the bloody door open. It had jammed itself shut. 'Oh my God, what else can you do to me this day?' I asked the unseen presence. My banging and thumping eventually led to my release, thanks to the efforts of an American gentleman of kindly disposition, who had his nose firmly pinched between two fingers. I went to the sink, turned on the tap and out rushed the water like a jet from a hose. Without any warning, it poured straight down the front of my beige trousers. I was utterly drenched. To even the most casual passer-by it was going to look like I had just had a major accident .

And so, with a bag hanging in front, I made a slow, soggy exit from the arrivals hall and into the bedlam that is Heathrow. The fact that I was so encumbered would have been enough to attract the attention of even the most uninterested traveller, but now attention would be riveted on my apparent incontinence as well. It was truly an awful experience and in that sorry condition, I had to find the check-in desk for the next part of my journey to Manchester.

Thank the good Lord and all his holy saints, the rest of the journey passed relatively uneventfully and we finally arrived in

Manchester, my two dogs intact but my nerves in shreds. There was the same agonising wait for baggage and dogs as in Heathrow and then, just as before, came the tortoise-slow, push-pull routine out of the arrivals hall. When we emerged from Manchester airport, I was overjoyed to see Phil waiting for us, wearing his usual sardonic grin. He walked over saying, 'You bloody took your time! I've been fooking stood here for ages!' There was absolutely no point in trying to tell him about my journey and the disaster in Belfast because he was already on his way out the front door, pushing Cracker towards the car. But then he stopped and, turning round very quickly, said, 'Hang on a minute! There's no fooking way this fooking load is going into my car, Volvo estate or no Volvo estate. You'd best find somewhere to leave them fooking sky kennels!' That was my mate Phil – direct and straight to the point.

As usual when I find myself in trouble in an airport, I looked for the nearest policeman, but this time I was not on my own. Phil launched one of his very rarely seen charm-offensives and managed to completely disarm one of the lady airport staff members. I don't know what he said to her but, whatever it was, it worked a treat. I was allowed to store the kennels behind a door marked 'Staff Only' until Sunday afternoon, provided it did not become a regular habit. Job done.

Training the next morning, a Saturday, was supposed to begin early, but it didn't for me. It couldn't. Phil and I did not arrive in Leyland until much later because I couldn't get out of my sleeping bag. I was physically and mentally drained and, on top of that, Phil could talk for England, which he did that Friday night and into the early hours of Saturday morning. Eventually we were ready to work. Bodies had been 'buried' and dogs were sent to search for them. Critical eyes were watching from various vantage points and the standard of searching scrutinised in detail.

Dave Peplow, although never a search and rescue dog handler himself, knew whether a dog was any good or not. He could also spot the shortcomings and strengths of the handlers. Very little escaped Dave and, by putting us under pressure like that, he helped everybody improve. The day wore on – burying casualties, finding them, burying more – until it was time to quit.

We were shattered and needed a rest. But our timetable said that after a break for something to eat, we were due to get a very special presentation by Patrick, the boss of a London-based rescue organisation. His team had already been abroad, we were told, and were apparently very good at what they did. Patrick, however, was known to take no nonsense and to rule with an iron fist.

Rodney, Phil and I decided to nip around the corner for a curry before the talk. We had a few drinks and the craic was ninety. When it came, the meal was hot and spicy, and between that and the fact that the three of us have very low alcohol tolerance, we became well pissed. When we arrived back at the fire station, where the presentation was to take place, it was a struggle trying to remember the combination for unlocking the door, but we got in eventually. By that time we were already late, as we bumped and crashed our way into the lecture room.

Patrick, our guest speaker, was about six foot three and was wearing severe black overalls and long paratrooper-type boots. There were tools, torches and little black bags dangling from his black leather belt. He was clearly upset that we were late. 'What time of the day do you call this?' he demanded, glaring at the three of us, his face suffused with anger, his eyes popping and the veins in his neck standing out like knotted ropes. We were all a bit taken aback.

I tried to pass the blame on to Rodders, who in turn tried to pass it on to Phil who, in turn, was having none of it. 'Shut up, the whole lot of you, and sit down!' roared Patrick, now almost apoplectic. He struggled to breathe for a second and then, regaining his strength, roared, 'Right! I'm not putting up with this. I'm off!'

'No, no. Don't go. We're very sorry, Patrick,' Rodders pleaded, abject sorrow in his voice. 'We won't make another sound. Please carry on.'

Patrick thought about it for a minute and then, placated a little, turned to the rest of the group. But unfortunately Rodders, Phil and I messed up again. You know that feeling when you are in church, or at a funeral or some other sombre event – the last place you should be laughing – and the more you try not to laugh, the more you do. Well that was how it was with us that night.

Patrick continued, 'As I was saying before that interruption, when we are on a mission, we don't sleep, we don't eat and we don't drink! Why? I'll tell you why. Because sleeping takes up time when you should be out there rescuing someone. Eating and drinking mean you have to shit and piss. That also takes up valuable rescue time! That's why we don't bring food or water with us! We haven't a minute to waste. It's all or nothing.' Patrick waved his finger in the air and his neck stretched out belligerently.

That was it. He had pushed our boundaries too far and all efforts at respectful decorum were gone. Phil, Rodders and I exploded into hoots of laughter, spluttering and choking. I was laughing so much that I felt I was seriously in danger of having a heart attack. It wasn't just what Patrick had said – it was the way he said it, with such intensity and passion, marching to and fro in his black gear, the bling on his belt clanking loudly and punctuating each step.

He stopped and stared venomously at the three of us. 'What the hell would you lot know?' he threw at us. 'None of you has ever been to one of these disasters, have you?'

'No, Patrick,' I managed to blurt out. 'Sorry, Patrick! It's just that we had a few beers and we're being stupid. Sorry. It won't happen again.'

'Well then,' he said, slightly appeased. 'All right. But you'll see. When you get out there, you'll see!'

He carried on with the lecture in his dogmatic, forthright way and, of course, some of the things he said were very sensible. But then he started explaining about the medical bits and pieces his team carried with them on deployments. 'There's a doctor among you lot, isn't there?' he demanded. 'Which one of you is the doctor?' he asked, staring at the lads in the front rows. Everyone turned around to look at Rodders. Phil and I pointed at him. 'He is,' we both said at the same time.

'You?' demanded Patrick. 'You? You're not fit to be a doctor!'

That was it. Suppressed hysteria burst the floodgates and we laughed and cackled and hooted, mainly at Rodders, who was doing his very best to look indignant. It was really bad. Down at the front of the lecture hall the door slammed shut as Patrick stormed out. The lecture had ended.

Training the next day was slow to start because everyone wanted to talk about the previous night, but we got going eventually. The training site was in a disused factory with about three floors and millions of hiding places. Phil was in charge of training and of placing the 'bodies'. It came round to my turn to do a search with Cracker. Phil followed very close behind, watching everything. For the first few minutes, we found nothing and I began to believe that Phil was up to his usual tricks and hadn't actually hidden anyone. I panicked a little because, if there was a body there and I didn't find it, I would have failed that search and I hated losing to Phil just as much as he hated losing to me.

Cracker kept on searching and then suddenly stopped. We were in an empty corridor and he was staring at the floor. He circled round and round, sniffing the floor. I couldn't understand for the life of me what he was doing because the floor seemed fully intact.

'Well?' Phil asked innocently. 'What's to do then?'

'I don't understand him,' I said. 'He's never done that before. What the hell's got into him? He's definitely telling me he's found someone but where the hell are they?'

'Well, where do you think they might be, you daft bugger?'

'Under the floor?' I answered weakly.

'Correct!' he chortled.

He bent down, inserted a knife between the boards and prised up a section of flooring to expose the grinning face of Uncle Ray Jones, one of our regular Welsh 'bodies'. Phil had won our un-spoken competition and he proceeded to make hay out of it. To everyone he met afterwards he would shout in glee, 'Hey! Do you know what happened in there? That pillock ...' nodding towards me, 'that numbskull were searching in't corridor. His bloody dog barked and what does he do? Bloody nothing, that's what he bloody does. Calls hisself a bloody search dog handler? Honestly, my little six-year-old lad could do better.' On and on he went in the same vein, milking my crap performance dry. The shame of it! It was going to be very hard to live down.

Chapter 23

Training finally over, it was time for me and my two boys to start the journey home. Phil drove us to Manchester airport, where the whole check-in thing started again. It went fairly smoothly but, unfortunately, takeoff was delayed by thirty minutes, and that would have disastrous results for me in London.

By the time we had touched down in Heathrow and I had pushed the two boys to the check-in desk for Belfast, I learned that the last flight had gone. However, the airline accepted that the delay had been wholly their fault and kindly offered me overnight accommodation in a hotel near the airport.

They even booked Cracker and Dylan into boarding kennels at the edge of the airport. Great stuff, I thought. For once this travelling nightmare was not going to end in tears.

Unfortunately I was wrong. The boarding kennels in question were actually official quarantine kennels, run by DEFRA (the Department for Environment, Food and Rural Affairs). When we got to the kennels, they looked very nice indeed. The two dogs were duly checked in and I arranged a time to come back for them in the morning. I gave the kennels the number of the hotel where I was staying (I didn't have a mobile phone in those days), said goodnight and was driven away. God seemed to be smiling on His humble and lowly servant and everything was running smoothly. But I should have known the axe was about to fall.

At 2 a.m., the phone beside the bed shattered my sleep with incessant ringing. The voice on the other end was that of a woman from the kennels sounding most officious and very much awake.

With no apology for disturbing me, she said there was a serious matter she needed to discuss with me straight away that could not wait until morning. It transpired that she had measured my sky kennels and found that they did not meet the required dimensions (she said they were two inches lower and one and a half inches shorter than the specified size). She said that she could not allow the dogs to fly until the matter had been resolved.

'Is this a wind up?' I asked hopefully.

'It most certainly is not, Mr Powell,' she replied icily. 'Unless you provide kennels which meet our requirements, the dogs will be staying here.'

'Are you not just being a little bit extreme? I mean the kennels are not restricting their movements in any way, are they?'

'I'm sorry, Mr Powell, but it's more than my job's worth to allow your dogs to travel in the crates as they are.' Then she repeated loftily, 'As I've said, they're two inches too small in height and one and a half inches too small in length.'

'But the dogs were allowed to travel from Belfast to here with no problem,' I said.

'That's as may be, Mr Powell but, as I've said, it's more than my job's worth to let them leave here in kennels which are not the required size.'

She advised me that I could get new kennels made and that they might be ready the day after tomorrow. 'The day after tomorrow!' I ranted. 'What do I do between now and then? Who pays for my hotel? My God! Who pays for the new kennels? How much are they going to cost anyway?'

'I'm afraid I don't know who's going to pay for your hotel, Mr Powell. As for the kennels, they can be made for around one hundred and fifty pounds each, I believe,' she replied glibly.

'That's three hundred bloody quid I have to fork out plus the hotel bill and, no doubt, you'll be charging me for their extra stay at your place too, won't you?'

'Yes. There will be an additional charge for their stay with us, Mr Powell.'

I tried reasoning with her, hoping to tug at her heartstrings, explaining that Cracker and Dylan were search and rescue dogs, trained to work in earthquake conditions to find survivors. But she was having none of it.

I leapt out of bed, sleep forgotten, and threw my clothes on. I couldn't possibly afford to stay in the hotel, let alone pay for two new sky kennels. I went back to the airport not knowing what to do. Suddenly, the answer to my prayers drifted into view: a Metropolitan Police dog handler standing there, guarding the nation, with his very fine-looking German shepherd dog. I almost broke into a run to get to him. 'Excuse me, officer. Can I have a word with you please?'

'Certainly, sir. How can I help?' All very polite and businesslike. I told him my name and then blurted out what had happened.

A knowing smile spread across his face and he said, 'She's a fucking jobsworth, mate!'

'A what?' I asked.

'She's one of these bloody people who say, "Ooooh it's more than my job's worth." A jobsworth, see?'

'I've never heard of that but I know what you mean. Yes, that would definitely sum her up. Can you help me at all?'

'I'm sure I can, mate. Hang on a sec,' he said, reaching for his radio. I heard him report what I had told him and the sympathetic-sounding voice of his desk sergeant responding at the other end. Then the knight in shining armour smiled and said, 'Right! Let's go and see what we can do.'

As he led me out to his police dog van, he told me his name was John Allison. On the way to the kennels, he must have concocted a scheme to spring Cracker and Dylan, but he said nothing about it to me at the time. He did suggest, however, that we should give the DEFRA tyrant a chance to redeem herself – to realise that she had perhaps been just a bit over-zealous.

The kennels, now looking truly joyless in the dim light of dawn, were locked when we got there. My new friend rang the doorbell and we waited. From the depths, we could hear its clamorous ringing, and of course it set all the dogs off. The barking rose in a crescendo, each dog no doubt thinking and praying that the time of its release was at hand.

The door opened and, although I hadn't met the lady who had

phoned me, I knew her immediately. This overbearing, intrusive creature barring our way, was indeed the archetypal 'bitch from hell'.

'Can I help you, gentlemen?' she asks, in a manner that clearly expects the answer to be 'no'.

'Good evening, madam. My name is Constable Allison and this is Mr Powell. I believe you are detaining two of his dogs, is that correct?'

Again she went through the supposed problem with my kennels.

'I see. Look, miss …' Constable Allison began a reasoning ploy, 'these are professional dogs who are clearly loved and well cared for. Can you not make an exception in this case?'

'No, officer. I'm sorry but I can't,' she replied firmly. 'They stay here until bigger crates are provided for them and that's final.'

'Right. I believe you said that he can get new kennels made somewhere near here?'

'Yes – just a few miles down the road. If you like, I'll give you the number and you can speak to the people yourself.'

'May I use your phone then?' he asked.

'Certainly, officer. It's this way, in my office.'

While he followed her, I waited outside, exasperated and feeling very sorry for myself. Nothing happened for a while and then, astonishingly, my new friend walked out the front door with Cracker and Dylan bouncing around on their leads, and their sky kennels being pushed behind them by another DEFRA employee.

'Thanks very much indeed, miss,' he shouted over his shoulder. 'Don't worry – I'll take full responsibility for them. I'll see to it that Mr Powell gets the new crates. I'll drive him there now myself,' he promised.

'Thank you, officer,' she said, sounding mollified, but not comp-letely convinced. 'I'll come to see the dogs loaded on the 7.30 flight to Belfast myself. You're sure that's the right time?'

'Correct, miss,' said my new friend. 'I'll have the dogs and their crates ready for your inspection before they're loaded.'

Cracker and Dylan were overjoyed as we put them into the van. The sergeant shoved their 'too small' sky kennels in through the side door of the van and, with a cheery wave to the lady, drove us away. 'Now, Neil,' he smiled. 'That gives us forty minutes to get you on your flight and away home before that bitch knows you've gone! I'll ring ahead and let the staff know we're on our way.'

'I don't believe you,' I gasped.

He replied, laughing, 'I hate people like that. They're so far up their own rear ends that they're looking out their own mouths.'

'Outstanding,' I said, in sheer admiration.

At 6 a.m. we were pulling up at the front doors of Heathrow, where two guys wearing the uniforms of airport staff were standing waiting. As quick as a flash, they took the dogs out of the van, crated them and whisked them away to the inner depths of the airport. My new mate beamed at me and told me to run in case I missed the plane. I had fifteen minutes. I thanked him from the bottom of my heart.

I ran as fast as I could to the boarding gate, where I was waved down the corridor and on to the plane. Relieved, I threw myself into a seat, and in minutes we were roaring down the runway and away home. I never saw or heard from the woman again, but I did make sure that from then on whenever I flew anywhere, the sky kennels were always bigger than necessary.

Chapter 24

On a rainy windswept afternoon in March 1999 four teenagers from Banbridge in County Down were reported lost in the Mourne Mountains during their Duke of Edinburgh gold award expedition. According to their assessors – who had contacted the police – the students should have been at their agreed rendezvous point twelve hours ago and there was now great concern for their safety. The point towards which the young people should have been heading was a well-known ford at the top of the Trassey Track, a rough path that leads to the foot of Slieve Bearnagh. It is a point where three valleys converge to form a 'Y' shape, the two upper arms lying in a south-east and south-west direction respectively, joining the base, which runs due north.

Since the morning the weather had deteriorated badly, shrouding the mountains in dense swirling mist and heavy rain. The conditions were so bad that even an experienced well-equipped mountaineer would have been tested. Concern for the young people was growing by the minute – both hypothermia and serious injury were distinct possibilities.

The police officer who had taken the initial call from the students' assessors was a friend of mine, so once he had alerted the local mountain rescue team, he rang me. Quickly he outlined the situation, gave me the contact number of one of the kids' teachers and asked me to phone right away for an update. As soon as he put the phone down, I rang the number and was greeted a very distressed voice. When I had explained who I was, he told me that, as per their emergency protocol, the assessor had rung him at home to tell him there was a problem. He had then travelled directly to the rendezvous point and was now waiting there with the two assessors.

I said I would be with them as quickly as I could and that I was bringing a mountain search dog with me. 'I know this is really hard for you but hang on until I get there,' I said. 'Don't go on the hill because that'll make it very hard for Dylan – he will get confused by your scent.'

'We'll wait here for you,' he assured me.

'I'll be with you in twenty minutes, so you won't have to wait long. See you shortly.'

I then phoned one of the mountain rescue team leaders to explain what I was going to do. Like me, he felt that Dylan was the kids' best hope.

I got to the top of the track in about twenty minutes and, parking beside the school minibus, could see two adults sitting in the front seats. I opened the driver's door and after the usual pre-liminaries learned that, unfortunately, two of the assessors had felt unable to wait and had already gone up the hill to search for the missing children. It was a bit of a setback but, given that they had both taken the left-hand valley, I reckoned Dylan could still do a good job on the valley to the right. It led south-west, to what is known locally as Pollaphuca col – the very heart of the Mourne Mountains.

As we set off, the wind was varying in direction from dead ahead to over on my left-hand side, where it was blasting straight down from the steep sides of Bearnagh. Unfortunately, that was where the two teachers might have been by then, so there was an outside chance that Dylan could pick up their scent. All I could do was hope that he didn't.

I put his search coat on him, patted his side and sent him off with, 'Find him, Dylly.' As usual when he heard the command he ran for about fifty metres, stopped, threw himself on to his back, waved his legs in the air for a bit, stood up, shook himself, looked at me and then carried on. He never failed to follow that ritual and it was very embarrassing when people were looking on. In seconds, the swirling misty tendrils had reached out and swallowed him up. I kept walking up the path, moving about thirty metres off it at intervals in case the kids had wandered in that direction. Dylan could not have found them over there because their scent would have been blown to the other side of the valley, well away from him. In about twenty minutes I reached the halfway point to the col but there was no sign of Dylan. Visibility was down to around thirty metres in any direction, but I knew he would be somewhere ahead of me, cutting across the wind, giving himself the best chance of finding the youngsters.

Normally at night or in bad weather, having swept ahead for a missing person, Dylan would come back to find me. He had developed his own system for this – he ran in a huge loop downwind until eventually he cut across my scent cone which he then followed back to wherever I was. Given that he'd been gone so long, I felt it was probably time for him to find me now, so I stopped walking and waited for a few minutes. Almost on cue, he appeared. I was delighted to see him and was about to carry on up the valley when he ran in front and stopped me. He began to bark that peculiar bark of his: 'Agh uff, agh uff.'

My God he's found somebody, I thought, but the problem was knowing who. It could easily have been the two teachers out there searching, but then it could also have been the missing youngsters. Whoever he had found, Dylan was going to have to take me to find out so I said, 'Show me, son.'

He turned and ran off to my left, heading towards the steep ground of Bearnagh Slabs, a well-known climbing area about eighty metres in height. I blundered along behind him, slipping and stumbling over the greasy wet peaty ground that covered the area. The angle started to increase steeply as he led me into the wind and up towards the ridge. Carefully he picked his way upwards, waiting every now and again for me to catch up, then climbing again. His bright orange coat was only just in view as he cautiously made his way through gaps in the boulders and small slabs of granite. Higher and higher we went into the cloud and the hammering rain.

I guessed we must be very near the top and as I strained to look upwards for the hundredth time, to my amazement I could make out the form of a person standing up. He – or possibly she – was on a ledge and was shouting, but the words were being swept away by the wind. But as I got closer I heard a young man's voice shouting desperately, 'Up here! Up here!'

'I see you,' I shouted back. At that point I had no idea then whether we'd found the missing kids or their teachers.

I climbed the last few feet and could see that we had struck gold. Dylan had indeed found the four youngsters and against all the odds.

'See, I told you,' he seemed to say, as he barked excitedly.

'Good lad, Dylly,' I shouted in relief and delight, and tossed his yellow tennis ball into his open mouth.

'Am I glad to see you guys,' I said. 'Is everybody okay?'

I could see that, very sensibly, the three girls were lying close together in bright orange bivvy bags, but the boy was the one who had been standing. His clothes were soaking wet from his having braved the elements hour after hour, calling for help. His face was blue with cold and he looked well on the way to becoming hypothermic. The kids said that they still had all their emergency food and kit – they had been conserving it all in case they were stuck on the ledge for another night. So it was a matter of persuading the young lad to get inside his bivvy bag and to eat something sweet.

'The team is not far behind,' I assured them. 'They'll soon get you off and down to the minibus.' I radioed to advise them that the kids were located and were safe, and I gave our position. All we could do then was to sit tight and hang on a bit longer. While we were waiting, the kids told me that they had become disorientated in the bad weather and found themselves on the steep ground of Bernagh Slabs. They were too frightened to go down and could not face going back up, so they elected to sit it out and wait for help. In the circumstances it had probably been the right decision and I made sure they knew it.

Meanwhile Dylan, being a retriever, had dropped his beloved tennis ball and the kids' food became his focus. His big brown eyes were asking them, 'You can't possibly be intending to eat all that yourself can you?'

He did not have long to wait; indeed, they all spoiled him rotten.

At last the team arrived and the four kids were on the move again. The descent was slow and careful and in about forty minutes they had got back to the minibus. As so often happens at times like that, the clouds were suddenly swept aside and the rain stopped. The youngsters were greeted with open arms by their hugely relieved and very happy teachers and were soon drying out in the warmth of Newcastle police station.

Kate, the dogs and I were on holiday in Sligo in August that year when we went on a day's shopping trip to Tubercurry – or rather, she went shopping while I hung around outside the shops, bored sick. What a joy, therefore, when my brand new mobile phone rang and I heard the cheery voice of Phil Haigh on the other end.

'Phil, you bollocks, it's great to hear from you but I'm shocked, what with the cost of phone calls and all,' I said, knowing how much Phil hated spending money.

'Aye – you're right. Listen! There's been a fooking great earthquake in Turkey and DFID want to know if we can deploy. Are you available?'

DFID is the Department for International Development, and one of their responsibilities is the deployment of UK search and rescue teams abroad.

'Of course I am. How long have I got?'

'About twelve hours, mate. We'll be leaving from RAF Lynham. Okey doke?'

'Bloody hell! I'm on holiday in Sligo but I'll do my best,' I said in shock.

'Let me know how you're getting on. I'll speak to you in a bit,' he said and was gone.

I blundered into the shop to tell Kate that my part of the holiday was over. 'Erm, Katie …' I started weakly.

'I'm nearly finished,' she said as she carried on staring at whatever it was in her hand.

'Kate, look … I need to get home to Newcastle fast with Cracker. Phil wants us at this big earthquake in Turkey. The problem is the rest of the dogs. How will you manage them here in Sligo if I bugger off?' I asked.

As usual Kate took it all in her stride and calmly answered, 'Look, you get yourself and Cracker sorted out. Leave me to worry about the rest of the dogs.'

'Wow,' I thought.

Then she asked, 'How are you going to get there?'

'I'll ring Sean Rodgers,' I said in a moment of inspiration. 'He'll know what to do. He knows people in the Air Corps.'

I dialled Sean's work number, never thinking for one minute that he'd be there because he was always on the road.

'Sean Rodgers here,' came the reply.

'Sean! It's Neil Powell. Sorry for bothering you but I'm in the shit.'

'Why? What have you done now?' he asked.

'I haven't done anything, Sean, but I've been called to help at an earthquake in Turkey. The trouble is I'm in Sligo on holiday. Do you know anyone in the Air Corps who might bend a few rules to get me home to Newcastle quick?'

Sean never flustered about things and in an unhurried calm voice said, 'You wait there and I'll ring you back.'

Rather than waste time hanging around Tubbercurry, we decided to drive straight back to the holiday house we'd rented. We had to get packed up quick. Twenty minutes later, as we were hurtling along the narrow roads that twist and weave their way over the hills, my mobile phone rang again.

'Neil, Sean here. Can you get to Sligo airport for 2.30 this afternoon? The Air Corps have agreed to send a Dauphane helicopter to take you to Newcastle.'

'My God, Sean! You don't frig about, do you?'

'Yeah, I'm some pup, aren't I?' he replied, the delight in his voice obvious.

'I'll be there in time, Sean. Thanks very much – I owe you.'

Kate and I bundled the dogs into the car and gunned it to Sligo airport, a journey of about twenty minutes.

When we arrived, I immediately and inadvertently caused a bit of a stir with two of the staff in the reception area. I told them I wasn't booked on any flight but that I was expecting an Irish Air Corps helicopter to pick me up in a few minutes.

'An Air Corps helicopter, is it?' one of them enquired with unctuous interest. 'A helicopter is coming to pick you up from here is it? And what about the dog?'

'He's going too. We're both off to Turkey.'

'To Turkey? Well now, is that a fact?' she said, looking knowingly at her colleague.

'Yes. But first I have to get home to get my kit.'

'Oh! You have to get home for your kit, is it?' Her eyebrows lifted a bit higher and her unctuous tone deepened. 'And where might home be?'

As I was explaining, I heard the noise of a helicopter landing outside and of course the members of staff heard it too. 'Well, there's a helicopter landed, right enough,' one shouted over his shoulder as he stared out the window.

'Now do you believe me?' I asked the one nearest.

'I do, sir, I do,' came the contrite reply. 'This way, sir …' She directed me to the No Exit door which she opened with a key.

I asked Kate to phone our daughter Clair, who I hoped would be at home in Newcastle.

'See if she'd get my kit gathered up for me, Kate. Say I'll meet her at the football pitch in Donard Park. If she rings the cops at Newcastle police station they'll be able to tell her when I'm going to get there.' I knew we would land there as it's the landing place in Newcastle for all search and rescue operations.

Kate nodded in resignation. 'I'm sorry to drop you in it like this, love. Thanks for what you're doing. See you in a week or so,' and I left her with a hurried kiss and a hug. As I ran to the helicopter with Cracker, I turned to see that Kate, standing all alone and faced with a long journey home by road, her holiday in tatters, could still wave and manage a smile.

The blast of air from the rotating blades hit me and threatened to knock me off my feet. The noise of the helicopter engines was deafening and Cracker was not at all impressed. He hated flying as much as me. The crewman beckoned me towards the open door of the aircraft. Cracker fought against me and pulled on the lead and my bag slipped off my shoulder. 'Oh for the love of God, Cracker, you bollocks,' I shouted, but he couldn't hear me – indeed, I couldn't even hear me! We wrestled and struggled to the door where we were blasted by hot exhaust gases and deafened by the noise of the engines just above our heads.

The crewman told me to chuck my bag in the back, Cracker was trying desperately to make a run for it, and I was fighting to stay upright. I swung my bag off my shoulder and chucked it inside the neat little six-seat aircraft. Next I climbed in with Cracker. I was strapped into a seat, while Cracker jammed himself underneath it. I was handed a pair of earphones with a microphone attached and I heard the pilot asking, 'Where to?' like it's a taxi service.

'Newcastle, County Down,' I answered. What else could I say? I was blown away by the whole thing and my heart was threatening to leave my body at any moment.

'On our way,' came the calm reply.

The engine noise increased, the vibrations became more severe and we were airborne with the speed of an express elevator. 'You're off to an earthquake in Turkey, I hear,' said the metallic voice of the winch-man in my ear. He sounded confident and professional which, in my state of panic, I found calming. I explained that Cracker and I belonged to an international search dog team based in the UK and that this would be our first deployment overseas. I told him I was going to have to get all my survival gear and a change of clothes from home before trying to get a flight from Belfast to RAF Lynham. We skimmed along, following the main roads from Sligo to Enniskillen. I knew them well, having trundled up and down between Newcastle and Sligo for years – I almost forgot my fear of flying as I marvelled at the speed of the helicopter.

'Is there someone at home to help you with the kit part?' he asks.

'Yes. My daughter Clair will be at home. She'll meet me.'

'So, all you need to sort out then is how to get to England?'

'Yes. The cops might be able to find out from Aldergrove if there are any military flights going.'

'Right. I'll get on to that through the coastguard,' he offered helpfully.

I was amazed at the cooperation being shown to me by the Irish

Air Corps, who, I later learned, had to get special diplomatic clearance for what they were doing. They were, in effect, flying across an international and highly sensitive border into an area caught up in a contentious armed struggle.

And then we were coming in to land at the football pitch on the edge of Newcastle town. I saw blue lights flashing here and there and the place was awash with people gathered around the perimeter fence. There were members of the coastguard and police, dressed in bright yellow jackets, keeping everyone back from the cordoned area. There was an orange smoke flare to show our pilot the wind direction.

The helicopter swept in and touched down, and the winch-man gave me the all clear to get out. I stopped in the doorway to thank him, and the pilot and for getting me here so fast, but they dismissed my thanks and then blew me away by offering to fly me to Aldergrove once I'd gathered my kit. I tried to protest but they said they were going there to refuel anyway.

I jumped out with Cracker, who was only too glad to get away from the deafening noise. He was pulling frantically towards open space when I saw Clair and her husband Raph waving at me from behind the sea of yellow high visibility jackets. They'd managed to bring all my 'emergency-going-away-to-foreign-places gear', which I always have packed and ready, just in case.

After the briefest of thanks and goodbyes, I ran back to the waiting helicopter. My gear was hauled aboard, followed by a protesting Cracker. I waved to Clair and Raph and was directed to a seat by the ever-attentive crewman. The engine noise increased, the aircraft trembled, fighting to overcome gravity and we were again soaring skywards. We swung north-west and Cracker and I were on our way to the next part of this incredible adventure. The flight to RAF Aldergrove was a short one and we were soon landing at the heavily protected British military base. Uniformed personnel marshalled the Irish Air Corps aircraft to a parking place and the pilot shut down the engines. I thanked the crew again for all their kindness and stepped down onto the tarmac.

I was immediately ushered away by an attentive RAF corporal who tossed my heavy kit bag on to a trolley as we headed off in the direction of a large hangar-like building. It turned out to be a purpose-built terminal for servicemen and -women, just like the civilian equivalent at Belfast International across the other side of the airfield. It had a check-in and X-ray machines and all sorts of notices advising caution to all personnel whilst serving in Northern Ireland.

I was taken through the security check and, emerging from the door, was confronted with the enormous bulk of a C130 Hercules transport plane. Its load bay door was open and personnel in military uniforms were busy loading the plane with baggage, freight and people. 'Get on board and find yourself a seat, young man. They're flying a crowd home for leave today so you're lucky. Better still, the plane is going to RAF Lynham.'

'I can't believe it,' I stammered.

What a stroke of luck. I'd had absolutely no idea where Lynham was so, without this lift, I would never have got there in time.

'These Hercy birds aren't very comfy,' my guide shouted, nodding towards the giant plane, 'but you'll get used to it.'

'Yes … thanks very much,' I managed, not at all convinced, but when I got up close to it, I could see that the C130 really is a huge aircraft and, with its massive four engines, looked reassuringly safe.

I made my uncertain way up the ladder on the port side and entered the trembling bulk of the aircraft. On my back I was carrying a large bag filled with my tent, cooking gear, spare clothes, dog food, sleeping bag and working clothes, including a pair of steel toe-capped boots. I was also hanging on tightly to Cracker who still hated flying. It was a struggle but everyone else was too preoccupied with their own business to notice.

My kit was tossed into a netted section towards the tail of the cavernous interior. I strapped myself into the metal-framed, canvas-covered seat and was handed the only luxury item of the flight – a pair of bright yellow earplugs. 'Makes things a bit less noisy, mate,' shouted the RAF crewman over the din of the engines warming up for takeoff. The ramp closed and I hung on tightly to Cracker, who was now puffing and panting at my feet. What does he know that I don't, I wondered.

We began to roll ponderously forward, the noise deafening, every bump on the tarmac thumping my bottom and hammering my back. It went on for what felt like forever until at last we turned, ready for takeoff. The bedlam increased to overwhelming levels. Cracker pressed himself against my legs so hard that I had to move before he broke one of them. Just when I thought the noise had reached maximum decibels, the clamour increased even more as we started the mad dash for the sky. The giant plane bounced, jolted and swayed her way down the runway and then, amazingly, we lifted off and the huge, ponderous, fully laden monster sailed upwards like a bird.

The engine note dropped to a comforting, steady roar and I felt it was safe to take a furtive look around. The seats were all occupied by very fit- and healthy-looking servicemen and -women, already dozing or reading books. Nobody looked anxious, and so I relaxed a little. Cracker, still under my seat, stuck his head out to look around him, clearly not convinced he should be there.

Then just as suddenly as we took off, we started the descent to RAF Lynham. Already I was starting to get panicky in case Phil and the lads had left without me. The landing was effortless and in a replay of the takeoff, we thundered and rumbled down the runway until slowing we swung round and headed for wherever it was that we had to disembark. The engines stopped, the ramp was lowered and we were waved off the plane. Cracker and I walked unsteadily towards a building close by, while someone shouted that my kit would be brought over directly.

I went into the terminal to find the place teeming with rescue guys from all over the UK – there were teams from fire and rescue, Rapid UK and international rescue and, in the middle of them all, Phil Haigh, scruffy as ever. On seeing me, he jumped up and said, 'About bloody time too, you Irish twat!' We shook hands, slapped each other on the back and then he was off on one of his mile-long soliloquies about who said what to whom, when we might be taking off for Turkey, what kit he forgot to bring with him (trust me to have everything I might need) and so on and so on. Meanwhile, we had to 'hurry up and wait' for whatever was going to happen next.

I cast my mind back over the last few hours and the mad dash to get to Lynham, while now here we all were twiddling our thumbs. Somebody told us that the delay was because we were waiting for approval from the Turkish authorities to land in Turkey. The usual self-reliant sort of blokes were already making themselves at home, having sourced tea, coffee and even sandwiches. True to form, Phil tagged along with some of them and, with me in tow, got fed and watered too. He is a master scrounger.

Eventually, a stir of movement and guys began standing up, reaching for bags and talking animatedly. It amazes me that after a period of waiting, some people always seem to know exactly when it's time to move – it's like they have a built-in radar that tunes itself to incoming messages from whoever is in charge.

Phil and I were told we'd be working with the Kent fire brigade when we got to Turkey. The team leader was a senior divisional officer called Ian Muir and his deputy was Divisional Officer Neil Hubbard. Phil made a wry face and a derisory crack about getting stuck with 'bloody water squirters' but I knew he was delighted – with the fire service, we would have the best support.

'Right lad! Let's make a move,' said Phil, grabbing the lead attached to his enormous German shepherd, Denke. He hoisted his fairly empty kit bag on to his shoulder and said, nodding at a group moving off, 'We'll follow that lot. They seem to know where they're going.'

They shuffled out and we followed, passing through a series of corridors and doors until eventually we crossed the tarmac towards another C130. Crates of rescue equipment and Land-Rovers were being ferried up the ramp and effortlessly swallowed by the cavernous opening. 'Fook me,' said Phil. 'Look at that lot! How the fook is it goin' to get off the fookin' ground carrying all that fooking shite?'

'Oh thanks, Phil,' I say. 'Thanks a bloody lot!'

'Oh we'll be all right. Trust me! I know these things. I'm English,' he smirked, rattling his top row of false front teeth up and down, a party trick he enjoyed. I had to laugh at him, the clown.

The inside of the Hercules was a cacophony of sound, caused by the idling aircraft engines, the orders being shouted by load masters and the growl of Land-Rovers as they ground up the ramp. Bright internal lights cast a harsh, unforgiving brightness on everything. Members of the various teams were finding seats next to each other and available spaces were disappearing fast. Phil and I found two canvas chairs towards the back of the aircraft on the starboard side. We were beside one of the Land-Rovers, now chained to the deck. A crew member gave us the usual safety blurb and then the ramp closed with a resounding thump. The noise became even more strident and we frantically fumbled for our yellow ear defenders and stuffed them into our ear canals as far as they would go.

Just as I finished inserting mine, I got a tap on the arm and Phil was signalling at me to remove them – he had obviously thought of something important to say. Leaning close to my ear he shouted, 'Ah were just thinking, mate … how does the fooker up the front that's driving know what weight this fookin' plane is carrying? After all, you've only fookin' guessed what you've got in that great bag of yours and all these water squirters probably guessed theirs as well. Then there's all those fookin' great boxes of kit they loaded on. How heavy are they? If you ask me, this fooker will never get off the ground! We'll probably run off the end of the runway. Shit the fookin' bed!'

'Fuck me! Thanks Phil, you bollocks,' I croaked. 'That's all I needed to hear!' I stuffed my defenders back into my ears and resigned myself to the fact that I was probably going to die horribly on this, my first flight to a major earthquake.

At 9 p.m., we started rumbling towards the takeoff point, stopped for a few (seemingly) endless minutes and then began the takeoff. We trundled forward slowly at first, then picked up speed until, in seconds, this leviathan was hurtling down the runway towards what I was now quite sure was certain death. After what felt like miles and miles of runway, we crabbed skywards, painfully slowly. The wheels came up with a thump, we banked to one side and we were on our way to Turkey. Phil dug me hard in the ribs. 'See!' he bellowed, smirking. 'Ah told you there were nowt to worry about, didn't I?'

Chapter 25

The flight was eight hours long and in all that time the dogs neither moved nor had a pee – how they hung on I do not know. The toilet provided for our use was a canvas screen around a toilet bowl bolted to the port side of the aircraft. As the ever-insightful Phil observed when I expressed some reservation about using it, 'It's shit or bust mate.' Looking from the windows of the aircraft I watched the lights of villages and towns drifting slowly past, thousands of feet below. When that became boring I tried to sleep, curled up under a Land-Rover with Cracker lying tucked in beside me. Some of the firemen had brought hammocks which they slung neatly from various anchor points above the loading ramp. No discomfort for them, I thought, as I watched them swing comfortably from side to side, apparently fast asleep. In God's name, how did they know to bring a bloody hammock, I wondered. The plane bucked and swooped in some turbulence and then droned peacefully on and on into the night sky.

Coming out of a restless doze I was amazed to notice that the very same group of all-knowing people who seemed to have prior knowledge of when we were leaving Lynham all those hours ago were beginning to make preparations for landing. How do they always seem to know these things before everybody else? I felt my ears popping, so even I knew we were starting our descent. Phil woke up and gave me a thumbs-up. It was about one in the morning as we landed in Istanbul.

The Hercules came to a shuddering stop and the ramp, stripped now of the fire brigade's hammocks, cracked open. The heat, even at this early hour, hit us like an oven. We were immediately bathed in sweat and the dogs began to pant. Everyone was talking and rearranging bags and clothing. Neil Hubbard and Ian Muir ushered everyone off the plane. We transferred our kit to one of three previously requisitioned buses with smiling, nodding drivers, who were now assured of at least a week's pay.

It took quite a while to pile everything on board, then we drove out of the airport and into what seemed to be the unscathed streets of a teeming metropolis. The buses wended their way slowly to a waiting ferry which took us across the Sea of Marmaris. On the other side, we headed for the town of Yalova, one of the worst-affected areas. We started to pass through scenes of devastation where people, too scared to sleep indoors, were camped at the side of the road. Some had even set up makeshift shelters on the central reservation between two busy carriageways.

As dawn broke the scenes became even more surreal. We saw families huddled around smoking campfires whose homes had become a collection of rugs and blankets draped over stretched ropes. Houses, once so lovingly cared for, were tilted, way off-plumb, waiting for the last push from the heaving earth's crust to bring them tumbling to the ground. Nobody spoke in the bus as we crashed our way along a road strewn with debris. The lads, all hardened firemen, were shocked as they gazed out at so many people sitting in deep despair by the roadside.

When we arrived in Yalova, our team was immediately tasked with the search of a particularly badly damaged apartment complex. We took the dogs from their sky kennels, gave them a few minutes to have a stretch, a pee and a drink, and then sent them on to the destroyed buildings to search for signs of life. Work had to start as quickly as that because, for those trapped under the rubble, time was slipping away.

Phil and I had already agreed a plan of one of us watching and one of us searching, which we put into action. First it was Cracker's turn. Then his dog Denke was deployed to the same area to confirm whatever Cracker found or didn't find. Cracker made his way up a steeply sloping concrete section with me behind him. I watched as he stopped, looked at something, paused a little and then carried on. I looked too and saw a human arm in silent supplication, sticking out from under the impossibly heavy and unforgiving concrete slab of what had once been an apartment ceiling. Like Cracker, I noted it and then carried on. We were searching for the living.

The heat of the day was making things difficult – the temperature was in the low forties and the sun was blazing down from a clear blue sky. Cracker – with his dense coat, designed to keep out the cold of a British winter – found it very hard going. Very soon his panting changed to gasping but he did not once stop work. The urgent need to find the living meant that resting was not an option. I suddenly remembered the talk we had been given by that strange man Patrick at the fire station all those weeks ago – or was it a lifetime? In many ways his words had been prophetic but because we were so full of our own self-importance (as well as curry and beer) we didn't listen.

It was becoming more and more difficult to ignore the smell of decay. My stomach was turning. I also got a growing anxiety about what new horrors we were going to be confronted with as we crawled through the collapsed buildings looking for survivors. I noticed that Cracker's nose had become coated with a layer of very fine dust and I started to worry that the dust might have penetrated his airway and lungs. I wondered if that was why his breathing sounded so rasping. He carried on searching as I sent him into a small hole, giving access to what was once somebody's bedroom.

Through the gaps, I watched as he worked his way around the room past the broken bed and through another gap into another room. Again the smell of death was overwhelming. There was no sign of him for a while and then I saw him coming back towards me. He was carefully picking his way over and around all the humble possessions of the occupant which were strewn about the floor.

He came to the small access hole, jumped out and wandered off a little way, then stood and waited. It was clear that he hadn't found anyone alive in there. Phil sent in Denke who, because he was such a big dog, found the going much harder than Cracker. He checked here there and everywhere and finally came out, confirming what Cracker had 'said' a few minutes earlier. Phil looked questioningly at me and we silently agreed there was no point in searching here any more. He called Denke back and we moved on.

Elsewhere the lads from the fire service were meticulously conducting their searches using thermal-imaging cameras, video probes, powerful lights, cutting tools and a highly sensitive listening device called a vibraphone. The vibraphone consists of six sound detector 'pots', all connected to the earphones and set out around the site. The 'pots' will identify even the tiniest noise from below ground.

At one point during the search the operator blew a whistle in a previously agreed sequence of blasts, which meant that we should stand still and be perfectly quiet. The fire service members listened intently on the earphones for a response to their tapping, but heard nothing. The whistle blew again telling us to carry on while they repositioned the sensors. Tragically, neither the fire service nor Phil and I found anyone alive in the entire complex of apartments. The earthquake took the lives of every man, woman and child.

From Yalova we were directed to the seaside resort of Aydin where we set up camp along with four other fire brigade teams. We marked out a secure area for holding all the equipment, food and water supplies. A cooking station was set up for the team. We ferreted around looking for space on the ground for sleeping bags and sleeping mats. Lastly, we constructed a makeshift toilet.

For toilet, read latrine — a deep hole dug in the ground over which we placed an old kitchen chair with the seat removed. We stretched hessian sacking over four poles hammered into the ground to make a screen. The luxury materials to complement our privy were a roll of toilet paper, a container of sanitizing hand-wash and a small shovel. When finished in the toilet, each person dug a scoop of soil from the mound beside the chair and tossed it into the hole. Disgusting I know but, despite this unpleasantness, It was amazing how fundamentally important and comforting that toilet became — it offered a tiny degree of privacy in an otherwise goldfish-bowl-like environment.

Very soon the camp was besieged by heartbroken fathers, mothers, brothers, sisters, uncles and aunts, all begging us to come here or go there, to places where they said they had heard cries for help from beneath the ruins of their houses and schools. Ian and Neil tried to impress on our team that all search and rescue work had to be coordinated properly and that the responsibility for making decisions as to where and when we would search rested entirely with them. Ian warned Phil and me to be especially careful not to get dragged into uncoordinated searches with Cracker and Denke. Then he and Neil left to carry out a detailed reconnaissance of the resort.

Aydin was just a collection of five-floor apartment blocks built on a narrow strip of land between the sea and a main road. Nevertheless, it turned out that there were about four hundred and fifty individual apartments to be searched. Ours were the only search dogs in the area and the fire brigade teams the only trained search teams. Just as Ian had warned, we found ourselves bombarded with requests for help from local people. The teams worked through the searing heat of the day until suddenly some of the fire crew located a woman alive, buried under the ruins of her apartment, with their listening devices. The fire brigade worked flat out and, with the help and great skill of the team doctor Iain McNeill, she was released and brought to safety. We were all ecstatic at this glimmer of hope in such a dreadful place of misery and despair.

We carried on working until, at one the next morning, Ian Muir called a halt – everybody was exhausted. We went back to the campsite and tried to sleep but the heat, still overwhelming even at night, made it very difficult. At five in the morning we were up again and back at work.

While we were getting ready to search another building, a man came up to me and spoke in Turkish. He was clearly pleading for something. He didn't understand English any more than I understand Turkish, so I tried speaking to him in German. I can manage a few words and I took the chance he might know a little too. I was delighted when he answered. He told me that before the quake hit, his brother had been in an apartment near where we were standing. He was certain he had heard him calling from below the rubble and asked me please to go with my dog to look for him. Please would I come quickly.

What a mess! Conscious of what we had been told by Ian, I explained that we were trying to finish a job where we were and that, after that, we had been asked to search for a missing child in the next block of apartments. I promised him that when that was done I would come back to help him. He told me that the other teams had told him the same thing, but that none of them had returned. They had lied to him. He started to cry and turned away, saying that I was no better. That was very painful. I tried to reassure him that I was not like that and promised to try and help him when I was finished with the current job. He seemed to believe me and smiled his thanks, saying he would be back shortly. I watched him walk away.

Cracker, Phil, Denke and I carried on searching the buildings. By one o'clock in the afternoon we were asked to move to a new area some miles away in a place called Cinarcik. It had been devastated by the quake and our help was urgently needed. The whole team boarded the three buses and we moved on. I never saw that poor man again and I still grieve over it and wonder if his brother survived. This was my first personal encounter with a survivor who had lost someone dear. What happened must only have confirmed the poor man's loss of faith in foreign rescuers and undoubtedly compounded his grief at losing a brother he felt might still have been alive under the rubble and in desperate need of our services.

When we got to Cinarcik we were met by the local mayor. He asked Ian Muir and Neil Hubbard if we could search one particular area of apartments in the town and showed us how to get to them. On the way dazed, shocked and frightened people watched us silently. We were the only real chance their buried loved ones had. The pressure to do something – anything – was huge. The destruction of the town was total; the power of a 7.6 magnitude earthquake staggering.

Fine choking dust coated everything. Houses, shops, offices, schools and hospitals were either flattened or leaning at impossible angles, defying gravity. Many kept losing the battle – without warning, huge piles of masonry broke off and came crashing to the ground. More plumes of fine dust were forced into the air before falling back to earth, adding to the already deep powder piles covering everything. The smell of decaying human bodies hung like smog, the intense heat accelerating the process of decomposition. It is a smell like no other. It was overwhelming.

I wondered how Cracker and Denke were going to find anyone alive in this. Both of them were struggling by this point, having been working almost continuously since we arrived. We met up with an Israeli search dog team and I sat with one of the exhausted handlers. He told me that his dog, a Rottweiler, was knackered too and had stopped working. We chatted briefly about how they trained their dogs and how we train ours. He was surprised that we only reward our dogs with a tennis ball or a ball on a rope. They had been told that dogs would only work for a food reward.

Then Phil and I got a request from a Turkish interpreter to search for a young girl whose parents were beside themselves with grief. He told us that their apartment was close by and that the teenager was in her bedroom when the quake struck. The parents had heard nothing since but asked that we please, please bring our dogs to search for her. Phil and I looked at each other, remembering the warnings we were given by Ian and Neil, but we said yes anyway. Denke was suffering badly and was struggling to keep going. He had done a brilliant job up to now but, because of his size, he had to work really hard to make progress over the loose rubble. He was completely exhausted

Phil turned to me and said, 'There's no fookin' way Denke can do anymore mate. He's fooked!'

'I know, the poor old fella. Cracker's the same. If we don't cool them both very soon, they're going to die. We need a bloody stream or something!'

The interpreter was listening and he pointed to a place about a hundred metres away in some trees. 'Over there, my friends! Over there is a stream. Quick! Bring your dogs.'

We followed him, the two dogs staggering behind. We broke through some bushes offering welcome shade and sure enough we found a stream. But a group of Muslim people were drinking from it. Our interpreter explained the situation and the people immediately welcomed us and invited us to join them. They told us to immerse our dogs in the water to cool them. I was astonished because we had been warned that many Muslim people consider dogs to be unclean and avoid them completely.

But these people were kind and gracious and helped us pour water over Cracker and Denke. I washed Cracker's nose out and as the cool water took effect, it brought his temperature down. Beside me, Phil covered Denke – stretched out now on his side in the stream – with handfuls of water. The water flowed over him, washing the white clinging dust from his coat in dense clouds. He was very weak but Cracker seemed a little bit stronger. 'Neil, mate,' said Phil, 'Cracker will have to do this one. Denke is finished.'

'I know, Phil,' I answered.

The interpreter was tugging at our sleeves and beseeching us to go back to the collapsed building where the young girls' parents were anxiously waiting. When we got there I saw two elderly people, a man and his wife, standing forlornly, supporting each other in the tangled mass of what was once their home. They welcomed us and the old lady gave me and Phil a hug. Through the interpreter she told us how grateful she was that we were there and that she hoped we could find her daughter for her.

I looked at the place we were being asked to search. It was a totally flattened building, from which a maze of reinforcing bars, all tangled and twisted were sticking in the air. Cracker was going to have to work his way through this steel cobweb, but I knew there was no way any scent was going to come out. The parents were looking at us expectantly. We had no choice but to at least give it a try. I pointed Cracker in the right direction and said, 'Find him, Crack.'

He picked his way through the reinforcing bars, twisting and turning through them, this way and that, sniffing at the solid ground. He was having a hard time and eventually he made his way back. He stood in front of me and looked up hopelessly, and it was clear he had found no trace of anyone.

I turned to the parents, who were in floods of tears. They nodded their heads as though to say they understood. The mother came over, kissed me on the cheek and hugged me tight saying, 'Thank you. Thank you.' The poor father was on his knees, distraught. We could do no more and, through the interpreter, we told them how sorry we were. With the two dogs on their leads, Phil and I walked away in bits.

Neither of us said very much as we made for the campsite, locked in our own thoughts. Our friend, Iain the doctor, magically appeared with a cup of tea for us. 'Well, lads,' he said, 'you both know that if you need to talk about anything you have seen or done, I'm here. Just don't brood over anything! Right?'

'Right, Doc. Thanks, mate,' we both replied. I meant it. Phil did too but he would never let on that he did, not to me anyway.

So that was it – after only two days of virtually non-stop searching, there was no more we could do. On 21 August, just as quickly as we had arrived in Turkey, we were on our way home.

We landed at Heathrow having travelled on a chartered flight. Phil and I were told to wait in the aircraft for the animal health people to arrive from the quarantine kennels. This was the part I had been dreading. We were then given permission to get off the plane with Cracker and Denke, but were told we had to remain near the bottom of the aircraft steps. A group of firemen, two air hostesses and the captain of the flight came to stand with us. Eventually, a dark-coloured van arrived and an officious-looking young lady accompanied by a scruffy-looking man stepped from the vehicle. 'Now remember what I told you, mate,' said Phil, 'they're only doing a job. They have to obey the law even though we all know it's a stupid one. The dogs are going away for six months and that's that!'

The two officials walked over and reached for the dog leads to take Cracker and Denke to begin a six-month quarantine without saying a word. I cracked up at that point, crying my lamps out. That started off the others who were standing around – firemen, air hostesses, even the captain of the plane. Phil walked off to the side. He hates showing emotion, but even he couldn't hide the shaking of his shoulders.

It was truly heartbreaking to watch our two brave dogs being taken away like convicts. What a way to thank them, and in truth it was all so bloody pointless, given the fact that both dogs had been fully inoculated against rabies. Their tests before leaving the UK showed that each of them had very high levels of antibodies against rabies in their blood. The minimum level they needed in law was 0.5 international units of antibody per millilitre of blood. Cracker had 25 international units per millilitre, which was fifty times higher than the required threshold. Furthermore, neither Cracker nor Denke had been near any other animal in Turkey and, even if they had, their high levels of antibodies gave them complete immunity to rabies.

'Come on, mate,' said Phil quietly, 'we can get through this.' He put an arm around my shoulders, which for Phil was way beyond proper behaviour among men. We walked over to the terminal building to continue our journey home. I was told later that day that Cracker had been flown home to Northern Ireland to quarantine kennels in Belfast and when I got back myself, I wasted no time in going to see him. I was delighted that the kennels were excellent and that I would be allowed to visit as often as I wanted. The trouble was that poor Cracker could not understand why I kept going away again after each visit.

In the months that followed, there was a great deal of publicity about the dogs being in quarantine. In fact our campaign became so strident that eventually questions were asked in both the House of Commons and the House of Lords. But it made not one jot of difference – the two dogs stayed for the full six months.

Chapter 26

Almost three months went by and then a second major earthquake hit Turkey. It was on 12 November and had a magnitude of 7.2. Its epicentre was near the city of Bolu in the Duze region, about forty-five miles to the east of the area hit by August's earthquake.

Phil and I were again asked to join the team being flown out from the UK. Our major concern, however, was what we should do about Cracker and Denke. The authorities had previously assured us that in the event of another disaster occurring overseas, they would permit us to take the dogs out of quarantine prematurely. The sting in the tail, however, was that on their return the two of them would have had to start quarantine all over again. That was not an option – I could not have inflicted extra time behind bars on Cracker – and so I went with Dylan, Cracker's twin brother, while Denke stayed at home.

The flight in the RAF Hercules was again a long one and, shortly after touching down in Turkey, the pilot made a shocking announcement. He said he had been informed by staff at the British Embassy that because this earthquake had not been as bad as first thought, our team might not be needed. In fact, he continued, we might just be turning around and going straight back to the UK. 'What?' I asked in astonishment. 'But if we just turn round and go home, the dogs will have to spend six months in quarantine for nothing, surely?'

'Not at all,' the pilot answered. 'After all, they never left the aircraft and so strictly speaking, they're still on British sovereign territory, for God's sake!'

'Is there any way you could check that with DEFRA in London for us, just to see what they say?' I asked him.

'I'll do it right now,' he answered, returning to the flight deck.

After five minutes, he returned and said, 'Well … I've spoken to somebody at DEFRA and explained the situation and do you know what they said?'

'Let me guess …' Phil answered.

With hands raised to heaven the pilot said, 'They said that since the dogs have left UK airspace, they will have to spend their full six months in quarantine on return. Now, how daft is that?' he demanded. How daft indeed – but DEFRA's response typifies the nonsensical draconian law which defines the United Kingdom's quarantine regulations both then and now.

'Now what?' Phil asked.

'Well, what have we got to lose?' I answered. 'We might as well take the dogs off the plane and try to do some good now that we're here.'

The fire service teams had already been assigned parts of the city of Duze to search, so we tagged along with one of them. They were delighted to have the dogs.

Setting up camp was the first priority. The fire lads unpacked their tents, which were fairly roomy sturdy things that gave loads of living space. I, on the other hand, unpacked the shelter tent Dylan and I were going to use. This was a very small one-man affair into which I would be cramming my spare clothes, a sleeping mat to insulate us from the ground, my sleeping bag, Dylan's warm coat and his food. Phil, for his part, decided to bunk in with the fire brigade lads, the crafty sod.

A team member was elected cook, so he was busy getting dinner ready – a mixture of 'boil in the bag' foods like Lancashire hotpot, chicken casserole, chicken and mushroom pasta, sausage and beans, beef stew and dumplings, and chilli con carne all mixed together. Yum. Unfortunately, as on any deployment, few things go according to plan and this one was no exception. The team leader received a request to search a collapsed structure nearby and was told that a guide had already been sent to take us there. Dinner could wait.

The way searches like this usually work is that dogs search the area first, because they still provide the quickest way of establishing if there is anyone alive under the rubble. If the dog indicates that he has found the scent of someone alive, then the specialist teams get to work to narrow the location down. They use their vibra-phones to search for the slightest noise from below.

When we got to the site, we were confronted by the remains of a very large building. I needed to get Dylan to the top but, because of the time element, the only way to get him up there quickly was to use a ladder. We found an old wooden affair that had already been propped against the wall by local people. I showed Dylan the first rung and said, 'Go up son.' To my astonishment, he put one tentative paw on the first rung and then slowly and carefully began to climb the ladder, rung by rung right to the top. How he knew he could do that still mystifies me.

When we got up, some local people were gathered around a hole they had dug. It was about four feet deep and, through an interpreter, one of the men said he believed there was a survivor trapped somewhere below. They weren't sure where he was and so asked if Dylan could narrow down the area for them. Dylan sniffed around the base and sides of the trench but, by his behaviour, I was quickly able to tell that there was no one there. I looked at the people who were anxiously standing watching, and shook my head. They were clearly disappointed but I told them I'd get Dylan to carry on searching a little further away.

He worked steadily over the nearby tangle of bricks, roof tiles, bedding, cooking utensils, broken television sets and broken toys, and then stopped. He was right at the bottom of a partially standing wall, sniffing intently at its base. It must have been about twenty feet high and it tilted at an impossible angle, towards the centre of the building. 'What the hell has he found down there and what is keeping that wall up?' I was thinking.

Dylan, meanwhile, clearly satisfied he had found the scent of someone alive, began barking and wagging his tail. He started to dig a hole. He stopped and pushed his nose into it and then barked again. 'Holy shit! He really has found someone alive down there,' I said, more to myself than anyone else. Some of the firemen working in the trench we had searched earlier climbed out and ran over to us.

'If he's not careful,' one of them warned, 'he'll bring the whole fucking lot down on himself.'

'Fuck me,' said another guy. 'How the fuck do we check down there? That fucking wall is very dodgy looking. It'd be impossible to prop.'

The leader asked for the trapped-person locator. Just then, a lady dog handler from another country showed up looking very professional in her immaculate, heavily badged overalls. Her dog began to bark and so she authoritatively asked someone what was going on.

One of the firemen replied, 'We think there may be someone alive under here. We're waiting to use the trapped-person locator to check it out.'

'I see,' she said perfunctorily. 'Then, I will search it with my dog.'

She gave a command, and the dog began to wander around the area, barking here and there at nothing in particular. After a few minutes the handler shook her head and said, 'There is nobody alive down there. My dog barks that way only when he finds dead people.' She said goodbye and walked away, her dog still barking as they disappeared into the night.

'What the fuck was that all about?' asked one of the firemen.

'I have no idea,' I said, stunned.

'Right, lads,' somebody said from behind. 'Here's the kit. Let's get started.' They opened the reinforced carrying case and took out the listening 'pots' and earphones. This time, an additional tiny two-way loudspeaker and microphone were lowered and manoeuvred into the void below. The whistle was blown to demand silence and a local man handed a second microphone. He was to use this to ask if anyone was alive down there. The little speaker now under the rubble would transmit his voice.

The operator wearing his headset listened intently, his face screwed up in concentration. The Turkish man called out to anyone still alive in the voids below to make a noise. He repeated the question and this time, the operator with the earphones stiffened. He tensely asked the Turkish guy to shout out again. The operator confirmed that he had heard somebody responding with tapping and calling. He handed the earphones to the local man and asked

Me and Dylan preparing to search in Turkey

The after-effects of the earthquake in Turkey

A family anxiously awaiting news of their loved ones

Dylan resting after a long day's work

DYLAN'S 2006 PDSA GOLD AWARD FOR ANIMAL BRAVERY CITATION

Displaying outstanding gallantry and devotion to duty while carrying out official duties with his handler, Neil Powell, as part of the Northern Ireland Search and Rescue Dog Association (SARDA).

In March 1999, Dylan saved the lives of four students lost for several hours on the mountains of Mourne. Despite exceptionally poor weather conditions, Dylan located the group stranded on a ledge 250 feet above ground level. He stayed on duty until the rescue team had lifted everyone to safety.

Later, in November 1999, Dylan worked in Duzce as part of the UK Fire Service Search and Rescue team and the International Rescue Corps following the earthquake in Turkey. Dylan located two people buried alive in the rubble. Crawling between floors, climbing ladders and spanning dangerous voids, this dog never wavered from his duties.

With Dylan in the Mournes

Me and Charco on our way to Pakistan

Searching for survivors in Muzafferabad, Pakistan

Taking a break between searches

Charco with local children in Algeria

Helpers from the fire brigade taking a break

CANINE-999

MAN'S BEST FRIENDS: Phil Shields with Charcoal, Neil Powell with Sammy and Raphael O'Connor with Jay, and (below) Phil and Eamon McKenna practise a rescue manoeuvre

PICS: Ian Magill

The dog rescue team always on alert just in case disaster strikes

BY CIAR EDGAR

MEET Charcoal, Jay and Sammy, the heroic four-legged members of Northern Ireland's specialist rescue team.

With a sense of smell 50 times better than humans, acute hearing and incredible agility, the dogs are crucial members of the local urban search and rescue team.

And when a concrete roof at the Law Society building in Victoria Street collapsed earlier this month injuring six workmen, the three black Labradors were off on their way to the scene within minutes.

The dogs live in Newcastle with their owner, renowned dog trainer Neil Powell.

Neil volunteers for the Fire Service's Urban Search and Rescue Team (USAR) with his son-in-law Raph O'Connor.

Once news of the incident broke the pair were taken from Newcastle Fire Station by Land-Rover to the city centre site where their dogs searched the building to ensure that no workmen were trapped.

Neil said: "Two areas were very hazardous to send people into. The whole building was in imminent danger of collapse."

The biggest challenge was searching the building's large underground car park. "It was pitch dark. We had to stay at the lift shaft which was the safest place to be," Raph explained.

"The dogs moved across a range of hazards and negotiated all of that movement of us in three or four inches of water."

It takes Neil and Raph about a year to train a dog to search for people.

Neil added: "You teach the dog one little piece of the overall exercise and you reward him or her with a ball or a tuggy toy.

"Basically the dog is taught 'if you do this for me, I will play with you and the ball', so the dog is really doing it to get rewarded.

"The first thing you teach them is the word 'find', and you use the toy and teach them that the person they are going to look for will always have that toy.

"Then you work on time and build up the degree of difficulty with the hides you use and get the dog used to negotiating rubble."

Once the dogs find somebody they bark to let their trainers know.

And if that happens, firefighters from the specialist rescue team move in.

A partnership that

THE close link with the Northern Ireland Fire and Rescue Service and NoII's search and rescue dogs is groundbreaking, according to the area commander for Belfast.

Chris Kerr heads up Northern Ireland's Urban Search and Rescue Team, which was officially launched in 2004.

His squad of 24 highly trained firefighters rushed to the scene when the Law Society building collapsed earlier this month.

As well as a team of search and rescue dogs available on call, the team also has specialist equipment including fibre optic cameras which can be fed through narrow tunnels and sound equipment which enables the operator to hear minute sounds clearly.

"When we were at Victoria Street we could hear the BBC cameraman and the reporter doing the piece to camera outside the bar at the end of the street," Chris said.

But as well as working in collapsed buildings, it's also equipped to tackle other highly dangerous situations.

Urban search and rescue was developed after 9/11 and Chris said climate change and resulting storms and flooding is also a major issue for the team.

As well as attending six building collapses in the last two years, the team has also been on hand to rescue people trapped in their homes or cars during the severe floods last summer.

"People don't realise that in

The *Sunday Life*, March 2008

Fern, one of my Drowned Victims Search Dogs

European first for local dog trainer

A NEWCASTLE dog handler and trainer is continuing with his record of firsts.

Neil Powell's water search dog, Fern, has become the first dog in northern Europe to gain an International Advanced Water Search Dog certificate.

Neill, who also trained the first sniffer dogs in the world to [...] out counterfeit CDs an[...] now be used anywh[...] world to help locate peo[...] in water.

Fern, a two-and-a-ha[...] Springer Spaniel an[...] Spaniel cross, played a c[...] in locating the bodies [...] Steele and Rory McAli[...] teenage cousins who dro[...] Castlewellan Lake over th[...] weekend.

Described by her ow[...] being "a gutsy wee dog," [...] assessed for the internatio[...] tificate by former Swedish [...] Forces officer, John Sjoberg[...]

Last week Mr. Sjoberg spe[...] days in the area assessing N[...] Fern as they worked tog[...] searching both fresh and sal[...] areas for specific targets [...] merged deep underwater.

The men, who have wo[...] closely together for over a dec[...] were both impressed with Fe[...] capabilities.

Neill explained that as par[...] the rigorous assessments he [...] Fern were given different scen[...] ios and had to perform searc[...] according to the various situation[...]

"John certainly made sure Fe[...] was tested to the full and at th[...] end of it all I was delighted whe[...] he said she had passed with flyin[...] colours. She is a gutsy wee dog[...] who loves to work and seems t[...] always strive to please," he said.

"Fern had a bit of a hard start in[...] life. Her original owner could not[...] cope with her energy and enthusi[...] asm and at one stage she faced a[...] bit of an uncertain future, but once[...] I found her I knew she has the[...] potential to become an excellent[...] search dog and this certificate[...] proves her capabilities."

Describing Fern as "a unique[...] and wonderful little dog," Mr.[...] Sjoberg said he could immediately [...] see Fern's potential.

"She is a very talented little dog with the right attitude and drive and these components are essential for a water search dog," he explained.

"During the assessment I could see that she worked h[...] the targets pinpointed and this i[...] essential as searching on water i[...] very different from land and aeria[...] searches."

He added: "Neil and Fern ar[...] confident pair and [...]

Down Recorder,
Mourne Observer,
October 2007

Photo: Chris Halpi[...]

Fern achieves a UK first

NEWCASTLE dog trainer Neil Powell's water search dog Fern has become the first dog in the United Kingdom to gain its Advanced Water Search Dog certificate.

Fern was involved in the search for the two Castlewellan teenagers, Rory McAlinden and Clare Steele, who tragically drowned in Castlewellan Lake earlier this year.

John Sjoberg, a former Swedish Special Forces officer who spent two days in Newcastle monitoring Fern before she was awarded the certificate carried out the assessment.

Neil told the *Mourne Observer*: "Fern is a great worker and I am pleased she has passed the assessment. She had a hard start in life but now she has this international certificate she can travel anywhere in the world that we need to go."

Lucky and Flo who were trained to detect and locate pirated DVDs

Toronto Sun, September 2007,
NY Post, August 2007

Cracker's burial

CRACKER'S 2006 PDSA GOLD AWARD FOR ANIMAL BRAVERY CITATION

For displaying outstanding gallantry and devotion to duty while carrying out official duties with his handler, Neil Powell, as part of the Northern Ireland Search and Rescue Dog Association (SARDA).

Cracker ... was also part of the 1999 Turkish earthquake search team locating bodies trapped in the debris. His ability to locate the deceased gave families the opportunity to pay their last respects to loved ones.

Cracker is the only dog in the UK trained to locate bodies in water. His skills have helped locate four people, bringing closure and peace of mind to grieving families.

Me and Cesar Millan

Trail dog Paddy in training

him to translate what the person was saying. The man listened and said, 'He says he is alone down there. He says the people around him are all dead. He is injured and cannot move.'

There was a buzz of excitement and a flurry of activity. Our team leader decided that the only safe way to rescue the person was by first supporting the leaning wall with a heavy lift crane. Some local men volunteered to run to a nearby site where they knew a crane was working. They would ask the driver to bring it here urgently.

Thirty minutes later we heard that the big crane was fully committed where it was but that the driver had promised to come to us as soon as he could. That was a real setback, a crushing disappointment. The local man let the trapped person know what was happening and then we waited. Somewhere else needed the trapped-person locator so it was taken away. I stayed and as the night wore on, I got Dylan to check that the man was still alive from time to time. He would go down to the base of the leaning wall, sniff and then bark as excitedly as he did the first time. I knew the man was still there but there was no sign of the crane coming to help get him out.

In the middle of the night another tremor hit the area. These aftershocks have a feeling and a sound which is hard to put into words. I can only describe it as being like some monstrous animal deep beneath the ground roaring and shaking the earth. When it stopped, I sent Dylan to check on the man again, but this time, he did not bark. The trapped-person locator was brought back and the whistle was blown for silence. They called to the man, waited, listened intently but got no response. They tried again and again, but still nothing. The last tremor had ended the poor man's life. None of us could speak. We packed up and went back to camp. It was devastating. We had been so close to saving him ... so close.

But we were hardly back in camp when yet another request for search dogs came in. A guide led Phil, Dylan and me through dark, eerie, silent streets to the place where we were needed. It had been a large building but the front had collapsed and the top floors had pancaked on to the lower floors. The whole structure had tipped forwards towards the front of the building and that was where we were wanted.

We could see in the harsh light of the hastily erected arc lamps that a trench had been cut through the rubble. The team heading the work was the UK-based, International Rescue Corps. One of the leaders detached himself and came and shook our hands. He indicated the building and said, 'Right, lads. There was a doctor, a nurse and an elderly lady in this building when the quake hit and, by the way, the son of the trapped woman is here so watch what you say. What I want you to do is to check with the dog for any sign of life at the far end of that trench.' He pointed it out. The son had told the team leader that that was roughly where their second-floor apartment had been.

Phil and I moved into the trench and I sent Dylan down along its length. He worked slowly and methodically, checking the left side of the excavated area and the ground below his feet as he went. I became acutely conscious of the people watching everything we did. It was very stressful. He reached the end of the trench but gave no sign that he had found anything. He turned, and started back towards me, checking the right side of the trench this time. Close to the start of this second sweep, he stopped, checked again and started barking. He pushed his nose into a small opening at ground level. His tail was wagging furiously and he barked continuously. He had found someone alive!

With that, a Turkish television crew suddenly appeared from nowhere and I heard someone asking if I would have any objection to a Greek dog handler coming to search the same place with his dog. 'Sure. Go ahead,' I said.

The cameras started whirring and the Greek chap went down into the trench. We watched as his dog made a half-hearted attempt at searching and then wandered aimlessly back towards him. The Greek handler shouted almost in triumph, that his dog had also indicated in the same place as Dylan. None of us had seen his dog indicate and we had all been watching intently. The television people didn't mind – they carried on filming. An interviewer collared the Greek dog handler for an interview. Somebody whispered to us that it was about politics. Phil and I walked away disgusted.

Thankfully, someone then asked us to go to the back of the building to carry on with the search. On our way there, we passed a family huddled in the dark in front of a camp fire, including an old man wrapped in a blanket, sitting on a piece of wood trying to stave off the cold of a November night. His daughter and her husband were there too and we learned they were relatives of the lady trapped inside the building.

The family had come in from the country, eight or nine hours away from the city, where they lived on a small farm. We wanted to sit with them to listen to their story and share some of their pain, but we were asked to hurry by someone shouting from the rear of the building. We rounded the corner and found a large group of local people and rescuers, lifting rubble. Again the place was illuminated by flickering arc lights powered by a spluttering, smoky petrol generator. One of the bosses of the IRC team was standing beside a small hole cut into what was once part of the apartment block. 'Good lads. Welcome. This is the son of the old lady we are searching for,' he said, introducing us. We shook hands with the young man who bobbed his head and thanked us for helping his family.

The IRC man continued, 'We aren't sure if she is alive, so that's why we wanted your dog to search at the front of the house. The son says she was in the bathroom when the quake hit. That would be just above where the dog was indicating. Follow me and I'll take you in the back here near to where the bathroom should be.' He made a beeline for the opening they had cut in the wall, ducked inside and was gone.

'Holy shit, Phil. This is getting a bit serious,' I managed, as I very carefully stooped to follow the guy inside.

'Fookin' right it is, mate,' said Phil from behind me. We were taken deep inside the building and could see that floors which had fallen from above had been propped with lengths of timber, jammed and braced to prevent any further movement. Holes had been drilled and tunnelled through partially collapsed walls – there were no doors. The place was enveloped in a cloud of thick dust, making breathing a chore. Face masks helped but they quickly became clogged with the stuff. Our guide led us on through three of these openings until we reached the point where their work was centred.

He stopped and pointed upwards to a neat, square-shaped opening in the ceiling above our heads. 'Take a look, lads,' says he, gesturing upwards. 'You'll see when you climb through that hole, there will be about eighteen inches clearance between the floor and the ceiling above you. You need to send the dog along the corridor which leads to the bathroom. According to her son, that's where the old lady was.'

I stood on a salvaged chair and peered through the hole but found it difficult to see anything. Dust was even worse up there and was effectively blocking the light from my torch. But I could just make out the corridor, which went round a corner. As our guide had warned, the space was indeed very confined. When I got back down I asked the IRC man how safe he thought this place was. 'Not very,' he replied. 'But your weight and the weight of the dog should not cause too many problems.'

By now the cold clammy sweat of claustrophobia was trickling down my face. 'Let's get outside then,' says the IRC lad, and you can sort your dog out. Okay?'

I was only too glad to escape and we followed him outside quickly. As we emerged into the glare of the lights, the crowd had swollen and there was a hum of talk. I noticed two Turkish men holding Alsatian dogs, standing close to the hole we had come out of. The men were speaking animatedly to some other IRC man and were waving their arms about, apparently remonstrating with him. 'What the fuck is this all about?' our guy muttered over his shoulder to us.

We crossed to the group and saw that a real tantrum was going on. It seemed that the two Alsatian dogs were cadaver trained and these Turkish guys were insisting that they and their dogs be the ones to go in to look for the old lady. After all, this was their country. The IRC man quietly pointed out that his team had been working on that site for hours and that it was only right that they, and we, should finish the job.

Now while all this was going on I said to Phil, 'I don't really want to go in there again, anyway. They can bloody have it. They're welcome to it.' I wasn't at all thrilled at the idea of crawling around a cramped and potentially lethal place like that. Dylan, of course, wasn't bothered one way or the other. He had found a nice comfortable place, as he always did at times like this, and was fast asleep. I never knew a dog like him. No matter where he was, he could magically find just the right spot, stretch out and it was 'good night from him'.

Meanwhile, the argument continued to sway back and forward, with neither side giving way. Coincidentally, some Eastern bloc volunteers decided this was a good time to set up a second generator to provide extra lighting, right next to the hole we were about to crawl back into. Very soon, the air had filled with petrol fumes and carbon monoxide. For a moment, the arguing stopped while the IRC guy shouted, 'For fuck's sake tell those bastards to move that fucking thing somewhere else before it kills us all.' The common language of whistles, shouts, pointing and 'slicing of throats' conveyed the message to the generator operators. The men understood and knocked it off, apologising. They pulled it to one side, but just as they were about to restart it, the dreaded rumble of yet another aftershock started to build beneath our feet. Phil grabbed my arm and shouted, 'Run!'

We legged it as fast as we could with Phil shouting in my ear, 'Keep well out from the fookin' walls.'

We emerged from the alleyway to the front of the building where the family from the country were still sitting by their camp-fire. They hardly took any notice of the aftershock, but it gained in ferocity, bringing huge pieces of bricks and plaster crashing to the ground. In seconds, the building we had been in a few minutes earlier seemed to jolt violently. Then, as suddenly as it had started, the shaking stopped and all was eerily still.

When Phil and I got back to the yard at the rear of the building, we saw that the entire floor below which we had been crawling, had dropped to the ground. We stared in disbelief and shock, realising that had it not been for those Turkish guys arguing with IRC, we could have been well inside the building and now dead.

Access to the building, or what was left of it, was going to have to be reopened, re-propped and re-shored. We were told that it would take hours, so there was no point in hanging around. 'That poor lady ... ' I began to think about what had probably happened to her, but had to stop, pull down the imaginary steel shutters and move on.

'Thanks, lads,' said our mate from IRC as he bravely and determinedly went back to work.

'Well, I think we might owe a big debt of gratitude to those two Turkish blokes for coming along when they did,' I suggested to Phil. He just shrugged and said, 'Happen we do!' and walked off muttering over his shoulder, 'Come on, lad! Let's find somewhere else to work.'

We walked around for a while but by then teams from all over the world were in the area, so we decided to go back to the campsite. Threading our way through the smashed-up streets, where the temperature had now plummeted to minus ten degrees centigrade, we met some of the fire brigade lads. They were also heading back to camp from their own particular part of hell.

As we walked along, a solitary figure came towards us out of the darkness. It was a teenaged boy carrying a flat loaf of bread, probably given to him by one of the relief agencies at the campsite. He stopped and, like so many other Turkish people we had met, wanted to shake our hands. He thanked us for being there and wanted to give something in return. He offered the loaf of bread, his only bit of food. I thanked him, broke a piece off and handed it back. He offered it to the others who thanked him also. It was a very moving gesture and, as we said goodbye and he walked off into the uncertainty of the night, I marvelled at the wonder of man's universal brotherhood.

Back at the campsite they had lit a fire and we warmed ourselves, sitting on salvaged chairs and sofas. Someone had had the great foresight to bring a bottle of brandy in his kit and this was passed silently around. The talk ebbed and flowed but it gave everyone a chance to slay their demons. When bedtime came around Dylan and I got into our tiny shelter. I fitted his warm coat on him, crawled into my sleeping bag and moved over to let him curl up beside me. In an instant we were both fast asleep.

At about three in the morning I became conscious of a lot of noise from outside but I decided I would find out what was the cause of it in the morning. I drifted back to sleep, listening to the unflappable Dylan snoring blissfully beside me, while the ground shook as another tremor reminded us that nature was not finished yet. When morning broke I wriggled out of the tent, leaving my mate Dylan still in a deep sleep. Outside, I was confronted with the most amazing sight – a village of huge tents had sprung up overnight, right up to my back door. The Yanks had arrived!

I stamped some circulation back into my legs and stared in amazement at the sheer size and luxury of it all. Inside the tents were rows upon rows of neat camp beds – or 'cots' as the Yanks call them – all set out on wooden floors. A doorway led to a bar-cum-coffee-place-cum-store. From nearby I heard the unmistakeable voice of Phil saying, 'Bugger my teddy! Look at this lot!'

'Hi, Phil. Now that's how to camp,' I said in appreciative awe.

'Look at it,' he choked in amazement. 'They even have a fookin' supermarket!'

Later that day the UN Relief Agency decided that the mission in Turkey had become a recovery rather than a rescue operation and so the search for survivors was stopped. For us, that meant packing up for the journey home. Nobody wanted to leave because the hope burned, albeit weakly now, that just one more person might be found alive. But the smell of death had become almost palpable and so regrettably it was time to go.

All the rescue kit was checked, packed and loaded on to the buses. We jammed ourselves around and on top of it, ready for the long journey back to Istanbul. When we arrived in that bustling city, we were taken directly to the British Embassy for what was called some rest and recuperation before returning home. The Embassy was in a walled and gated compound with armed guards, a proper guard room and a very posh reception area. It was very impressive.

The staff made all of us very welcome and, for the couple of days that followed, we were humbled by their generosity – even the dogs were given their own private bedrooms on the second floor, real bedrooms with double beds! We lived like kings for a short while but all too soon it was time for us to face the misery waiting in London – six months' quarantine for our wonderfully brave search dogs.

In a gesture of immense kindness, one very senior person at the Embassy contacted DEFRA officials in London to plead clemency for the dogs. But it was hopeless. Dylan ended up in kennels in Belfast sharing a cell right next to his brother Cracker, who still had three more months. Without doubt, the dogs were well looked after, but they didn't care, they just wanted to go home.

I went to see them each week, but every visit was heart-wrenching for them and for me. The routine was that my two boys would be brought out of their kennels and placed in two adjoining exercise areas. They were not allowed to mix in case one was carrying rabies, so I alternated between Cracker's enclosure and Dylan's. To help calm them, I'd lob a ball around, first for one and then for the other. If they ran around the concrete exercise yard too much, their nails would wear away and start bleeding. While I was with Cracker, Dylan would cry and stare pitifully at me through the bars. Then when I'd swap cages and go to play with Dylan, Cracker would take over staring and crying. When eventually they got tired, I'd sit and stroke them and talk to them and tell them how much I loved and missed them.

But worst of all was home time. That was truly upsetting. They would stand, forlorn and devastated, watching me leave through the wire mesh gates, completely unable to comprehend why I was going without them. I can still hear their pitiful crying and howling years afterwards. I hated putting my dogs in quarantine but it was the price of taking them abroad on search and rescue deployments. Was it worth it? I don't really know now.

Chapter 27

During our first trip to Turkey, Phil and I had struck up a friendship with Neil Hubbard and Ian Muir, the officers in charge of Kent fire service's search and rescue team. In 2000 they invited us to go to France with them on a joint exercise between Kent fire and rescue service and their French counterparts, also veterans of the Turkish earthquake. For us as dog handlers, it was an opportunity to test the effectiveness of the new pet passport scheme. One of the requirements of that scheme is that before returning to the UK, dogs must be treated for internal and external parasites by a registered vet no fewer than twenty-four hours before travelling to the UK.

We had all the dogs treated as required and then, just before boarding the Eurostar in Calais, we presented the veterinary papers for our dogs to the DEFRA official in her little cubicle. I knew instinctively that we were in trouble. The official studied them closely, frowned, studied them again and then imperiously announced, 'I'm afraid these papers are not in order, sir.'

Her tone was one so often displayed by minor officials, who always much prefer to apply the letter than the spirit of the law.

'Pardon?' I said. 'Not in order? What do you mean, not in order?'

'As I said, they are not in order. The time of the parasite treatment as listed here is one hour out, sir.'

'One hour out? Oh my God, no!'

'Look, there is obviously a simple explanation for this,' interjected the smooth-talking Ian Muir. 'Why don't you just ring the vet and he will confirm that he has made a mistake?'

'Sorry, sir. It's more than my job's worth,' she sniffed. Now, where had I heard that saying before, I wondered?

'So what do we do now then?' asked Ian.

'Well, sir,' she said with that irritating, complacent, supercilious attitude so often favoured by people like that, 'you will just have to go back to the vet and get him or her to issue new papers with the correct time on them.'

'But that will take bloody hours,' said Neil Hubbard, who had now joined the fracas.

'Well you had better get started then, sir,' she replied with a disarming smile that disarmed none of us.

And that was what we had to do – travel all the way back to the vet's place in Calais and get new papers issued. When we presented those, it was to an entirely different DEFRA official who was polite and helpful and even somewhat apologetic for the way we had been treated earlier. She waved us through to the Eurostar and we were on our way, bloodied but not defeated.

When I got home two days later, I was met by a very tearful Kate and our two girls, Emma and Clair. All three were in a terrible state. 'What the hell's happened?' I asked.

'It's Cuisle,' Kate whispered. 'He's dead.'

'Dead?' I shouted at her. 'What do you mean dead?'

Kate explained that after she fed the dogs on Friday, she went out to check on them and found Cuisle standing with his tummy in an arch, pulled up tightly underneath him. She knew right away what was wrong because she had seen it with our Doberman, Kelly. It was, she was sure, gastric torsion, also known as a twisted gut. She knew it was a potential killer so she rang the vet to warn him, then lifted Cuisle into the car and rushed him straight to the practice in Belfast. But they couldn't save him. My big boy died on the table and Kate couldn't bring herself to tell me until I had got back from France.

The two girls, Kate and I stood there crying at the front door of our house for what seemed ages. In the weeks that followed, life was so empty without him. Cracker and Dylan no longer had their pack leader to tell them what to do and they spent days searching for him, each of them badly affected by his death. For me personally, it was like losing a brother, just as it had been when I lost Kim, Kelly and Pepper and all the other dogs I had lived with and loved.

Cuisle, like Kim and Pepper, had been a groundbreaker in search dog terms – a wonderful rare and very special dog who allowed me the great privilege of trying something unique. And, as with the others, he is never very far from my thoughts and will always have a special place in my heart. But time is a great healer and little by little things got back to a sort of normal. I still had to train Cracker and Dylan so I put Cuisle behind the metaphorical steel shutter in my mind, and got on with it.

It is odd, but then perhaps not so odd, that in times of hurt something or someone will come along to help ease the burden. For me it was a friend called Davey Mayberry, a retired police-dog instructor. He introduced me to a whole new world of search dog work in which I became so engrossed that it took my mind off losing Cuisle a little. In fact, in his police career, Davey had been more than just a police-dog instructor. His last position was as a Home Office police-dog examiner and, whilst engaged in that role, he introduced one of the most effective changes in police search dog work in the UK – the 'passive indication'.

In the past, when an explosives search dog found a hidden cache of explosives, he had to be physically restrained from digging them out. The passive indication taught the dog to sit and point with its nose towards the stash rather than approach it. This development meant that handlers no longer had to work their dog on a line, so a potentially lethal search could be carried out much more quickly and safely.

Like Joe Boyd – my police friend who had found Kim for me – Davey was a master at getting dogs to work for him using a very gentle, patient and persuasive approach. To me, his work was little short of magical and, as I watched him train a black Labrador called Sport to detect hidden drugs on people, I was spellbound. From Davey I learned a new and very clever training technique which had as its basis the very precise timing of giving rewards, coupled with the scenting ability of the dog and its willingness to learn. Being a dog with a uniquely high drive, Dylan loved the challenge of this new work and, after eight weeks, became what is called a 'dual-trained dog' – he could locate hidden drugs but also, if asked, could switch to searching for hidden casualties. On finding a person carrying drugs he would sit in front of them and steadfastly refuse to move. In his other role, as you will remember, he barked continuously to let me know that he had found a casualty.

Davey and I formed a specialist company called Narco Dogs, with Sport and Dylan as our working dogs. We offered a service to nightclubs which had a drug problem – the dogs would check patrons for hidden drugs before they entered the venue.

Well this new vocation of Dylan's backfired on me in Heathrow airport one day. He and I were waiting at the airport for a flight home after a weekend's training with the international rescue dogs team. We went for a short walk outside the terminal building, to allow Dylan to stretch his legs and have a pee if needed.

He was on a long extendable lead as we walked along, minding our own business. Just to our right, I noticed a group of what looked like soldiers standing with their backs to us. They all had close-cropped hair, were neatly dressed and had their kit bags stacked beside them.

One of the soldiers was wearing his rucksack on his back and was standing at the edge of the group, near to where we were passing. As we walked by, Dylan stopped, checked the air and then astonished me by going over to this chap and sniffing very intently at his rucksack. Then, to my horror, he sat down and stared intently up at his bag. He was very clearly indicating that he had found drugs. Some of the other soldiers standing nearby noticed Dylan sitting there and one of them nudged the bloke carrying the offending duffle, whispering something in his ear. He turned, became transfixed by Dylan for a moment, then directed an anxious gaze at me. It was an instant frozen in time.

I smiled weakly, apologised and gave Dylan's lead a good yank to pull him away. But the little shit refused to budge. I pulled harder, but again to no avail. In the end, I had to drag him away, his nails scrabbling on the pavement as he resisted. He was furious and fought to get back to the rucksack as I was frantically trying to force a path through the crowds to safety, croaking, 'For fuck's sake,

Dylan. Not now, you cretin.'

By the time we reached the far end of the terminal building, he had calmed down and when I thought he had more or less regained his composure I decided it was safe to walk him back. As we approached the group of lads, still standing in the same place, I made dammed sure Mr Dylan was on a very short lead and could go nowhere near the possible drugs stash. Indeed as we passed them, I noticed that the suspect rucksack was no longer on the guy's back. It had been jammed securely into the middle of their large pile of bags, well out of Dylan's smelling reach. I also detected a flurry of elbows jabbing anxiously into the sides of group members as we passed by and saw that all their faces were studiously averted. Dylan sailed past them, his mind temporarily on other things. The automatic doors swished open, we passed through and the drama was over.

Inside I saw an armed police officer standing nearby so I went to speak to him. I told him my name and what I was doing there with Dylan, and then I asked him whether there were any drugs dogs employed at the airport. 'Well, not really,' he said slowly, an unspoken question hanging in the air. I could see I had no choice then so I told him what had happened outside. Straight away he spluttered, 'What? Where are they? I'll soon sort this lot out!'

'No, no!' I croaked, not wanting to get embroiled in a huge investigation. 'It's too late, officer. They all got on a bus as I was coming in so they've gone.'

'Oh!' he said, clearly disappointed.

Dylan and I were soon on the next flight home, but it would not be long before we found ourselves back in another airport for an even longer stretch.

On 11 September 2001, the Twin Towers of the World Trade Centre in New York were destroyed by two passenger jets flown directly into them by fanatics and, in an instant, the course of the whole world was changed. Humanity would never again be able to trust the stranger in light of this new and barbarous war against society.

At three o'clock that afternoon, I was about to go home from work, having been relief teaching in St Mary's girls' school, Newry. When I started the car, the radio came on and I found myself listening in horror to the news. I ran back to tell my colleagues what was happening and we all sat in front of the television, stunned, watching the atrocity take place before our very eyes. As more news filtered out, it appeared that Islamist extremists had been responsible not only for this outrage but for the others which followed soon afterwards. It was 'Killing for God', a travesty of Islam, of Christianity and of all other religious and secular norms.

I completed my journey home in a daze. As I opened the front door, Kate, who was clearly as distressed as I was, handed me the phone. It was Phil asking me to get to Heathrow as fast as I could. He said that the UK Government was putting together a team to help the hard-pressed New York emergency services in the search and rescue effort.

I said I'd get there as quickly as I could. I phoned my son-in-law Raph, who was our new international rescue team member, to ask if he would be willing to travel to New York. It was an idea Phil and I had discussed many times before – bringing new members to disasters as observers to better prepare them for the time when they would become dog handlers themselves. Raph readily agreed and so, at eight that evening, after hours of hectic preparation and Kate phoning to arrange our flight, we were on our way. British Midland most kindly agreed to fly us from Belfast International Airport free of charge and, even more generously, allowed Dylan to travel in the cabin with us.

When we arrived in Heathrow, the terminal was almost empty. It was eerie to be standing in a place normally buzzing with noisy passengers and tannoy announcements that was almost completely quiet and still. The silence spoke volumes about the shock everyone was feeling – as though travelling by air had become a taboo.

My mobile phone rang and it was Phil with another update. He told me that for now all we could do was wait, just as he and the rest of the team were doing at various places around the UK. Raph and I found an out-of-the-way place in the terminal and prepared to spend the night on the floor.

About twenty minutes later, two police officers – a man and a woman – sauntered across and asked who we were and what were we waiting for. When we told them, they could not have been more helpful. One immediately offered to contact the Metropolitan Police dog section to see if anyone there would be free to help us out. Not until morning, came the reply. So that was that. We shook hands and the two officers wandered off to continue their patrol. I walked Dylan outside for a breath of air, gave him his tea and then it was back to stretch out on karrimats and try to get some sleep.

Early next morning I suddenly remembered Myles O'Reilly, an officer I knew in the operational planning department of the London fire service. I rang him, told him our story and immediately he said, 'I'll send an appliance round to collect you at the terminal door. Be outside in about fifteen minutes. Talk to you later.'

It was very touching to think that here we were, two crummy civilian volunteers with a dog, and yet the London fire service were pulling out the stops to help us.

In fifteen minutes exactly, a large fire appliance pulled up outside the terminal. A cheery fireman ushered us on board, refusing to allow us to carry our own bags. He drove us directly to the Heathrow fire station where we were given a really warm welcome and a huge plate of chips, sausages, eggs and beans. Then we were given rooms where we were invited to get some sleep before the next part of our journey to New York. It was amazing.

Two hours later, we were woken up to be told that a police dog handler from the Metropolitan Police dog section was here to look after Dylan and to offer us whatever help he could. He introduced himself and then rumbled kindly, 'I suppose your dog could do with a bit of a run, mate. Put him in the spare cage and I'll take you to where I always exercise my lad.' He was kindness itself and, as we drove away from Heathrow, we felt as though we'd known him all our lives.

'Are you football fans?' he enquired casually as we glided through the morning traffic around Heathrow.

'Not really, but Raph is,' I answered lamely.

'Well, he'll like this place then,' he grinned, as we swung through the gates of Chelsea Football Club, no less.

'This is where I exercise my dog every day. Great, isn't it? I'm well known here, so let Dylan have a good run. He's quite safe. Just pick up any little deposits he might make.'

Raph was ecstatic at being on the hallowed turf.

An hour later we were back at the fire station and I was answering the phone to Phil. He told me that it had now been decided to hold the team in the UK for the time being because another immenent terrorist attack was feared – this time in London or Paris. However, twenty-four hours later, we were stood down. The threat had passed and we were allowed to go back home.

It was a little bit of an anti-climax, I suppose, but at least we had been privileged to play a part, however tiny, in the huge rescue effort of 9/11. The UK had demonstrated its willingness to offer help and, in so doing, sent a clear message to the extremists lurking in their shadowy hideouts, that the British people would stand firm against them.

As for us? Getting home was a much more complicated affair than the journey over, but Kate worked wonders and we were eventually on our way. And Dylan? Well he was stretched out fast asleep as usual, snoring gently, waiting for the next chance to show his love for all humanity.

Chapter 28

Going back a couple of years to September 1999, a field trials Labrador breeder called Brendan Mack had been watching the Northern Ireland BBC evening news when he happened to see me talking about Cracker. I was bemoaning the fact that he had had to go into quarantine after the heroic work he had done in Turkey. I got very emotional during that interview when I recalled the moment that Cracker had been taken away by the DEFRA officials.

Brendan, deeply affected by the interview, tracked down my home phone number and offered to give me the pick of a litter his champion bitch had given birth to a fortnight earlier. I was deeply moved that a total stranger could be so kind and I thanked him from the bottom of my heart – and of course accepted the offer.

Six weeks later Kate, Clair and I were standing in Brendan's kennels looking at eight beautiful black Labrador puppies. Any one of them would have been brilliant, as far as I could tell, but one stood out from the rest – Charco. He was slightly taller than the rest of the litter and was forward and inquisitive, with a beautiful sleek head. I just knew that he was the one for me.

We took him home and he was immediately accepted by the other dogs. They greeted him like their long-lost brother. He was easy to house-train and, at twelve weeks, was barking, sitting and lying down on command, and coming when called. Kate had even taught him to crawl along the floor on his tummy. He grew up with a real zest for playing and hunting a tennis ball, and went on to become a fully qualified collapsed structure search dog with British International Rescue and Search Dogs (BIRD) at eighteen months. In fact he was so bright that later on in his life I was able to train him to search for explosives. In that capacity, we worked at London's famous Canary Wharf, the O2 building and Lord's, home of Middlesex Cricket Club. During one of the test series between England and Pakistan, Charco and I were entrusted to do one final sweep for explosives on the route to be taken by the Queen. It was just a short section between the players' gate and the main pavilion, but he searched it perfectly and, thankfully, found nothing. When just a few minutes later the Queen herself swept past and smiled benevolently at Charco, he just stood there – proud, almost arrogant – as he surveyed what for him was just another car going by.

But I digress yet again. I had decided not to involve Dylan and Cracker in any more international work – I had no wish to put them through the stress and upset of quarantine again – so Charco was going to be the dog that would come with me when the BIRD team was called to the next earthquake. This was one call I fervently hoped would never come, but come it did. In May 2003, an earthquake of magnitude 7.3 struck Algeria in an area just west of Algiers, the capital. The UK offered the Algerian authorities the assistance of its specialist search and rescue team and they accepted. I was asked to bring Charco as part of the team and, while I hated the thought of the six-month quarantine sentence which awaited him when we got back, it was hard to say no. Dreadful pictures of the disaster were all over the news every hour.

Thanks to the generosity of British Airways, Charco and I found ourselves on the next available flight from Belfast to Heathrow. Once we got there we had to find a way to get to Stansted, the team's departure point. I had no idea where Stansted was, let alone how to get there. I rang Phil but was told that he was having his own problems getting to the airport due to horrendous traffic jams, so I would have to sort myself out. As usual at times like that I decided to look for the nearest police officer. I didn't have too far to look and when I had explained the situation to him, he directed me to one of the phones at a check-in desk. He rang a number and handed the phone to me. I was delighted to find that I was speaking to the sergeant in charge of the police dog section. I explained the situation to him and said that I was stuck with my dog and all my kit, including a dirty great wooden sky kennel, in Heathrow but that I needed to get to Stansted urgently. Without hesitation he replied that there would be a dog handler and van to pick me up at the front door in twenty minutes. Wow! In exactly twenty minutes, my police dog handler escort arrived in a brand new police dog van. I felt very important. Charco was loaded into one of the two cages; the other was already occupied by a very indignant police dog.

The police officer was a nice guy and we chatted on about doggy things for a while. We arrived at the airport very quickly and as soon as he dropped me off, I found a trolley and went inside to look for Phil and the team. Hours later, having been flown to Algeria in a specially chartered commercial aircraft, we found ourselves on the back of an open truck. It was preceded and followed by vehicles carrying police and armed military who told us to keep our heads down and our mouths shut. Our destination was a football stadium where we were told we would camp under the protection of armed guards. That really didn't make sense until we heard on the grapevine that some German bikers had been kidnapped two weeks previously and were being held hostage by a group of extremists. What the hell had we let ourselves in for?

Then we ran into a traffic jam in a village somewhere en route. As we sat there motionless, a sullen-looking group of young Algerian guys, muttering and staring daggers at us, began to gather. Darkness was falling and the atmosphere grew more and more tense. For some idiotic reason, I chose that very moment to use my new digital camera surreptitiously to take a photograph of them. The flash gave me away and it had the same effect as putting a match to the blue touchpaper. The crowd surged forward and menacingly demanded the camera. At the same time, there was a shudder from our truck and miraculously we shot forward. My camera and I were saved. Everyone gave a huge sigh of relief as we moved forward again, none more than me. At last, after a few more hours of travel, we passed through the high metal gates that guarded the entrance to the football stadium.

Next morning we woke to a warm sun and the surreal sight of armed guards standing on terraces normally reserved for adoring football fans. It seemed ironic that, in a country desperate for help from the outside world, the rescue teams needed protection from extremists, who clearly did not care for their countrymen. The morning dragged on a bit, but eventually we were told to get on the back of a lorry and be ready to move off. We lifted Charco over the tailboard, threw our gear and ourselves in after him, and the lorry shunted forward to fall in line behind the armed escort. We drove out through the gates and into the town, hoping to bring rescue to those who so urgently needed it.

It wasn't long before we got to a row of demolished houses and the convoy stopped. Some of the leaders went off to speak to an official but soon came back to direct our lorry further up the road. We stopped again and were asked to search some buildings but it very quickly became obvious that we were not doing anything worthwhile. Some suggested that all we were doing was window dressing, so to speak. In fact, we heard later that some French search and rescue teams had been quite busy that day and had effectively negated any need for us.

But in the end, we were tasked to go to another collapsed building in which a young girl had apparently been buried. It didn't take us long to drive there and the building was easy to find because of the large crowd that had gathered. Some people were taking a break in what shade they could find from the searing hot sun, while others were pulling away rubble with their bare hands. If the smiles of welcome we got were anything to go by, they were overjoyed to see us arrive.

We climbed down from the trucks and, while some of the team started to unload equipment, I brought Charco over to the remains of the house. Some of the men who had been digging stopped to watch, while others directed me to where they thought I should start searching. Through the interpreter, I requested that anyone standing on the other side of the site should be asked to move away while the dog was working. I explained that the scent of those people might be filtering through the rubble and could confuse the dog. They understood and a chorus of voices shouting in French told them to move back.

I put Charco in through a door to search what was left of the building. He picked his way across the devastation of a shattered home, the smashed masonry, the jagged remnants of living-room furniture, broken beds and scattered clothes. Eventually he came to one corner of the room where, low in the rubble, he started scratching and whining. On my knees, I could see a small hole that seemed to be sloping steeply downwards through the debris. Charco didn't bark, he just whined softly, staring down at the hole and pawing it. His behaviour was very odd, so I called him off to give him a short breather. When he went back a second time, he did exactly the same as before. Naturally, none of this had escaped the attention of the bystanders who were becoming increasingly convinced that he might have found the child alive. However, I felt uneasy about it and wondered whether he was reacting to scent coming from people who might still be standing too close to the other side of the house. I asked a man to check for me and sure enough, he found a relative of the child tunnelling just yards from where Charco had been working.

When he was asked to hang on for a few minutes to give the dog a better chance to search, he was very apologetic and moved away immediately. I sent Charco in again and for the third time he gave the same response. His strange behaviour had had nothing to do with the man we had asked to move. He was reacting to the presence of the missing child who must have been very near. When I looked around at the people watching, their faces said that they thought so too. Tragically she must have been killed in the collapse of her home, because that alone would explain Charco's odd reaction. Our job was done there and so Charco and I moved away to let the people return to their sad task, while we went back to join the others.

At the lorry we were told that someone somewhere had issued another warning that our safety could not be guaranteed and so we had to leave. We had been under constant threat since arriving in Algeria and now, because too much time had passed since the earthquake first struck, those in charge of the UK teams recommended we be pulled out. It was a hard decision and we all felt sorry we had not been able to do more, but it was the right decision. Next morning we broke camp and began the long journey to the airport and home.

Arriving back in the UK a couple of days later, we were again confronted by the spectre of quarantine as our poor dogs were confiscated and driven off to six months' detention. What a harsh reward for trying so hard to help suffering humanity. Little did I know that two years later we would be at another, far bigger earthquake in Pakistan.

But life at home went on and exactly one year after the Algerian earthquake, a very sad incident occurred at a beautifully scenic place in the Mournes. It was at one of the main reserve water supply reservoirs for the Belfast area. A man who had been employed there by the Water Board failed to come home. It was suggested that he might have fallen into the water while doing his routine checks. I was asked to help in the search for him and took both Cracker and my new drowned victim search dog CJ (Cuisle Junior), a German shepherd just like his namesake.

Within minutes of our starting the search, both dogs separately indicated a possible location for the man, very close to the dam wall. The search was being coordinated by the police and the duty inspector was watching us working from the nearby roadside. I shouted to him, 'I'm fairly certain he is here somewhere,' indicating the area in front of the dam wall. I continued, 'I can't say how far out from the shore he might be.'

'Right,' he replied, 'I'll let our guys know when they arrive,' referring to the team of police divers who were on their way.

A couple of hours later the police divers duly arrived. They pulled on their black diving suits and made ready to enter the water. I assumed they would start searching from the point indicated by Cracker and CJ but instead they launched their boat and drove to the far end of the reservoir, a good half-mile away.

'What are they doing, Inspector?' I asked in amazement.

'I'm not really sure,' he said, 'but I know they have their own systems for searching.' He seemed to be as mystified as I was.

The divers searched meticulously, metre by metre, marking each section cleared with a string of buoys to give them a visual reference. As darkness fell, they got out of the water, packed up their equipment and drove off. For two more days they continued diving the lake, progressing slowly along its length. Eventually, they reached the place where CJ and Cracker had been indicating, but still found no trace of the missing man. Just as it had been with the Garda divers, they probably felt that what I was claiming was so outlandish that it could not be taken seriously. No one had ever heard of dogs that could find people under the water. They quietly packed up their gear and took their leave.

However, the wife of the missing man was still there with her family. It was very sad to see them and I could not even begin to imagine how bad they must have been feeling. She walked over to me and asked whether I still believed her husband to be in the water. All I could say for certain was that both dogs were positive that something of real interest to them was near the dam wall. Two days later, as evening was falling, the body floated to the surface, right beside the dam wall and that poor family was given the closure it needed.

Chapter 29

On 8 October 2005, the north-west province of Pakistan-administered Kashmir was rocked by a 7.6 magnitude earthquake centred near the city of Muzaffarabad, the capital of Kashmir. Seventy-nine thousand poor souls died in the disaster, many of them schoolchildren who had been hard at work at their desks. Like everyone else, I was horrified at the television coverage of the disaster, but as a teacher I was even more appalled at the dreadful loss of so many young lives. The British government offered search and rescue teams to the Pakistan government, who readily accepted.

Charco and I went as part of the BIRD team, flying direct to Islamabad. I was paired with a great friend of mine, Brian Jones, the bloke who once described his hair colour on a passport application as being 'autumn blonde', only to have it returned to him refused. He is a real joker and totally laid back, but one of the most dedicated men I have had the pleasure to work with on search and rescue.

The outward journey to Pakistan was by charter flight rather than the Hercules of earlier deployments. It seemed to take just as long though, perhaps because sleep was impossible – everyone was too wound up, though nobody was letting on. After what felt like a lifetime, we landed in Islamabad, the capital of Pakistan. We had to go through the usual arrival procedures, when passports were surrendered and verified, then we just had to find somewhere to sit until some form of onward transport could be sorted out.

The epicentre of the earthquake was in Muzaffarabad, 105 miles from Islamabad, and that was where we were going, but the roads were apparently impassable. A few hours passed slowly and anxiously while we occupied ourselves with walking the dogs and dozing. At last there was some movement among the Pakistan officials. Of course, those people I mentioned before, who have this built-in early warning system that tells them they are about to move, had already gathered their kit and were standing at the exit doors. 'How the hell do they always know before the rest of us?' I still wondered in amazement.

We were directed on to the apron area of the airport and then ushered away to the end of the runway. Two Pakistan army helicopters were waiting for us, their engines ticking over noisily. They were the Huey-type helicopters, like the ones in films about the Vietnam war. Although they appeared to be of fairly advanced age, we were assured by some helpful officials that both helicopters were in 'tip-top condition'.

Dusk was falling. On the direction of one of the pilots, we loaded gear and dogs into the venerable aircraft. Apprehensively, we climbed aboard, strapped ourselves in and waited. After a cheery thumbs-up from the same pilot, the revs increased, and we lurched and strained upwards. Jauntily, the helicopter tilted its nose and turned north, making for the high mountain passes which led to Muzaffarabad. Brian said that the Huey had a cruising speed of around 106 miles an hour, so he thought we should arrive after dark in about one and a half hours. The pilots looked relaxed as they chatted away, but I did not like the fact that the light was fading fast. The tension in my stomach was mounting. I tried to look ahead and then wished I had kept my eyes shut, because right in front of us I saw a very high ridge looming closer and closer.

It looked to me as though we were making right for the centre of it and that we were about a hundred feet too low. One pilot started talking animatedly to the other and then the controls were handed over. Brian nudged me but he need not have bothered – I was already transfixed. Agonisingly slowly, we began to rise. The pilots put on their night goggles and the talking stopped. Both of them went very quiet. We watched, mesmerised, as the ridge towered above us. The engine noise was deafening as the helicopter clawed and struggled higher and higher. I have been to the site of a helicopter crash so I know what one looks like and now I was shitting bricks. It looked like our stay in Pakistan was going to be a short one.

Then we were skimming the top of the ridge by mere feet. Once over, we began a sharp, swooping descent into a long, winding valley with enormous, high walls on either side. I could hardly believe my eyes when, in the fading light, I saw houses perched on impossible-looking ledges thousands of feet up. The sight distracted me enough to enable me to forget about where we were. I became fascinated by how solitary they were, with no neighbours and no roads or tracks leading to them. How the hell did they survive away up here, perched at such dizzy heights with no shops for miles around? It was amazing. Brian pointed to a house and shouted, 'You would really hate to get home there and find you'd forgotten the bloody milk wouldn't you?'

We laughed a bit too loudly at that, as we let out some of the pent-up nerves.

The helicopter started to lose more height and began circling above a vast array of makeshift shelters and tents. Throngs of people were staring up at us, their faces illuminated by arc lights set up around the perimeter. We touched down at Muzaffarabad beside the Jhelum and Neelum rivers.

We unloaded the helicopter, dumping all the gear in a pile, before carrying it up a gently sloping field to the main campsite. Someone pointed us towards our campsite, about two hundred yards further away. It was a sea of tents housing search and rescue teams from all over the world. National flags fluttered in the light breeze, proclaiming national identities in a place where nobody really cared.

We wandered around and Russ Vaughan, our team leader, spotted a vacant area of concrete. We threw down sleeping mats and sleeping bags and waited. I used the time to feed a very hungry Charco and then took a seat beside the fire someone had thoughtfully lit. All the lads drifted towards the fire, dressed in their protective overalls, some carrying helmets and gloves, and all anxious to get started.

Russ stood on the edge of the group and told us there was a problem with transport: 'Look, lads. This is a delicate situation we are in here. There are dozens of vehicles belonging to the Pakistan Army parked just at the gateway of the campsite – the ones we saw when we came in. But I'm told that they are not going to be made available to any of the visiting teams because they have not been given orders to assist yet.'

We were all outraged, having come all this way and then being made to sit and wait.

'For fuck's sake, Russ, that is a huge crock of shit,' piped up someone from behind me.

'I know, I know,' he said, shaking his head. 'I think that we'll just have to go over to the gate and ask for help from the locals. They're thronging everywhere out there.'

And that is exactly what we did. We passed the shiny new four-wheel-drive jeeps and lorries of the army and went outside the gates. Everyone with a car or a van wanted to bring us wherever we wanted to go. Through our interpreter, we were ushered into a fleet of ancient cars and driven off into the night. We were immediately immersed in a mêlée of people and vehicles and noise. Our driver picked his way through the narrow streets, where we continued to be passed by hundreds of dazed survivors caught in our headlights and winding their way past destroyed buildings that had tumbled out on to the narrow streets. We arrived at what remained of a large technical college. We heard that it had been full of students when the earthquake struck.

We could see parents standing everywhere, distraught, waiting and hoping to have their child found alive somewhere beneath the devastation in front of them. I was aware of the awful realisation that they were looking to Russ, Charco, me, Brian and the rest of the team to perform some sort of miracle.

We all wanted to give them what they so desperately hoped for. I had to be careful not to let my nerves affect Charco – it would have been so cruel if he had given a false indication and raised the hopes of devastated parents, only to dash them again as quickly.

'Right, lads – here's what we're going to do,' said Russ, quietly enough to be heard only by us. 'Neil. You and Brian fuck off over there with Charco,' pointing to his left where a huge mound of collapsed building had been floodlit. 'You start searching there, while the rest of us start right here in front of us.' He rattled off another string of orders to the tunnellers, the guys who go in under the rubble, propping and shoring as they go, looking for the slightest sign of life below ground.

The pile of debris Brian and I had to search with Charco was enormous. The smell of death hung in the air like a cloud. We picked our way respectfully over a line of dead bodies, neatly laid out along what had once been a corridor. They looked so sadly surreal beneath their brightly coloured shrouds. It did not feel right to be stepping over them, but there was no other way to get to our search area. I was very mindful to keep Charco beside me, to avoid giving any offence to grieving relatives watching from nearby.

We climbed on to the torn remains of what was once a humming, thriving, vibrant school. Signs written in English were hanging forlornly, a testament to the once flourishing bilingual infrastructure, now shattered and in ruins. We went around, under and over the ruined building, Charco searching, checking, re-checking and then moving on. He stopped beside a human head, looked at me and walked away to focus on the living.

Brian acted as 'spotter', and got me to give a bit more attention to this or that section, making certain that Charco thoroughly covered as much as he possibly could. We got to the end of the search but all we found were human remains, unidentifiable as adults or youngsters.

We made our way back to the start point and then worked in the opposite direction. We mainly encouraged Charco to search from the surface of the huge rubble pile but sometimes he could get underneath, although not very far. I came across a teacher's desk – a high, old-fashioned one – and could see the remains of the teacher sitting, lifeless, a pen still held in his hand, his upper body crushed by what had once been the upper floor. We moved on and on but we found no one alive – just deathly silence. Brian peered through a small hole in the debris of what was once a classroom and turned away in tears, unable to tell me what he had seen there.

We eventually made our way back to Russ and told him that we could find no signs of life. It was the same for the rest of the lads and we all stood there in shock. Even the hardened firemen who made up most of our voluntary team were suffering.

Russ explained what we had done to the interpreter who in turn spoke to the people gathered around. He told them that nobody had been found yet but that we would come back and try again when more material had been removed. He pointed at the enormous diggers and crane that were clearing layer upon layer of destroyed buildings. Then we said goodbye.

There was a bit of a hubbub among the crowd as someone pushed to the front. We were targeted by an Englishman whose uncle lived in the city. He asked us if we would go with him to search his house for the man's son. He took us to what was obviously the home of somebody important, with a walled and gated garden. The house had collapsed completely on one side but on the other side some of it remained relatively intact and we saw that there was an attached garage still hanging on. Various people were standing around and, speaking to them, we learned that the son had been upstairs in a bedroom ironing a shirt, when the earthquake struck. We got started at the intact side and as Charco made his way to the garage door he became very agitated and excited. He stretched upwards towards the corner of the door nearest the house, his nose craning as high as he could push it. Brian and I watched him, mystified. There was nothing that was obvious to us that would have made him behave this way. I brought him to the rear of the garage where we could get inside though the big hole made by the collapsed wall. Immediately Charco ran to the wall nearest the house and started barking and looking up towards the ceiling.

'What the fuck is that about?' asked Brian. It was really strange behaviour and not at all like Charco.

'I have no idea, mate. Maybe we need to get inside the house and search this side of it. What do you think?'

We decided that this was a plan and we could see that if we got on to the balcony just above us we would have fairly straightforward access. I got up first and then Brian pushed the squirming Charco up to me.

'What's the floor like?' asked Brian. 'Here, let me have a quick shufty while you hold the boy here.'

He took a look inside the bedroom and tried to estimate how safe the floor was. He gave me the thumbs-up and I sent Charco inside with a quick 'Find him, son' and me close behind. Brian watched from the window so that he could go and find the cavalry if we got ourselves in the shit.

Charco picked his way past the bed and sniffed his way over to the corner of the room, roughly above the point where he had been barking in the garage. I looked all around but could see nobody. Why the hell was he barking?

Brian, watching from the window, suggested, 'Go over to that doorway. It looks like the other half of the house has collapsed behind it.'

Sure enough, we again got the barking response from Charco. Someone from below shouted up, 'There's going to be nobody alive left in there! From where I'm standing, the destruction looks to be absolute.'

Dejectedly, we climbed back down to ground level. Charco was well pissed-off at not being rewarded for what he obviously considered to be a find. We had to say to the people standing nearby that we believed it actually *was* possible that the missing lad was still alive in there but that we could do no more because we did not have the tools. They thanked us and shook our hands and we told them we would be back again in daylight. There was nothing left for us to do now. Charco needed a rest so we headed for the camp-site, gave the boy a feed and then fell asleep on the concrete for a couple of hours.

After a quick breakfast, we returned to the house. The rising sun imperceptibly began its daily routine of baking the region bone-dry and when we arrived in the garden, the smell of decay hit us like a wall. It was clear that there would be nobody found alive here.

Then Russ got word over the radio that we had been reassigned to search a primary school in the city itself. A primary school! It was to the right of the shattered road we were walking along – not a stone standing, a tangled mess of roofing slates and splintered timber. Where to begin? Charco, eager as ever, launched himself onto the pile, watched expectantly by all the people standing around. Many had been pulling the rubble away with their bare hands, desperate to find any of the children still hanging on to life in the void below. He showed a lot of interest in one place but then we received an urgent call over the radio to go straight away to yet another location further down the street.

'But we've just started here,' Brian shouted into the microphone.

The guy on the other end fired back, before breaking transmission, 'This is urgent. Get down here now! Out!'

We told the interpreter what had happened and asked him to explain to the people why we were leaving. We promised them that we would get back as soon as we could.

Chapter 30

Our guide led us into a maze of alleyways. He was a local man who, like so many others, wanted to help, to do what he could to ease the pain of his people, floundering in the hell they had been plunged into.

We found ourselves running behind him as he weaved and ducked his way through the warren of narrow side streets. People we passed were engrossed in their efforts to find the living or just to recover something of the lives they once had – anything at all. No one really noticed us. The passageways we plunged along were so narrow that it was possible to stand in the middle and touch the walls on either side. All of the buildings were leaning at seriously precarious angles and many had huge lumps of masonry hanging from them.

At last our headlong dash stopped. We arrived at a building where the floors at the back had all pancaked on top of each other. The front half was still perilously teetering beyond the vertical, with a huge crack running all the way to the top. Somewhere in the rubble below, the voice of a man had been heard calling for help.

Russ Vaughan and the lads from BIRD were there already. Russ asked me to search with Charco on the pile of bricks and crushed furniture to the rear. In seconds the dog found live human scent filtering from the void below. He started to get very wound up but couldn't quite pinpoint where the man was. We made our way towards the front and went into the building itself. After a few seconds searching, Charco focused on a small borehole someone had made in the floor. He checked it again and again and then started to bark. He danced around looking from the floor to me, and back again: there was no doubt about it. The young lad was right below, but where exactly?

The lads brought in a local man who had been doing a great job as the team's interpreter. He called down through the hole and after a few seconds, got a weak answer from somewhere in the darkness beneath. The man had been found. A thin rubber pipe was lowered and water dripped down it to give him his first drink since he had become trapped.

He called weakly that he had been trapped there since the earthquake first struck. 'My God … that was thirty-six hours ago!' someone muttered. The interpreter held up his hand for silence. He listened carefully and then turned to Russ and told him, in shock, that the man was lying underneath his dead uncle and that there were two other dead relatives next to him, one on either side of him. That explained the smell of decay filling the room. Charco and I stood back to give the lads space to get on with trying to dig the young man out.

Suddenly, the ground shook violently as yet another aftershock hit the city. We dived for cover but the teetering walls of the badly damaged building stayed up. The team got back to work, sweat coursing down their faces and bodies. They wrestled with the debris, cutting it away piece by piece. They knew that at any moment a false move might send tons of rubble crashing down on the survivor below them.

Brian was asked to go back to camp for spare batteries for the cutting tools. It was a long way off and he would have to walk through all those backstreets and alleys by himself. Given the fact that we knew we were being targeted by extremists, I marvelled at his courage when he immediately said he would go.

Another big tremor hit but nobody stopped. The work went on and everyone put their trust in the Man above.

After an age, Brian got back with the much-needed batteries. He told me that on his way to the camp, a bloke had stopped him and said, 'We know you're here to help our brothers and sisters. If it were not so, you would now be dead!' Brian had carried on to camp in a state of shock.

As he had made his way through a side street just outside camp, he had come across a doctor working on a badly injured woman. Her leg had been shattered and the doctor was trying to do what he could for her but had no anaesthetic. She was being held down by some of the local people. 'It was horrendous, mate. I can still hear her screaming,' he told me quietly, visibly upset.

The work to free the young man went up a gear with the help of the replacement batteries. It was an unrelenting task of cutting, shoring and removing debris as the team inched their way closer and closer. After five long weary hours, the trapped man, a twenty-year-old tailor called Tariq, was pulled from the tiny hole and laid out on the floor, his face covered in fine dust, eyes staring in a mixture of shock and relief.

A local made reassuring sounds as he wiped away some of the dirt from the young man's mouth and nose, while someone else held a cup of water for him to drink. Dazed and in deep shock, Tariq started to recount the nightmare he had been enduring for all those lonely hours in the darkness. I had to leave, knowing that it was best for me and the way I worked in these situations that I didn't hear the detail. For now, the main thing was that the young man was safe. Was this rescue a miracle? I don't know. But was it bordering on incomprehensible? Most definitely.

We were not long back in camp when a small local man approached us and began to implore our help. We had no idea what was wrong.

'I'm sure that interpreter is still around somewhere,' said Brian. 'Look! Keep the bloke here and I'll go and find him.'

I asked the man to sit down. He was very distressed and started wringing his hands, pointing at Charco and then pointing and nodding his head towards the city. Brian came back with the interpreter and very soon we learned that the man had a brother who worked as a book-keeper in a set of offices close by. He had been there when the earthquake had struck and demolished his entire building. He had not been seen since. When the man had gone to look for him he had found the place in ruins. He had begun calling for his brother and he swore he had heard him answering and calling for help. The poor man begged us to go with him to search for his brother.

We had a quick chat among ourselves and decided to go and look for Russ. Any decision about any of us leaving the camp to search for someone had to be his to make. We found him sitting with some of the team who had just got back from another search operation in the city. We told him the story and he immediately said that we would help. He went to the control centre and informed the UN search managers that he wanted to take his team out to carry out another search. Nobody objected and so he called our whole team together.

Although Russ was the undisputed leader of BIRD, he always gave us the respect of inviting our opinion about incidents like these. He told the others what the man had said and everyone agreed that we should help look for his brother. The decision made, we told the man, who became ecstatic. We gathered the equipment we needed and followed him out of camp.

We cadged a ride on an ancient bus which was parked outside the camp. The driver was having a smoke and a chat to some locals. He ushered us on board and in minutes his venerable single-decker was struggling purposefully through the clogged streets of the city. It was almost sunset and we learned that the end of Ramadan, the Islamic month of fasting from dawn to dusk, was upon us.

In a hopelessly blocked street choked with traffic our bus shuddered to a stop. People were milling about and calling out good-naturedly to each other. It was total gridlock. I got out of the bus, partly to cool off from the oppressive heat and partly to absorb some of the atmosphere. Beside me was a lorry packed with men, women and children, all waving and smiling at passers-by and at me. Some passengers were crammed on the roof, others were on top of the cab, and a few were perched on the bonnet. It was complete and utter bedlam, with everyone shouting and laughing and waving at each other.

As the last rays of the sun disappeared, a young man of about twenty jumped from the roof of the lorry and landed in front of me. For a second I thought I was in trouble but he smiled and offered me his hand saying, 'You are a rescue man. Welcome!

Welcome! Thank you for coming to help my people. Here my friend – eat...' He extended a hand holding some bread. From above, someone else dropped an apple to him and that was offered to me as well. 'These are my family. We have come to the city to find our cousins,' he went on.

Now food was virtually raining down from the roof of the lorry to the people on the pavements – the place was awash with good-will and neighbourliness and I could only marvel. It was a surreal moment of joy in a sea of misery and it was hard not to get drawn in to the warmth and good cheer.

My new friend shouted above the din of car horns, revving engines and people calling out to one another, 'We have come in from the country to visit our families here in the city. We stop fasting now. Please eat with us. Where are you from, my friend?'

'Ireland,' I replied, thinking he would never have heard of it.

'Ah! North or south?' Before I could answer he went on, 'You know Belfast?'

I was blown away by that. Here in the middle of Muzaffarabad a young man from up-country Kashmir knew about Belfast!

'Belfast is forty miles from where I live,' I shouted back in amazement.

'Ah,' he nodded excitedly, 'I am going to go there soon. Perhaps we can meet?'

Was this real? Was I actually having this conversation with a complete stranger in the depths of a devastated city, about him visiting me in Belfast?

Our bus revved its engine and began a shuddering forward movement.

'Get on the bloody bus, Neil, or you'll be walking,' bellowed Brian.

'I have to go,' I shouted to my new friend, offering my hand. 'Thank you for the bread and I hope you find your family.' We waved to each other and then he was swallowed up by the shunting, struggling sea of traffic and people.

'What was that all about?' Brian roared at me as I climbed back into my seat.

'I'll tell you later,' I shouted back.

It had been a fleeting moment of brotherhood and would have been very hard to explain right then.

After a while, the lights of the bus showed that we had stopped outside a walled courtyard that was surrounded by a huddle of buildings, some collapsed and others completely intact. The man whose brother we had come to search for took us to an almost totally collapsed building where the missing man had been working.

Using his powerful torch, Russ peered through a glassless window. He called me over and pointed inside. I could see a ceiling hanging down, bits of furniture scattered everywhere and on the far side, a partly collapsed wall. I could also see a door and I could just make out a set of stairs almost completely covered in fallen masonry.

'Right then,' announced Russ. 'You wait here a sec. I'll go in first for a quick recce, and then I'll come and get you.' He scrambled through the window and gingerly made his way across the room and into the next one. He reached the stairs and made his way cautiously upwards. He checked for hazards and listened all the while for sounds of life. Five minutes passed and he came back to the window, gave me a brief run down on what he had found and said, 'Search as far as the stairs. Now listen to me – if another tremor hits, get out fast.' Then he stood aside to let me and Charco in.

'Okay. Find him, Charco,' I said. The dog launched himself through the window and, with nose scanning the ground and tail wagging, meticulously worked his way across the tangled room towards the stairs. It was much harder for me to get through the window, and by the time I did, Charco was already hunting around the pile of masonry stacked at the bottom of the stairs. He became very focussed and stretched up high, smelling the actual wall itself. He craned ever higher and sniffed intently. He started barking but I couldn't see why.

I looked back to the window to see Russ staring at me, his eyes silently asking if we had found the bloke. I called him in. 'Russ, Charco's barking here. Look,' I pointed to the wall. 'It must be that he's picking up scent lifting from somewhere but I have no idea where. I can't see where the guy might be unless under that pile over there,' I say, pointing to the rubble scattered over the stairs.

'It's possible that he might even be back there in that part of the building,' I suggested, pointing to an adjoining room where the upper floors had fallen to ground level.

Russ thought about it for a second or two, then said, 'I'll get the lads in and we'll cut a trench down into this lot under our feet.' He issued a series of orders to the team outside and they came pouring in, armed with shovels, picks and a vibraphone, the highly sensitive listening device also known as the Trapped Person Locator (TPL). In minutes, they were piling into the debris, pulling away big pieces of masonry. I called Charco and we went back outside – the team needed all the room they could get.

This was one of the worst parts of being a search and rescue dog handler – the anxious wait. As always, I found myself asking, Is the bloke there at all? Is the dog right? Did I commit these lads to a highly dangerous situation for nothing? It was very stressful – almost like being in suspended animation. Time dragged on forever and the suspense grew.

Night had fallen. I looked around, and saw in the beam from my head torch that the missing man's brother was still there. He was talking to another guy, much bigger and heavier than him. It turned out that this was another brother. Through the interpreter they asked if my dog's barking meant that their brother had been found.

I answered carefully, 'Not necessarily ...' How could I tell them that Charco might have got it wrong, and for any number of reasons. 'The dog is getting a scent, all right, but it might be because he is confused by the people standing around out here. It's very hard to know...' I finished lamely. They both nodded, trying to understand what I had said.

After an age, Russ and the lads crawled back out of the window and Russ said quietly, 'We've cut down into the rubble and have reached ground floor level. I can't see how the bloke can be there. I don't think there's anything more we can do tonight. Sorry, Neil. I think Charco might have got this one wrong.'

I was stunned. A whirl of questions flew around in my head. I was sure that Charco was right, but Russ and the lads were very experienced and they thought he was wrong. What the hell could I do now? Why was Charco barking? He never ever barked unless he had made a find. Perhaps he was getting scent from people outside the building as it filtered through, carried on the light breeze.

My confidence in Charco was badly dented and I felt sick inside because I knew that if he was wrong, I would find it really difficult to trust him on the next search. I decided to ask for another dog to check what he had done. Russ was talking to some of the locals, so I caught his attention. He excused himself and walked over.

'Russ, is there any chance of getting one of the Fire lads to double-check the place with his dog before we give up?' I asked him.

'Why not? Let's give it a try. Give me a minute ...' He turned away and radioed back to camp. After a brief conversation with someone at Control he said, 'Right, mate. One of the fire brigade dog handlers is on his way. We'll hang on here till he comes. Okay?'

'Thanks, Russ,' was all I could manage, a great weight lifting off my shoulders.

While we were waiting, I saw in the glow of our torches men of all ages starting to drift into the compound. They were dressed in the traditional woollen gown of the area, known as the 'phiran'. Russ's radio squawked. He held the speaker mic close to his ear and, after a short exchange with the person at the other end, called the team together and said, 'Gather round. Right now, Control is telling me that a specific threat has been made against us. They suggest strongly that we get out of here and leg it back to camp right now. What do you guys think? Do we go or do we take a chance and carry on with what we're doing?' I caught sight of the two brothers standing forlornly nearby, staring at us. Someone piped up, 'We finish what we came here to do and bollocks to it.' Everybody nodded at that. We were all agreed – we were here now, so we were staying. We tried to look unconcerned and got on with the job.

Small camp fires had been lit and in the darting light of the flickering flames we could see that the crowd had grown to quite a size. Some of the team tried talking to the men standing nearby but the language barrier ruled out any serious conversation.

After about twenty minutes, there was a stir and we saw the cavalry arrive in the form of Fire Officer Neil Woodmansy and his little collie bitch. He was accompanied by a few of his fire brigade colleagues.

'Hi, Neil. Over here, mate,' I said, leading him to the window and shining my torch inside. 'That's where Charco was indicating.' I directed the beam onto the far wall. 'The team have dug down into the debris but can't find anything. I don't know what the hell to think!'

'Well, I'll give it a rattle and see what she says,' he answered quietly.

He pointed at the window and his little collie jumped through it like a shot. She quickly searched the rubble and was soon at the place where Charco had shown such interest. Neil now crawled in after his dog. She stopped and did a double take at the wall, but didn't indicate. I could see Neil watching her closely.

'What do you think?' I called to him.

'Don't know, mate,' he shouted back. 'She's definitely showing interest but not enough to convince me there's someone alive in here. I just don't know,' he said, scratching his chin in thought.

'Maybe the bloke has only just died and that's why the dogs are doing what they're doing,' said Russ, who was standing close by.

'That's possible,' I replied because it's true that dogs can't really distinguish between the scent of a recently dead person and a live one.

Someone nearby muttered, 'The thing is, I've heard that sometimes people will say anything just to get us to dig a loved one out so they can bury them. They know we're here to find the living and that we aren't going to waste time digging out the dead. That's for somebody else to do. I think there might be a possibility that the guy heard nothing, but he's saying he did, just to get us to find the body, the poor sod. I'd do the same.'

I looked from Charco to the two brothers and then to the collapsed building and finally to the lads in the team. Russ had made the decision that this was a no-hoper and so, with heavy hearts, we had to pack up. He told the two brothers. They were torn between grief for their missing brother and gratitude for what we had been doing to find him. The decision to walk away felt like a complete contradiction to everything we were here for. Russ, like the rest of us, was not finding it easy, but he was the team leader and led from the front.

When we got back to camp I had time to reflect on what had happened. It was so unlike Charco to give what we call a 'false indication'. In fact I had never known him to do that. Yet the boys were not able to find the man in any of the places they searched. In the privacy of my tent, I agonised over the events of the last few hours. Did they fail to find the missing man because they were searching in the wrong place – because Charco and I had made a mistake? I knew I shouldn't be brooding on what had happened because I couldn't do anything about it now. My fretting intensified and I started panicking over Charco. Had he become unreliable? What would I do when he indicated on our next search? Could I trust him enough to direct our search efforts to the place he indicated? What if he was wrong again? On and on the negative thoughts bombarded my mind. Then another thought. What if Charco was right but the lads themselves had got it wrong?

The thoughts and worries built and fed on themselves until, mercifully, Brian poked his head through the tent door and said, 'Neil, mate. What the frig are you doing in here?' Not waiting for an answer, he went on, 'Come on ... there's a cup of tea waiting for you out here.' Brian is a good bloke and I could read in his eyes that he knew what was going on. 'Come on, mate,' he repeated. I shrugged off the negative thoughts and dragged myself outside. It was time to pull down the steel shutter in my mind and lock the thoughts behind it.

Waiting for me at the door, Brian nodded towards the place where we usually sat around the fire. He had this mischievous grin on his face as he pointed towards the Doc – the medic appointed to the UK international rescue team, civilian and fire service – who was sitting, large as life, enthroned in his usual seat. Now, the Doc was a really good bloke, always boosting morale with his bantering and leg-pulling, but he was a terrible 'wind-up' merchant. He never tired of practical jokes and the really annoying thing was that nobody was ever able to turn the tables on him.

I then spotted the reason why Brian was struggling to contain himself. Charco was wandering around the edges of the group carrying a toilet roll in his mouth. He had a habit of carrying things around like that, and on this particular occasion he'd obviously mooched into someone's tent, found the roll and nicked it. Oh my God … that was it, we had the Doc. Clearly Brian was on the same wavelength because he was nodding enthusiastically and grinning even more widely. All I needed to bait the hook was for Charco to come to me now with his prize.

Moments later, my prayers were answered and Charco spied me, making a beeline for me immediately right through the group of amused watchers. He wanted me to throw the toilet roll for him – he did this all the time with things he picked up, but the Doc didn't know that.

As Charco got closer, I said in a loud exasperated voice, 'Oh, for God's sake, Charco, not again … you've just been a few minutes ago.' I saw that this had caught the Doc's attention and he took the bait.

'What's Charco carrying that for, Neil?' he asked innocently.

'Oh, he's just telling me he needs the bog,' I said as matter-of-factly as I could.

'He never is!' gasped the Doc in amazement.

Brian chirped up, 'It's true, Doc – he does that every time he needs to go.'

'Bloody hell,' said the Doc, staring in wonder at Charco, still standing with the toilet roll in his mouth and staring at me, his tail wagging, silently pleading with me to throw it so he could run after it, fetch it and bring it back. 'Oh all right then, mate. Come on,' I said and we walked out of the group and over to the side of the campsite where the makeshift toilets had been constructed.

Now I should explain that Charco was taught from a very early age to piddle on command. It's quite an easy thing to do. As a pup he would always hear me say 'Hurry up, hurry up' while he was piddling. I would say it over and over. Very soon he had formed a mental bond between his action of piddling and my words, 'hurry up'. Simple.

I knew the Doc was still watching intently so I whispered to Charco, 'Hurry up', and of course he obligingly did a pee. I took the toilet roll from him and we nonchalently walked back to the fire. The Doc was clearly gobsmacked by this and began talking animatedly to the lads on either side of him. They had twigged what I was up to and started playing along, nodding in agreement.

As I got back to the group the Doc said, 'Well, I'm buggered! I thought you were joking, Neil. He really did need to go to the toilet. Bloody hell, that is one very clever dog!' He was caught, hook, line and sinker.

We kept him going for a few days longer until the farewell function at the embassy in Islamabad. The Doc was at the bar, engaged in animated discussion with some important-looking people in suits. He spotted me and introduced me to his companions. Then, joy of joys, he glowingly announced that I was the owner of a very clever dog called Charco. He relayed the whole toilet roll incident while I struggled to keep a straight face and look serious.

Some of the BIRD lads who had been watching and waiting slipped a toilet roll to Charco and sent him over to me at the bar. Ever the one to be the centre of attention, Charco paraded around through the crowd of rescuers and posh people, toilet roll clamped firmly in his jaws. I positioned myself so that Charco would see me and that the Doc would see Charco approaching.

'My God,' gasped the Doc. 'Look. Would you believe it … here he comes now. See what I mean?' he said to his new mates. 'Bloody hell, Neil,' he said, not taking his eyes off Charco, 'he needs to shit a lot doesn't he?'

Everyone in the bar had stopped talking and were waiting to see what would happen next.

'Well not this time, Doc,' I explained. 'You see, when he holds the bog roll end on like that it means that he wants a pee. If it was broadside in his mouth, then he would be saying he needs a shit.'

'Good God!' he gasped.

The wind-up was almost complete. 'What? What?' said the Doc to no one and everyone, hands outstretched in supplication. Then the penny dropped.

'Oh no! NO! Oh you bastards!!!'

The place erupted in hoots of laughter and cheering. We had him at long last. We all loved it – and no one more than the Doc himself.

Chapter 31

Next morning, the sun came up and the heat of the day began again. I was still in a turmoil about Charco apparently getting it wrong the night before. We were sorting ourselves out for the day ahead when one of the brothers of the man we had been searching for the night before appeared and begged us to go with him to carry on the search. It was truly heartbreaking but he was told by the team leader that we could do no more. There were just too many other emergencies for the team to go to. He got into a terrible state and pleaded with the interpreter to make our search managers change their minds. He was convinced his brother was still alive under the rubble and that Charco had indeed found him, so he couldn't understand why we weren't going back there to find him. A young officer in the Pakistan Army, having heard the commotion, came over and in fluent English said that he would try to explain it to the distraught man. He put his arm around him and walked him away and we never saw him again.

We had been asked to go to the city of Balakot, north-west of where we were. We heard from people who had survived and had made it on foot to Muzaffarabad, that Balakot had been almost totally destroyed and that no rescue teams had been there. Russ appeared with a British Embassy Land-Rover and a local driver to take four of us on a recce of the area.

We had not travelled very far when we came to a section of road which wound its way around a very steep set of cliffs with yawning drops beneath. Half of the road had just collapsed into the river and the remaining half seemed to be suspended on nothing at all. The driver stopped and was not too thrilled about the idea of going on. We got out and checked the road more closely and we saw that it was just hanging there and every now and then large pieces fell off and crashed into the river a long way below.

Then to cap it all, the temperature dropped dramatically, the sky grew black with ominous-looking clouds and they emptied a freezing mixture of rain and huge hailstones on us that bounced off our helmets and shoulders. In seconds, we were soaked to the skin and very cold. Now what? Nobody had brought wet-weather gear or warm clothes because we had set off from camp in blazing sunshine. If we wanted to go on to Balakot we would have to walk, because there was no way that the road in front would support the weight of a five ton Land-Rover.

And what if we did finally make it to Balakot on foot? We would have no equipment – we would have nothing more than our bare hands and Charco. What those poor people needed was a team fully equipped with tools for cutting and drilling, shoring and propping. We would be able to offer no more than the local people who had survived and were digging with their bare hands. The decision was clear. We had to turn back and report the situation to the controllers.

When we eventually got back to camp and Russ made our report and requested another search area, we were told to wait. But the wait lasted the whole day and then we were told that time had run out. The search and rescue operation had to stop so that the body recovery phase might now get into a high gear. We had to pack up and get ready for the long journey back to Islamabad. What a shambles!

All our tents and cooking gear were left with a local man who had been working with us and he was asked to give them to the people that needed them most. We piled ourselves into the ancient buses, their engines coughed into life and our convoy jolted forward on the 125-mile journey back to Islamabad.

The roads, already narrow and tortuous, were virtually impassable because of the enormous lumps of mountain that had been shaken loose by the earthquake. Local people had been working non-stop to clear them, using spades and picks and, very occasionally, they were helped by people operating big-tracked cranes and other types of earth-moving equipment. We met convoys of vehicles coming towards us, laden with food, shelter and clothing. Medical teams too, in their Red Cross-emblazoned four-wheel-drives, were converging on the area and, at last, we could see that the Pakistan Army had started to help.

Here and there, a few enterprising individuals were selling bottles of Coca Cola and Sprite, spicy food and bits and pieces of clothing from makeshift stalls. The most striking thing for me was that even though so many had died or were seriously injured, the surviving people were still able to smile and wave at us as they walked by, many carrying all the possessions they had in the world.

Our convoy drove slowly on and on through mountain villages, hanging precariously from ledges and apparently untouched by the earthquake. There too the people seemed to almost shine with a mixture of energy, friendliness and an old-world sense of community. We stopped off at a couple of these villages to stretch our legs and buy food and bottled water. Everywhere we went we received the same wonderful open welcome.

About ten or twelve hours later, we rolled into the suburbs of Islamabad and finally arrived at the place where we could get some rest before the flight back to the UK. Was our trip a success? Well, if you looked at the overall cost to deploy us and to sustain us while in the country, and asked if it stacked up financially, the answer would probably be no. But, on the other hand, if you were to ask the young man saved by BIRD, or to ask the ten or twelve people who had been saved by the other British teams, the answer would probably be a resounding yes.

On returning to England, Charco was immediately locked up for six months and, except for those of us closest to him, who visited him three or four times a week, nobody wanted to know. The press were very good in trying to highlight the plight of dogs returning from overseas deployment in the service of humanity, but it felt like no one really listened or even cared.

Charco has never been the same since his two sessions in quarantine – even now, he still has serious issues about eating his food from a metal bowl. Every mealtime for him has become an ordeal, taking twenty minutes or more for him to finish his food. He is panic-stricken during the entire process, snatching mouthfuls of food and then backing away from the dish, terrified. It is really sad to watch such a beautiful, noble dog behaving like this. Recently, CJ, now ten years old, took Charco under his wing and encouraged him to eat. He nibbled a few nuts from Charco's bowl as though to say, 'Look, mate! It's okay. I can do it – so can you!' Meanwhile, if any of my other six dogs happen to decide to sneakily take advantage of Charco's terror, CJ stands beside him, stares at the would-be thief, lowers his head and gives a warning growl as though to say, 'Go on, punk! Make my day!'

The funny thing is that while Charco is clearly terrified of eating and is in no way an aggressive dog, he does make threatening moves at any of the others who come too near his bowl. None of them takes his bluster seriously though and they try to nick it anyway. Mr CJ, however, is an entirely different matter. Him they respect and when he says leave Charco's food alone, they do.

In 2010 Charco and I were invited to appear on the Cesar Millan show in Belfast and Dublin. Cesar has always been a hero of mine and I felt greatly honoured to meet him. We discussed Charco's bizarre behaviour and when I told him about the way CJ had taken him under his wing he turned to the audience and said, 'Now do you understand what I mean when I speak about the power of the pack?' Rock on, CJ.

Chapter 32

In April 2005, having retired from full-time teaching, I had time on my hands. To supplement my income, I began training explosives detection dogs for a commercial kennels near my home. The proprietor sold the dogs to security companies who were responsible for protecting the interests of oil companies in the Middle East. At the kennels, I met Fern, a little black-and-white 'sprocker'. She was just six months old and I fell in love with her the moment I set eyes on her. She was the most adorable little dog I had ever seen.

Fern was the accidental progeny of a cocker spaniel mother and an English springer spaniel father, both of whom had been working trials champions. But, because she was a mixture, a 'Heinz 57' so to speak, the kennel owner had considered her to be worthless and had therefore given her to a family as a pet.

For a short while everything had gone well but after four months the family brought her back, 'before she got herself killed on the road', they said. Apparently, she would never return when they called her and even though they had tried very hard to cure the problem, they had got absolutely nowhere. Reluctantly, they finally concluded that her one chance of living to a ripe old age was to start afresh with a new owner who could sort out her disobedience.

Knowing Fern as I do now, I am not at all surprised they ran into a brick wall. She is a dog with an exceptionally high hunt drive and could never have settled down to become a normal family pet – she would have withered away and indeed might one day have bitten someone out of pure frustration.

I took her home to join the rest of the tribe – Cracker, Dylan,

Charco, CJ and little Milo (a black and white collie that we had adopted a few years previously and had intended to train as a mountain search dog, but he sadly lacked the intellectual credentials necessary to achieve that lofty status) – and just as I had done, they fell in love with her. She was a big hit and settled in as though she had been with us from the start. She particularly latched on to CJ, who, though pretending to object with a grumbled throaty protest, nevertheless allowed her to share his mat. That place was normally reserved for Charco but he managed to jam himself on to the end and peace reigned.

The day after I got Fern, I set about teaching her to come back when she was called. I got a long line that I attached to her collar, took her into the forest and let her run around to do whatever she wanted. But every now and then I'd call her name and give the line a sharp jerk. Getting down on one knee I'd then encourage her to come back – if she hesitated, I'd give the line another jerk. When she eventually returned, I'd praise her lavishly and let her go again. I kept this up every day for a week and she got better and better until, by day seven, she was coming back with hardly any reminders.

In the second week, I let her run free, but still kept the long line attached to her collar. Whenever I wanted her to come back now, I'd wait until I could see the end of the line and could stand on it. I'd call her as before, praise her and let her go again. If she decided to disobey at any time, my foot, firmly anchoring the line, prevented her escape. This routine lasted for a further week, after which time the problem of Fern ignoring recall had disappeared completely. Only then could I begin to train her as a drowned victim search dog – she took to it like the proverbial duck to water.

Fern was a real joy to work with and after eighteen months of hard slog, I invited John Sjoberg to come to Ireland to assess her. The assessment lasted two days. She passed and was awarded the drowned victim search dog certificate. However, while part of me wanted to rejoice in her achieving it, another sincerely hoped she would never be needed. Tragically though, she was and just a few short days later.

In April 2007, in the middle of the night, Max Joyce, leader of the NI Fire and Rescue Service specialist rescue team rang. He said they had been called to search for two teenagers who had vanished during a boating accident in a lake outside Castlewellan and he needed Fern. Apparently, two boys and a girl had been enjoying some end-of-term high jinks in a Canadian canoe on the lake, when it suddenly capsized, plunging all three of them into the dark, icy waters. The girl had been unable to swim and so one of the boys, her cousin, had stayed to help her. Sadly, they had both drowned, but the other boy had managed to get ashore to raise the alarm.

Fern and I arrived at the command post shortly after dawn and, with a cox from the fire and rescue team, began to search. About twenty minutes later, Fern indicated a possible location for the youngsters. We checked it from various directions but she always indicated at the same place. A buoy was dropped to mark the spot for the divers. A few hours later, the teenagers were recovered by the Mourne underwater search team.

The entire community was devastated by the loss of the two young lives, and a huge funeral followed. It was a shattering day for the distraught parents. In the weeks that followed, the families organised a massive fundraising drive for the dive team and for the search and rescue dogs. The generosity of people in the area was staggering, prompted as it was by their desire to lessen the suffering of other families blighted by similar tragedies in the future.

An invitation to the two families and the rescuers to attend a reception in Dublin Castle came from the President of Ireland, Mary McAleese. I had the great privilege of attending with my wife Kate and it was a very moving occasion – the kindness Mrs McAleese and her husband showed to the grieving families still leaves me at a loss for words.

In March 2009, Fern and I were asked to assist in another search, this time for a man who had been seen falling into the River Boyne. Raph, Adrian and I arranged to meet John Higgins, the search and rescue coordinator of Lough Ree Sub Aqua Club, at a hotel in Navan town, for a briefing. John is a dedicated voluntary diver whom I had met in Leitrim in 2003 during another search. He was heading the volunteer divers for this operation.

He outlined in detail those parts of the river where his team and the Garda dive team had already searched. Then he took us to the place where the man had last been seen. It was a beautiful stretch of river, where the wide grassy banks give the people a wonderful location to enjoy long tranquil walks. As is always the case when I do jobs like that; it felt so at odds with what we were there to do.

We launched the boat and while Adrian prepared the engine, I secured Fern's life jacket and safety line. With a final check, we pushed off into the slowly moving waters of the Boyne. Fern immediately assumed her position on the bows and, unbidden, started searching. With Raph walking the bank to observe and offer assistance if needed, Adrian crabbed the boat across the slow-moving waters of the river, aiming for a point on the other side. He then manoeuvred us back again, setting up a zigzag pattern to cover as much of the river as possible. We went along like that for about half a mile before gliding around a sweeping bend where we encountered a small weir. It looked innocent enough with the water cascading down its gentle rocky gradient for about ten feet before continuing its journey to the sea. We judged that it posed no danger to us and so, while I took a firm hold on Fern, still clamped in the bows, Adrian tilted the outboard engine out of the water and the boat slid over.

On the lower side of the weir, a small rocky island split the river in two. The water on one side was clearly too shallow to hide a body so we concentrated on the other side. We allowed the current to push us past the little outcrop and had only gone fifty yards further downstream when Fern stiffened. Then, just as Cuisle and Cracker had done when they picked up scent, she defied gravity and leaned right down to the water surface, sniffing intently. She hesitated, then sitting bolt upright, looked over her shoulder and barked excitedly.

Quite carried away now, she hung back over the bows, her bottom in the air, her safety line taut, and still barking intensely. I was positive she had found the missing man, but I wondered why his body was right in the middle of the river. Bodies are generally found near the banks, either because the current is slower there or because branches of fallen trees catch and hold them.

On the radio, Raph asked if Fern had made a find. Adrian,

guessing that others might be listening, replied carefully that she might have, but that we needed to check again. We drove back upstream and repeated the search, starting just beside the weir. As we drifted back down past the spot, Fern did the very same thing in exactly the same place.

Meanwhile, John Higgins, who had been watching from a high point on the other bank, decided that we should pass on what Fern was doing to the Garda divers. He informed them over the radio and they replied they would be happy to check the location for us. In twenty minutes, they were at the scene and, as per protocol, they concentrated on the edge of the river near the banks. They found nothing. I was deeply disappointed and could not understand why Fern seemed to have got it so wrong. Although it is obvious now, I never really thought about checking the centre of the river. After all, bodies were never found there, were they?

We did the search all over again, but this time we started away downstream and made our way back up towards the weir. Just as before, Fern indicated at almost precisely the same spot. Unfortunately, it was starting to get dark by then so we had to stop and get the boat out of the water. We packed up and after another lengthy debrief with John, we headed home.

On the way, we talked a lot about what Fern had done. We went over and over everything, looking for an explanation and then the penny dropped. Yes, the divers had thoroughly searched the edge of the river, but they had not searched the middle! It was so obvious and yet we had all missed it.

I rang John and suggested that, next morning, he ask the divers to search again, but this time to concentrate on the middle of the river and work up towards the little weir. Having great faith in Fern, John said he would certainly get a team to do it, adding, 'What do we have to lose?'

The following afternoon John rang to say they had found the missing man. He had been trapped under a large boulder right in the middle of the river and was being held there by the pressure of the water. It was to the credit of the dive team that they located him where they did. Without their tenacity, the poor man might well have been held there for many more weeks and his family left in limbo, waiting for the return of his body. And as for Fern, I was so pleased with her. What a wonderful little dog she was turning out to be.

Almost a month later, a good friend of mine, Dave Marsh, honorary secretary of the National Search and Rescue Dog Association (NSARDA), rang to tell me about a tragic drowning incident that had happened in Loch Awe, a huge body of water in Argyle and Bute. He said that sixteen weeks previously, a fishing trip had gone very wrong on the loch when four friends drowned. I had heard of the tragedy on the national BBC news of course, but had no idea of the details.

Dave said that the men had been out for the evening in the village of Loch Awe, but when they were returning to their camp-site, their boat mysteriously sank. A fifth member of the group had not gone to the pub that evening, electing instead to stay at the campsite for a quiet night. It was he who had raised the alarm, having heard his friends' cries for help somewhere out in the darkness.

Dave went on to say that a huge search for the men had been going on since then, involving police divers and local search and rescue teams. Two bodies had been located, but there were still two men unaccounted for. He asked whether I would be prepared to take Fern across to help in the search, were he to offer our services to Strathclyde Police. Of course, I said yes, but I knew that since I was a completely unknown quantity, the police would want to check me out first. Dave said he would fill in the necessary details as to my credibility but that I could probably expect a call from them sometime soon.

Days later, I was contacted by the sergeant in charge of Strathclyde Police dog branch. He said he had been asked to act as liaison between me and the police. He was clearly knowledgeable about dogs and I was happy to answer all his questions about my background and about Fern's capability and so on. Satisfied, he set about arranging for us to travel across.

However, the weather was not good for the next few days and the strong winds would have made searching impossibly difficult for Fern. It was decided that we should wait and that the police would keep in close contact with the Met Office. After another week, a short period of light winds was predicted and we were asked to go to Loch Awe as quickly as possible.

For anyone who may not be familiar with that part of the world, Loch Awe is the longest freshwater lake in Scotland, being almost twenty-six miles long. It has an average width of half a mile and in places is over ninety-six metres deep. Some people might recall that, for a while, the BBC had used a film clip of Kilchurn Castle, which sits at the picturesque and beautiful northern end of the loch, to introduce some of its programmes.

Raph, Fern and I were met in Oban by a young police sergeant who was in charge of the Strathclyde marine policing unit. He brought us to a local hotel which was to be our base during the next couple of days. We were then given a detailed briefing on the history of the accident. He said that a senior police-dog instructor from their cadaver dog unit would accompany us on the boat – no pressure then! As it happened, the instructor turned out to be very supportive.

On the first morning of our search, as we crossed to the far side of the loch in the police boat, we were shown the campsite where the friends had been staying. It was an idyllic spot on the bank, shaded by trees, and with an uninterrupted view of the loch the men had been there to fish. But it was also a poignant reminder of how quickly fun can turn to tragedy wherever deep water is concerned. I shuddered at the thought of what those poor men had experienced that night.

After an hour or so of criss-crossing the slightly choppy waters, Fern gave a very strong indication. It was at a point roughly halfway between the quayside at Loch Awe village and the campsite, and was on a direct line between the two. The depth of water at that point showed as thirty-two metres. That, I was told, was going to present the police with a real problem. Diving to such a depth could take up to two weeks to arrange because of the challenges it presented. However, while it was impossible for the police to search with divers that day, they could and did use a sonar device to check the loch bottom for clues. Unfortunately, that didn't reveal anything useful. We did two days' searching in total, checking and re-checking what Fern had done, but then Raph and I had to go home. As usual the period of waiting was agonising but two weeks later I heard that the bodies of the two men had surfaced following a storm. They were picked up very close to the point that Fern had identified.

A few months later I was contacted by the Procurator Fiscal and asked to attend as an expert witness in an inquest on the tragedy. On the date in question, I was unable to travel, but in our lengthy discussion about the part Fern and I had played, he did say that the records indicated that she had indeed been very accurate in her indication that day. Thank God. We had done something worthwhile after all.

Chapter 33

The Motion Picture Association of America (the MPAA) is a representative body whose primary purpose is to advance the business interests of its members: Walt Disney Motion Picture Group, Sony Pictures, Paramount Pictures, 20th Century Fox, Universal Studios and Warner Brothers.

In 2005, in a brief interlude from search and rescue, I was invited by Davey Mayberry to conduct a feasibility study on behalf of this august body. Davey, who speaks in a deep rumbling measured voice, perfectly reflecting his six-foot-something height and his matching physique, said he would be a sounding board for me and would offer constructive criticism and advice where it was needed. The purpose of the experiment was to see whether dogs could be trained to locate optical discs – or DVDs as they are better known. The initial concept was the brainchild of John Malcolm, head of the MPAA's worldwide anti-piracy unit. John had once been a Department of Justice deputy assistant attorney-general, and was now a high-flying demanding executive, known for thinking outside the box and totally committed to taking the fight to the pirates. No dog had ever been trained to find DVDs before, so this was a unique opportunity, not to be missed by any committed dog trainer. Of course I jumped at the chance.

Once the formalities of terms and conditions were out of the way, my first task was to find two dogs with exceptionally high play and hunt drives who were also people-friendly. Fortune smiled and led me to Lucky and Flo, two black female Labradors, both of them crazy about playing with and hunting for tennis balls. To me, they were the perfect choice. For a start, they were environmentally sound – a dog-training term meaning that the dogs can tolerate loud noise, are comfortable around traffic, will climb on or under furniture, can travel on escalators and elevators and so on. In addition, they were quick to learn and, for the most part, were happy around people.

Physically they were not so perfect though, being small for Labradors and not particularly pretty. Flo had bandy back legs and her ears were chipped and torn from being attacked by other dogs in the crowded kennels where she had been living. Lucky was overweight, short-tempered and had been owned and completely spoiled by a lovely lady in her seventies, who was quite unable to cope with her. Lucky had a terrible habit of chewing things and once ate an entire Christmas cake along with the candles, candleholders and most of the cake stand. As well as that, Lucky's people skills weren't as fine-tuned as I might have liked. A glaring example of this occurred soon after we arrived in Los Angeles where, in the head offices of the MPAA, she took a serious dislike to the woman who was the company paymaster. The poor woman had put out her hand to say hello to Lucky, who decided she was having none of it and backed away growling. The woman either didn't hear the warning or perhaps hoped Lucky didn't really mean it, so she kept reaching forward to stroke her head. This pushed Lucky's aggression button and she snapped but, thankfully, missed biting the woman. It had been a warning and the message was clear: 'I will decide if I want you to touch me, not you'.

Having found suitable dogs, my next task was to establish whether they could actually detect an odour from optical discs. That took about a week of experimentation, and after one particularly productive training session, it became obvious that DVDs did indeed have a unique odour. Next, helped by suggestions from Davey, I had to ensure that the dogs were only detecting the odour of the polycarbonate of the discs and were not being confused by the scent from packaging or the glue used, or the marketing labels on the discs. After a short period of further experimentation I eventually confirmed that they were indeed detecting the basic polycarbonate material, rather than anything else.

The next eight weeks of intensive training passed quickly, after which the MPAA were informed that Lucky and Flo could positively detect single DVDs or packages of hundreds, in sealed containers or mixed in with other products. That news went down very well and to my great delight, the MPAA asked me to continue training the dogs until they were deemed by Davey as being at an operational level. That took me four more weeks and then the dogs were formally assessed at the DHL warehouse in Belfast, an enormous building filled with parcels and packages of all sizes and shapes. It was a vibrant busy place with the constant movement of staff, some on forklift trucks, others walking around the huge floor area checking this and that.

Lucky and Flo were each set the task of individually locating three packages containing discs, varying in quantity from two to hundreds. The entire assessment was recorded and the film eventually sent directly to the MPAA bosses.

I hated assessments, but I need not have worried because both dogs were brilliant and located the boxes without a hitch. However, since John Malcolm was determined to beat the disc pirates and just to be quite sure, another test was arranged for the dogs. It took place a few weeks later in the much bigger DHL and Federal Express warehouses at Heathrow and Stansted and was observed by top brass from the MPAA and from HM Customs and Excise. Just for good measure, it was also televised by a national television network.

A consignment of parcels had just arrived from Europe in three large container lorries, and the dogs had to search the delivery for hidden counterfeit discs. This was a task that hitherto would have been done by spot-check search teams with no means of verifying their effectiveness. Routine spot-checking of consignments is, by its very nature, a hit-and-miss affair. All it can do is sample a very small part of any shipment where customs officers will open a few packages, selected purely at random.

I began with Flo, always my favourite, and very shortly after starting along the first row of shelves lined with boxes, she stopped beside one labelled 'Sports shoes'. One of the customs officers slit it open and as he delved inside I anxiously held my breath. He found not just fake sport shoes, but also a hoard of pornographic DVDs, some of which were child-related. It was a stunning result and a severe blow to the perverts for whom the discs had been destined!

Then it was Lucky's turn. She was asked to search parcels as they passed along a moving conveyor belt, something I had not trained her to do. I need not have worried – she jumped straight on to the belt, steadied herself and got to work. Very quickly, she picked out a number of packages and, just as before, a customs officer slit them open. The first one was found to contain tins of dog food. But, as he removed each tin one by one, all the while failing dismally to suppress a somewhat cynical smile, he found at the very bottom of the box, one solitary disc. As it happened, it was a legitimate advertising medium but Lucky had proved the point. She could undoubtedly detect concealed optical discs!

The other boxes the dogs detected were also discovered to contain discs, all of them counterfeit. Everyone was ecstatic. The dogs had proved themselves effective beyond a shadow of a doubt and so were formally accepted on to the MPAA worldwide anti-piracy team.

Over the next year the two girls and I were flown around the world: Los Angeles, Washington, New York, Hong Kong, Dubai and Toronto. In every city, the MPAA arranged demonstrations of the dogs working and they were closely scrutinised by the local law enforcement agencies and by television networks from around the world. We even did a live 'bust' in Chinatown, New York, where, under the watchful eye of the NYPD, the dogs found hundreds of boxes of counterfeit discs in a basement store. Everywhere they went, the two little labs from County Down in Ireland were winning hearts and minds in the fight against global optical disc piracy.

A few months later, Lucky and Flo were sent to Malaysia, which, at that time, was one of the main sources of production of counterfeit optical discs. For personal reasons, I couldn't go, so Davey Mayberry went instead. While there, the dogs located discs and burners worth many millions of pounds sterling and in so doing, severely upset the pirating operations. The criminals were so ticked off with Lucky and Flo that they placed a bounty of £10,000 each on the dogs' heads and they had to be brought back to Ireland until the dust settled.

A few months later, I was asked to train two more dogs for the MPAA, Manny and Paddy. They were eventually presented as a gift to the Malaysian authorities, but unfortunately, soon after arriving in Malaysia, Manny died under what were described as mysterious circumstances. A truly sad ending to what had been a wonderful story.

These days many dog training companies are offering to train dogs to detect optical discs and some even claim to have been the first in the world to have done so. That, unfortunately, is the nature of so many in the commercial dog world and is the reason I have stepped out of it, never to return.

During my time working for the MPAA, I was fortunate to meet some truly lovely people, driven by high idealism in the fight against optical disc piracy. They were inspirational and, to me personally, were kindness itself and I will always remember them with gratitude.

Chapter 34

My old mate Cracker had begun to slow down during my daily walks with the dogs in nearby Moneyscalp Forest. On one particular day, I turned to check on him and he was nowhere to be seen. I walked back down the track and had almost arrived at the Land-Rover, when I found him sitting off to one side, on the grassy bank. He was delighted to see me, but he was panting a lot, which, given the fact he hadn't been anywhere and it was not a warm day, was strange. I called him and as he came towards me, I saw he had developed a limp. He didn't show any signs of pain but it was clear that the last thing he needed that day was a long walk in the forest. He would be better off at home.

So I loaded all the dogs into the Land-Rover and a few minutes later, we arrived back at the house. When I opened the door and said 'Okay, lads', the rest of the dogs leaped out but Cracker, usually the first out, wanted to lie where he was. I eventually had to lift him down, much to his annoyance because he always hated being fussed over. All his life Cracker would recoil at anyone putting their face next to his. He would pull away and act disdainful and tense until the moment of forced affection had passed and then he would relax again.

When I got him into the house, Kate and I checked him over. There were no cuts or tears anywhere, but it looked to us as though he might have strained a muscle in his left shoulder. Next day, he was no better. When we went for a walk, he showed no interest in charging off to do the usual sniffing thing with the rest of the team. It was clear that what he really wanted was to have his lead on – he kept biting it and holding it in his mouth, looking up at me as though to say, 'Would you please put this bloody thing on me?'

The rest of the dogs ran around the forest, hunting and chasing each other as usual, but Cracker just watched them stoically. He contented himself with checking out the grassy areas beside him as he walked along slowly with me.

When we got home, I said, 'Right, mate. No more walks for you until Friday.' Cracker, always a great one for making the most of things, was content to just lie in the sun, with Charco dozing beside him. And Charco, never quite the same dog since quarantine, possibly saw in Cracker a fellow casualty. He often lay with his head on Cracker's shoulder and from that position of comfort, they watched what was going on around them.

In the next week or two, Cracker's condition worsened – he developed a problem balancing himself. I could also see that his limp had become more pronounced. In fact, he didn't seem able to walk at all but would stand there panting as he watched me going outside. I had to carry him out to his favourite place in the garden where he would flop down in the sun and not move any further.

He watched me as I cut the grass or he studied the sparrows as they hopped around, searching for peanuts that might have dropped to the ground from the feeder above his head. He would bark at me if he wanted to be moved into the shade, or if he wanted a drink or a piddle. Clearly the time had come for me to take him to the vet, something I had been dreading and trying to avoid.

John Heatherington, who was Cracker's vet, is one of the best in Ireland, a young man with real expertise and a great love for his job. After a very thorough examination, he asked us to leave Cracker with him overnight so that he could do some X-rays first thing in the morning. And so, with a really heavy heart, I gave Cracker a kiss and watched as he limped after John into the back of the surgery. It was the last time we ever saw him.

Later that evening, at around ten o'clock, John's senior partner in the veterinary practice, Gilbert McKnight, a canine orthopaedic surgeon rang me and said, 'Neil, I've X-rayed Cracker myself and I'm afraid I've got very bad news for you.'

I couldn't answer him and so he went on, 'Cracker has a huge tumour on his left leg which has eaten into his bone and actually broken it. He is sedated at the moment, Neil, and I am going to help the poor old fella on his way. I am so sorry, Neil.'

'Thanks, Gilbert,' was all I could get out. And so Cracker was gone. Just like that!

All those weeks, the poor old fella had been trying to walk around with me and go to the toilet and eat and so on, while all the time one of his legs had been broken! That was the true measure of Cracker.

Kate later asked Gilbert to have him individually cremated and days later she brought him home in a wooden casket, his name on a brass plate on the top. I couldn't bring myself to look at it for weeks. It was so painful and sad without him.

Then a crowd of my mates from BIRD came over to Ireland to visit and do some search dog training. In a quiet moment, Brian said, 'Neil mate. It's time to bury Cracker. We're all here and we'll give him the send-off he deserves. What do you say, mate?'

'Okay, Brian,' I managed.

We all drove up to the top of Moneyscalp Forest, Cracker's favourite place, where the high ground gives beautiful views out towards the mountains beyond. We held a short ceremony there and then Kate and I buried him. It was heart-wrenching stuff.

Then, we all went back home to our house and got well and truly lamped.

But a week later, on a wet cold dark miserable day, I began to imagine Cracker lying up there in the sodden muddy grave and I thought, 'No way!' I went out, got into the Land-Rover, drove up to the grave, dug up the casket and brought it home. I washed it off and it is with me still and will stay with me until the day I die when, I hope, it will be buried with me.

Dylan was clearly suffering too. He moped about looking for his big brother for days. He was showing his years and by then had become as a deaf as a post. The only way I could get his attention was by sign language – when I wanted him to come, I would wave at him to get his attention and then give him a 'come here' sign. We still went for long walks in the forest but I had to watch him carefully because every now and again, he would wander off and get lost.

One day, while I was moping at the place where Cracker had been buried, all the boys were sitting around and I got sort of carried away remembering the good times we had had. Still thinking about Cracker, I got up and walked on for about twenty minutes. Then it hit me – where was Dylan? I looked round to check but there was no sign of him. 'Christ, where the hell is he?' I shouted. I ran back down the track but I could not see him anywhere.

Completely distraught, I phoned Kate and within minutes she was on her way. I met her at the gates of the forest and as she scrambled into the Land-Rover, I blurted out what had happened. We drove straight back to where I had last seen Dylan and then inched around the paths where we normally walked, she checking on her side and me scanning the other, but there was no sign of him. Calling his name was useless because of his total deafness, so I put my trust in the hope that the wind might carry my scent to him, but that didn't work either.

We spent four hours searching without a sign of him but one thing was certain – neither of us was going home until we found him. We were stumped. Then we came to a track that I never walked with the dogs because it was at the far end of the forest and led to a dead end. Kate suggested I should search it anyway, just in case, and because all else had drawn a blank.

'Why the hell would he go that way?' I shouted, in sheer frustration. 'He'll never be down there!'

'Look,' she said patiently, 'we've searched everywhere else, so just do it, for God's sake.'

Reluctantly, because I was convinced I was wasting time, I set off down the hill, following a path that led to the far end of the forest. I walked for about half a mile but, finding nothing, turned back dejected. When we met up again, Kate demanded to know if I had gone as far as the bottom of the track, right to the boundary wall.

'No, because he'd never go away down there,' I said.

'Please go back and go right to the bottom,' she insisted.

'Oh, for God's sake. All right!' I said in bad temper.

Back down the track I went. At the very bottom, I spotted the barest of movements off to one side, right next to a gate. I went to investigate more closely and, joy of joys, I found him – there was our boy. He had somehow walked all the way here and having found his way blocked by the gate had decided to stay where he was. Typical of Dylan, he had made the best of a bad job and had formed a sort of nest in the bracken. Judging by the way it had been churned up, that was where he had spent the last few hours, waiting for me to find him.

Beside myself with relief and happiness and pointlessly shouting his name, I ran to him. He was completely unaware of me until I got closer, then he lifted his head, possibly having felt the vibrations of my pounding feet. He turned, looked at me in surprise and then in so far as his elderly frame would allow, jumped with joy. We were both ecstatic with excitement as I hugged and kissed him and got plastered by his tongue.

Kate and I had been using two small radios to communicate with each other so when I pressed the button and bellowed that I had found him, she screamed, 'Where? Oh thank God. Thank God. Where is he?'

'At the end of the path,' I shouted back, proper radio procedure now completely out the window. 'I can't believe it. I found him,' I shouted again and again.

I lifted Dylan onto my shoulders and carried him up the track to where Kate was waiting. What a welcome she gave him and what a fuss he made of her.

But only a few short months later and exactly one year since Cracker's death, Dylan stopped eating. He spent a lot of time sleeping and when he was awake, he would find me and lay his old head on my knee for me to stroke him and tell him how much I loved him.

Eventually, the dreaded time came when we had to bring him to the vet. I went into the surgery, not wanting anyone else but Gilbert McKnight to look at Dylan. Thankfully, he was on duty that evening and I could tell that he sensed what was coming as he glanced down at my old mate. I told Gilbert about Dylan's total lack of appetite and of his restless panting and copious drinking of water.

He sighed and sat on the ground beside Dylan. He put his stethoscope in his ears and listened intently. He probed for a few minutes and then, with great sadness, took out the earpieces, looked up and said, 'Neil, I'm going to tell you the truth. Dylan is dying. There's no other way to say it. I'm so sorry.' Then he almost whispered, 'It would be better to let him go now.'

Dylan looked round at me and I couldn't bear it. I stood up and walked out of the room, leaving poor Kate to make the decision. I went out as far as the car, but then went back in. I opened the door of the surgery and saw Dylan still lying there, Kate kneeling over him.

She looked up in floods of tears and said that Gilbert had left her with him for a while and that he would come back in a few minutes to sedate him. She choked that when Dylan was asleep, Gilbert would send him to join Cracker. I looked down at him, my heart breaking in bits, while he gazed back with those deep brown eyes so full of trust and devotion. I held him tight and told him I loved him and would never ever forget him and that I would always miss him. Poor Kate stayed a while longer but I couldn't bear it. I got to my feet and walked blindly out of the surgery.

And now, one year later, I can think of no better tribute to Dylan than to end this book with him and to say that apart from Kate, he was my best friend, my trusted ally and so many times, my personal counsellor.

Back in 2006, both Dylan and Cracker had been awarded the PDSA gold medal for animal gallantry and devotion to duty – the animal equivalent of the George Cross. It was a grand occasion in which the chairman of the PDSA, Freddie Bircher, flew over to Northern Ireland to present the awards at Belfast Castle.

The PDSA website describes the award to the two brothers as follows:

> Dylan & Cracker: For displaying outstanding gallantry and devotion to duty while carrying out official duties with their handler, Neil Powell, as part of the Northern Ireland Search and Rescue Dog Association (SARDA).

> In March 1999, Dylan saved the lives of four students lost for

several hours on the mountains of Mourne. Despite exceptionally poor weather conditions, Dylan located the group stranded on a ledge 250 feet above ground level. He stayed on duty until the rescue team had lifted everyone to safety.

Later, in November 1999, Dylan worked in Duzce as part of the UK Fire Service Search and Rescue team and the International Rescue Corps following the earthquake in Turkey. Dylan located two people buried alive in the rubble. Crawling between floors, climbing ladders and spanning dangerous voids, this dog never wavered from his duties.

Cracker, Dylan's brother, was also part of the 1999 Turkish earthquake search team locating bodies trapped in the debris. His ability to locate the deceased gave families the opportunity to pay their last respects to loved ones.

Cracker is the only dog in the UK trained to locate bodies in water. His skills have helped locate four people, bringing closure and peace of mind to grieving families.

And for his work in Turkey, Cracker was awarded the UK Canine Global Hero Award, sponsored jointly by Pedigree Chum and Asda. I was asked to bring him to New York to have the presentation made and to have his paw print permanently displayed in a 'sidewalk for heroes'. Unfortunately, quarantine restrictions at the time prevented him from going. However, a very generous and specially commissioned award ceremony was set up for him in London. He and I were flown over, picked up at the airport by limousine and taken to a hotel. There then followed a series of television and radio interviews, one of which was with Simon Weston – Falklands burns victim – a true gentleman and a genuine hero! We were escorted by a stunning-looking PR lady, and travelled to venues all over the UK, where Cracker was photographed and feted by the press. He lapped it up.

These were truly fitting tributes to two wonderful dogs who I loved and with whom I had the honour to live for sixteen years.

★

I cannot find words to describe how I feel about their deaths or indeed the death of my other dogs, and so I have borrowed these beautiful verses from the poet, Vicky Holder:

> If tears could build a stairway
> and heartache make a lane,
> I'd walk the path to heaven
> and bring you back again.
>
> Our family chain is broken,
> and nothing seems the same.
> But as God calls us one by one,
> the chain will link again.

Thank you so much to all my wonderful dogs, thank you for letting me be a part of your lives. And to the ones that have gone before me, I'll see you later guys.

Epilogue

There will always be people who, for whatever reason, get lost and need to be found, and dogs are still the most effective means of finding them. Therefore, despite the pain of losing my old mates Dylan, Cracker and all the others, I am still a dog handler and honoured to be able to work with the Search and Rescue Dog Association (Ireland North) and the specialist rescue team of the Northern Ireland Fire and Rescue Service.

Charco, Sam and Fern are as eager as ever to hunt for those who are missing, and now they have a new brother, Paddy, a nineteen-month-old bloodhound-springer mix, who joined us in October 2009. By pure good fortune, Paddy became available for re-homing and was given to me by Tom Middlemas, a friend of mine for many years. From our frequent phone calls, he knew that I had become very interested in trailing as an alternative method of using dogs to find lost people. Paddy had already done the basics in this exciting new discipline and so it seemed like a match made in Heaven.

Trailing is relatively new in search and rescue dog circles in the UK and Ireland, but it has a long history of success in the United States, where films often portray the relentless bloodhound tracking down fleeing slaves or escaped convicts. Trailing involves giving a dog an article of clothing belonging to a missing person to smell. The dog is then asked to 'find' and it will only search for that one individual. If a person goes missing in parkland or in a forest, ordinary air-scenting dogs can become confused by the scent of volunteer search parties already on the ground, but the trailing dog, which is scent specific, will have no such problem.

When he spoke to me on the phone Tom said, 'I have the very

boy for you. His name is Paddy. He's three quarters bloodhound and one quarter springer, so he won't have the usual short lifespan or the health issues of the bloodhound but he will have the nose and the drive to follow a trail. If you want him, he's yours.' And that was it. Soon afterwards, Paddy joined our tribe, bringing the number of dogs in our house to eight. They were delighted to welcome the newcomer and he appeared to be just as pleased.

Unfortunately, I very soon discovered that young Paddy was not only a very headstrong young man, but also as mad as a box of frogs. I also learned that he had serious issues around food guarding and about a raised voice should I catch him misbehaving in any way. Two or three times in the first week, he planted his front paws on my chest, snarling because I gave him a telling-off about something. And If I approached him when he was eating, he would growl a low threatening warning and bare his teeth. He was, to put it mildly, very challenging and I was on the point of sending him back to Tom on a number of occasions.

Not only did he have aggression problems, he also had that peculiar hound trait of running off on an animal trail and disappearing for ages in hot pursuit. This would be accompanied by loud whooping, baying sounds to let the whole world know how clever he was. The difficulty with this kind of thing was that in a rural setting like ours, farmers with sheep and lambs were not going to be too tickled.

It all came to a head one day when Paddy took off over the wall, his nose pressed to the ground, to follow the smell of two ewes who had just legged it from the neighbouring field. It was on a bitterly cold February morning and I was clad in wellies and wrapped up from head to toe in warm clothes. I yelled at Paddy to stop, but I might just as well have shouted, 'Go on, my son! Run away as hard as you can.'

Meanwhile, the other seven dogs were all crowding around my feet telling me that they were all good boys and would never do anything as bold as that.

Knowing that this latest stunt of Paddy's could well be the final straw, I scrambled over the stone ditch and gave chase. The crazed baying of Paddy as he charged headlong after the fleeing sheep was getting fainter. I shouted desperately, 'This is it, you bastard! You're out of here!'

Over one field we scrambled, then another, across a road, over a gate into another field, through a barbed-wire fence and down to the river. At that point, the sheep had come to a standstill on the riverbank and Paddy, satisfied he had found them, had lost interest and was poking around for some new quarry to pursue.

'Paddy, you absolute bloody moron!' I shrieked. Of course that was enough to make the two ewes fling themselves into the river. One chose the shallow end and crossed easily to the other bank, but the other plunged into the deepest part. I watched in horror as she sank and bubbles began dribbling to the surface from her nose.

'Oh my God, look what you have done now!' I roared at an uncaring and otherwise preoccupied Paddy. There was nothing for it – I would have to get the ewe out. I estimated the water to be about waist deep and she was right in the middle. With the rest of the dogs watching with interest and Paddy secured to a tree to prevent any similar sorties, I stepped into the water. I thrashed towards her disappearing form, the boulders under my feet slimy with years of aquatic growth. The ewe was by this time a foot below the surface. As the water level reached my waist I lunged for her, only to find that I had seriously misjudged the depth. The bottom plummeted into what I later learned was a twelve-foot deep hole.

The cold was horrendous and as it wrapped its fingers around my body, I was paralysed, unable to move my arms or legs. My God, I thought, here I am, five hundred yards from home, and I'm going to drown in this stupid river and nobody will know why. I felt the horns of the ewe brush against my hand and I grabbed hold. I gave a last almighty push against the bottom with my boots and mercifully shot to the surface, dragging her with me. Still unable to move, the river pushed me to the bank and, at last, my feet scraped against the bottom. I dragged myself and the sheep out of the water and we both collapsed in a heap on the bank.

I got unsteadily to my feet and saw that the ewe was okay. I was freezing cold and knew I had to get home quick. Calling the boys and girls to me, I staggered back to the road. It was a slow, cold, wet, miserable walk home. Paddy walked beside me, anchored by the belt that I had relieved of its customary function of holding my trousers up.

It was an eternity before I got home. I opened the back door and made a soggy entrance to our kitchen, close to exhaustion and freezing cold.

'What the hell happened to you? You're dripping all over the floor,' Kate said, pausing from her task of emptying the dishwasher and stating the obvious.

'It was that bastard, Paddy,' I said, shivering. 'I almost drowned because of the lunatic.'

'Tell me about it later,' she ordered. 'Get out of those clothes and get into the shower before you get hypothermia.'

When I had dried out and was able to think straight, I phoned Tom and told him he could take Paddy back as quick as he could manage before he killed me or somebody else. I told him that, apart from nearly drowning me, I was having a daily battle, with him sometimes clearing off for anything up to an hour doing God knows what. 'The other day,' I added, 'he arrived home with a chicken carcass in his mouth. Okay it was rotten but would he give it up? Not him – talk about a wrestling match.'

'Right, Neil, let's get him back then,' he said.

'I'll get him across to you on the "greyhound transporter",' I said. This is a van that plies between Ireland and the UK carrying greyhounds and other dogs and provides safe and cheap transport.

'Let me know when he's coming and I'll pick him up.'

But the next day, Paddy was watching my every move from his kennel and I had second thoughts. How could I give up on him now, especially after we had gone through so much together, and what would his future be? So I phoned Tom and told him I had changed my mind and that I was going to try to sort him out once and for all.

It took me about six more months, but now he is brilliant fun and well behaved and his sheep-trailing days are well and truly over. He sits back from his food bowl when I go into the pen and he will let me pick up the dish without showing any sign of aggression.

He excels at trailing work – once given an article to smell, he will happily search for the owner of that article through crowds of people, down roads, over fields, wherever, certain in the knowledge that he will be rewarded with some cooked chicken. His enthusiasm for food knows no bounds!

In July 2011, following our successful assessment by the two of the UK's leading trailing dog experts – Tom Middlemas and Iain Nicholson – Paddy and I were awarded our Novice Trailing Dog licence. That makes Paddy the first dog in Ireland to have achieved the NSARDA Trailing Dog qualification and of that I am immensely proud. It's a terrific milestone in my search and rescue work – and hopefully not the last!

Acknowledgements

I have to thank so many people for the love, support and patience they showed me while I was learning to be a search dog handler, but I especially want to thank Kate, my devoted and loving wife who has stuck by me, and encouraged, listened and cried with me during my forty year journey. I want to thank our two beautiful daughters Clair and Emma, from the bottom of my heart for their patience and love while I was off on rescues or training dogs somewhere instead of being with them a little more.

I am so grateful to Joe Boyd and Davey Mayberry, two wonderfully talented dog trainers who taught me what I know about training, working with, and understanding dogs. I want to honour Phil Haigh, my old friend and now sadly deceased, a man who dedicated his life to helping those in trouble on the mountains or the caves beneath and who helped me personally through so many difficult times. Then too, I want to thank Hamish McInnis, Kenny McKenzie and Teddy Hawkins for their support when I first started training search dogs, as well as John Magin for his advice and help when I was teaching my dogs to ignore sheep. John Sjoberg my friend and mentor in drowned victim search dog work, deserves special mention for sharing with me his calm manner and profound understanding of dogs. Thanks are also due to my friend Pete Brown for his support and wise counsel, and to Adrian Mussen and my son-in-law Raph O'Connor for accompanying me on so many rescues.

I want to pay a particular tribute to all the wonderfully dedicated men and women of the Search and Rescue Dog Association throughout the British Isles who – with their dogs, the silent unsung heroes – tramp the mountains, hills and forests of Ireland, Scotland, England, Wales and the Isle of Man, in the worst of weather and often in the dead of night, in search of the lost and the wounded.

I want say a huge thank you to the staff of Blackstaff Press, Helen Wright, Patsy Horton, Sarah Bowers, Kate Shepherd and Anna Robinette, for taking a chance on me, an unknown author and for their advice and help in getting this work completed. Thanks too, to my friend, Angela Locke, author of *Search Dog* and *Sam and Co.: Heroic Search Dogs of the Fells*, for her encouragement and many offers of help as I struggled to put my story on paper.

Finally I want to thank my mother and father, Cynthia and Con Powell, and my sisters Pat and Cynthia for their love and support while I was growing up.